In Search of Return

Psychoanalytic Studies: Clinical, Social, and Cultural Contexts

Series Editor: Michael O'Loughlin, Adelphi University

Mission Statement

Psychoanalytic Studies seeks psychoanalytically informed works addressing the implications of the location of the individual in clinical, social, cultural, historical, and ideological contexts. Innovative theoretical and clinical works within psychoanalytic theory and in fields such as anthropology, education, and history are welcome. Projects addressing conflict, migrations, difference, ideology, subjectivity, memory, psychiatric suffering, physical and symbolic violence, power, and the future of psychoanalysis itself are welcome, as are works illustrating critical and activist applications of clinical work.

See https://rowman.com/Action/SERIES/LEX/LEXPS for a list of advisory board members.

Titles in the Series

In Search of Return: Mourning the Disappearances in Kashmir by Shifa Haq
Trauma and Repair: Confronting Segregation and Violence in America by Annie Stopford
Psychoanalysis as a Subversive Phenomenon: Social Change, Virtue Ethics, and Analytic Theory by Amber M. Trotter
A People's History of Psychoanalysis: From Freud to Liberation Psychology by Daniel José Gaztambide
Rethinking the Relation between Women and Psychoanalysis: Loss, Mourning, and the Feminine edited by Hada Soria Escalante
Lives Interrupted: Psychiatric Narratives of Struggle and Resilience edited by Michael O'Loughlin, Secil Arac-Orhun, and Montana Queler
Women and the Psychosocial Construction of Madness edited by Marie Brown and Marilyn Charles
Revisioning War Trauma in Cinema: Uncoming Communities, by Jessica Datema and Manya Steinkoler
Women & Psychosis: Multidisciplinary Perspectives, edited by Marie Brown and Marilyn Charles
Psychoanalysis from the Indian Terroir: Emerging Themes in Culture, Family, and Childhood in India, edited by Manasi Kumar, Anup Dhar, and Anurag Mishra
A Three-Factor Model of Couples Psychotherapy: Projective Identification, Level of Couple Object Relations, and Omnipotent Control, by Robert Mendelsohn

In Search of Return

Mourning the Disappearances in Kashmir

Shifa Haq

LEXINGTON BOOKS
Lanham • Boulder • New York • London

Published by Lexington Books
An imprint of The Rowman & Littlefield Publishing Group, Inc.
4501 Forbes Boulevard, Suite 200, Lanham, Maryland 20706
www.rowman.com

6 Tinworth Street, London SE11 5AL, United Kingdom

British Library Cataloguing in Publication Information Available

Library of Congress Cataloging-in-Publication Data

Names: Haq, Shifa, 1985– author.
Title: In search of return : mourning the disappearances in Kashmir / Shifa Haq.
Description: Lanham : Lexington Books, [2021] | Series: Psychoanalytic studies: clinical, social, and cultural contexts | Includes bibliographical references and index. | Summary: "Shifa Haq traces the dynamics of mourning, collective trauma, and political resistance in personal accounts of mourners of the disappeared persons, providing insights into psyche-polis connection. By using a psychoanalytic lens, this book turns to individual cases to throw light on claims of affect and memory to re-imagine social suffering"—Provided by publisher.
Identifiers: LCCN 2020039178 (print) | LCCN 2020039179 (ebook) | ISBN 9781498582483 (cloth ; alk. paper) | ISBN 9781498582490 (ebook)
Subjects: LCSH: Disappeared persons—India—Jammu and Kashmir. | Disappeared persons' families—India—Jammu and Kashmir. | Political violence—Psychological aspects—India—Jammu and Kashmir. | Bereavement—Psychological aspects. | Collective memory—India—Jammu and Kashmir.
Classification: LCC HV6322.3.I4 H35 2021 (print) | LCC HV6322.3.I4 (ebook) | DDC 362.870954/6—dc23
LC record available at https://lccn.loc.gov/2020039178
LC ebook record available at https://lccn.loc.gov/2020039179

For G
whose love is unknown
and the unknown
a kind of love

Contents

Foreword ix

Preface xvii

Acknowledgements xxi

Introduction xxv

1 The Work of Mourning 1

2 The Disappearing Act 27

3 Tracing Back, Moving Forward 49
- A House with No Doors 53
- Comb Gently 66
- Three Days in the River 76

4 Bearing Witness, Imagining Disappearance 89

5 The Shape of Mourning 103

References 115

Index 129

About the Author 135

Foreword

Vamık Volkan[1]

During its last three decades of armed conflict Kashmir experienced thousands of extra-judicial killings, torture, rape and fear of losing its culture. More than 8,000 persons have disappeared in Kashmir since 1989. The author of this book, Shifa Haq, psychoanalytic psychotherapist, visited Kashmir many times between 2010 and 2018, and, interviewed family members of disappeared persons. She sat with these mourner-survivors in their kitchens, abandoned childhood homes, ruins and city parks. She noted that those who were left behind continued to wonder, throughout decades, if the disappeared individuals might one day return.

There is a difference in human response to not knowing if a disappeared person is dead or alive and knowing that someone is physically gone through death. This difference, as well as Kashmir's collective, horrible traumas, has complicated its mourners' lives in special ways. In this book Shifa Haq tells the moving stories of three of them. Our understanding of these three individuals' internal worlds is enriched by the author's extensive understanding of the mourning process, gleaned from the study of the psychoanalytic literature on this topic, starting with Sigmund Freud's.

This book also examines how societal remembrances and mourning are expressed. As Shifa Haq states, horrors endured by the land of Kashmir cannot be undone, and 'the genie cannot be put back in the bottle; it is through containing, surviving and remembering historical trauma that we can hope to move forward and give the dissociated specters of violence a place in lived history'. Her references to poems and paintings linked to disappearances in Kashmir illustrate that there are also creative ways of remembering losses and horrors. She also lets the reader know that the long-lasting effects of disappearances and other traumas in Kashmir will carry forward, influencing generations to come.

During my long career as a psychoanalyst, I left my office many times, just as Shifa Haq has done, to study human psychology. I visited different countries and spoke, often assisted by a translator, with many survivor-mourners, not only in conference rooms, but also in streets, parks, elementary schools, cemeteries, ruins and while going somewhere in taxis or trains. As I was reading her book, I had a sense of walking side by side with Shifa Haq, witnessing with her the routes mourning takes when it is a shared experience and how shared images of external historical events intertwine with humans' internal worlds.

I am writing this foreword during a time when psychoanalytic and psychotherapeutic organizations, along with others in physical and mental health fields, are intensely preoccupied with an unseen threat to every person the world over: the COVID-19 pandemic. In the past, psychoanalysts and psychoanalytic therapists have shied away from paying professional attention to collective external events in the clinical setting. Although Sigmund Freud and several pioneering analysts wrote papers on history, culture, religion and other shared external topics and examined them from a psychoanalytic angle, it was not until recent decades that psychoanalysts and psychoanalytic psychotherapists began to dwell much on the impact of such events on their patients' internal worlds. Furthermore, we have rarely heard of these professionals carrying out serious work in societal and political arenas by leaving the confines of their office. Psychoanalysts' and psychoanalytic therapists' in-depth studies of shared external events and the appearance of their impact not only in the clinical offices, but also in societal settings, has an interesting history. I offer a short summary of this history in order to illuminate the importance of Shifa Haq's book.

In psychoanalytic literature there are many studies of a long-lasting dispute between Freud and the Hungarian psychoanalyst Sándor Ferenczi that began in 1925 concerning the influence of actual trauma—actual sexual abuse—on individuals' internal worlds (for recent studies of this dispute see: Haynal 2005; Hoffer 2010; Mucci 2013). Freud never denied the existence of *actual* sexual seduction. But after he developed new theories on infantile sexuality and the internal worlds of children, he wrote: 'Obviously seduction is not required in order to arouse a child's sexual life; that can also come about spontaneously from internal causes' (Freud 1905, 190–191). Focus on the stimuli that come from the child's fantasies for the formation of psychopathology became a key element of the new science called psychoanalysis. In 1932, Freud's followers blocked Ferenczi from delivering a paper that focused on the truthfulness of seduction.

This long dispute played a role in the path taken by other pioneer psychoanalysts, as they continued to follow Freud's lead, placing less emphasis during psychoanalytic treatment on the impact of actual seduction coming from the external world. This attitude was generalized and led to a de-emphasis on the impact of other external real events in the appearance of analysands' symptoms and character traits.

In 1932, Albert Einstein wrote a letter to Freud asking the following questions: 'Is there any way of delivering mankind from the menace of war? . . . How is it possible for [a small group hungering for political power] to bend the will of the majority, who stand to lose and suffer by a state of war, to the service of their ambitions?' and 'Is it possible to control man's mental evolution so as to make him proof against the psychoses of hate and destructiveness?' (Freud 1933, 199–201). In his response to Einstein, Freud suggested that anything that encourages 'the growth of emotional ties' through loving and identification with others operates against war. 'This, however, is more easily said than done' (p. 212). He expressed little hope for an end to war and violence or the role of psychoanalysis in changing human behaviour beyond the individual level. Freud's response to Einstein further discouraged his followers from pursuing the impact of historical, political and international events on their patients' internal worlds. For example, John Bowlby (1988) described that when he became an analyst in 1937 in Great Britain, psychoanalysts were only interested in the internal worlds of their patients; paying attention to historical events surrounding patients was considered inappropriate. In another example, Melanie Klein (1961) ignored the influences of war while treating one of her patients, a ten-year-old boy named Richard, whose analysis took place while World War II raged, literally overhead, during the London Blitz under which they both lived. This circumstance was not examined during Richard's analysis.

After World War II, it took some time to notice that many Jewish psychoanalysts in the United States and elsewhere interfered with verbal and affective expressions of Holocaust- related issues. Such expressions would induce anxiety; they were shrouded in silence (Blum 1985; Rangell 2003). Also in post-World War II Germany, there was both German and German-Jewish analyst-supported resistance to exploring the influence of Nazi Era traumas on German and Jewish analysands' psyches, even though the intertwining of historical external traumas with internal conflicts was certainly present (Jokl 1997; Opher-Cohn, Pfäfflin, Sonntag, Klose and Pogany-Wnendt 2000; Volkan, Ast and Greer 2002). This situation as well supported a bias towards a theoretical position called 'classical psychoanalysis' that focused primarily on the patient's conflicts linked to sexual and aggressive fantasies.

As we might expect, there were exceptions to this trend, and some well-known psychoanalysts such as Géza Róheim (1943) and Edward Glower (1947) turned psychoanalysts' attention to the role of cultural and societal issues in human psychology, in sadism, pacifism and war. Erik Erikson (1950, 1959) became a key figure in exploring child-rearing practices and psychosocial development. Róheim, Glower and Erikson's work, however, did not substantially change the practice of psychoanalysis. Generally speaking, psychoanalysts' attention to the intertwining of external and internal events in their analysands' psychological make-up evolved slowly.

In the 1960s, with the works of Henry Kristal (1968), William Niederland (1968) and others, the 'silence' around the impact of the Holocaust on human psychology began to fade. More studies of the influence of the Third Reich on the psyche of the survivors, both victims and perpetrators, surfaced (for a review of this literature see Brenner 2020). The inability to mourn after shared massive traumas at the hand of the Other was examined (see, for example, Fornari 1966; Mitscherlich and Mitscherlich 1973; Laub and Podell 1997). In spite of these changes, those working in the clinical setting generally continued to bypass the impact of historical external traumas.

Beginning in the 1980s, our world saw profound and rapid changes, such as the collapse of the Soviet Union and the incredible evolution of communication technology. This sparked a surge in new consideration of mass psychology and political violence seen through the analytic lens that became rather routine. There are noteworthy examples: Raphael Moses (1982) examined the Arab-Israeli conflict; Michael Śebek (1994) studied societal responses to living under communism in Europe; Sudhir Kakar (1996) described the effects of Hindu-Muslim religious conflict in Hyderabad, India; Nancy Hollander (2010) explored surviving political terror in South America; and Mitch Elliott, Kenneth Bishop and Paul Stokes (2004) and John Alderdice (2010) examined the troubles in Northern Ireland.

As a psychoanalyst, my involvement in political and societal conflicts started after Egyptian president Anwar Sadat visited Israel in 1977. During this visit, at the Knesset, Sadat referred to a psychological 'wall' between the Israelis and the Arabs—a wall that he stated accounted for 70 per cent of the problems between them. The American Psychiatric Association's Committee on Psychiatry and Foreign Affairs, of which I was a member, responded by bringing influential Arabs and Israelis together for unofficial dialogues for six years to find out if this 'wall' could be made permeable. In 1988, at the University of Virginia School of Medicine, I opened the Center for the Study of Mind and Human Interaction (CSMHI) with a faculty of psychoanalysts, other mental health professionals, former diplomats, political scientists, historians, an environmentalist and a linguist. This interdisciplinary team and I visited many areas of the world where international conflicts existed and brought together representatives of opposing large groups, such as Soviets and Americans, Russians and Estonians, Croats and Bosnians, Georgians and South Ossetians, Turks and Greeks, for years-long unofficial dialogues. I also observed various individuals and groups who were traumatized. I observed the impact of ethnic conflict in Cyprus, which began in the early 1960s. In 1990, I spent one week in an orphanage in Tunis with Palestinian children who had lost their parents, and later, in the 1990s, I talked with adults and youngsters in Kuwait who were adjusting to life following the withdrawal of Saddam Hussein's forces from their country. I interviewed Romanians and Albanians who had been tortured during the dictatorial regimes of Nicolae Ceaućescu and Enver Hoxha. In the late 1990s and early 2000s, I often visited internally displaced ethnic groups in the Republic of Georgia and South Ossetia following ethnic conflicts in this part of the world. Most recently, I went to Colombia and learned a great deal about the impact that 'war' between the government of Colombia, paramilitary groups, communist guerrillas and crime syndicates has had on individuals there (Volkan 1997, 2004, 2006, 2013).

My work away from my psychoanalytic couch allowed me to contribute to ethnic, national, religious or dialogical large-group psychology *in its own* right (Volkan 2020). This means making formulations about the conscious and unconscious shared past and present historical/psychological experiences that exist within a large group. My term 'large group' refers to thousands or millions of individuals who share similar sentiments and the same historical images from their past. Making such formulations enlarges our understanding of the emergence of present-day societal, political, religious events and leader-follower relationships, and allows us to look at the interactions between opposing large groups in-depth. This is similar to a psychoanalyst making formulations about an analysand's developmental history associated with various conscious and unconscious fantasies in order to understand what motivates certain behavior patterns, symptoms and habitual interpersonal relationships.

At the present time, in light of the globalization of religious terrorism and refugee crises, as expected, the number of people looking at societal traumas from psychological angles has grown (for a review of the literature see: Suistola and Volkan 2017). Now that COVID-19 is threatening all human beings, I am sure that the impact of this danger on individuals and societies everywhere will be examined from a psychoanalytic angle. It will be interesting and important to study how this unseen 'enemy' shared by all the ethnic and religious groups in Kashmir will affect relationships among these groups.

Some massive traumas are results of earthquakes, tropical storms, floods, forest fires, volcanic eruptions, and other natural causes. When nature shows its fury and people suffer, those affected tend ultimately to accept the event as fate or as the will of God. Following man-made accidental disasters, survivors blame a small number of individuals for their carelessness. Both natural and accidental catastrophes usually do not evoke our ethnic, national or religious identity issues. We do not become preoccupied with thinking that these tragedies occurred because we are Apaches, Tamils, Lithuanian Jews, Polish, Sunni Muslims or communists. Neither do these events initiate large groups' preoccupation with physical borders unless the disaster is like the 1986 Chernobyl accident that spewed tons of radioactive dust into the atmosphere. Sometimes, the murder of a 'transference figure' for the members of the large group, such as John F. Kennedy in the United States, Yitzhak Rabin in Israel, Olof Palme in Sweden, Giorgi Chanturia in the Republic of Georgia, or Rafik Hariri in Lebanon, provokes traumatic societal responses. If the murderer and the murdered leader belong to the same ethnic, national, religious or political large group however, there is not much impact on the large-group and border psychology.

Other massive traumas are due to the *deliberate* actions of an enemy group, as in ethnic, national, religious and political ideological conflicts, racism, terrorism, wars and genocides. All *deliberately* induced social traumas by the Other inflame large-group identity issues and preoccupation with borders as soon as they occur.

Individuals, in general, who study to be psychiatrists, psychologists, psychologists or other mental health workers end up working in their offices, hospitals and other care-giving facilities until their retirement. But those professionals who have seriously studied historical traumas have helped us realize that we cannot understand internal worlds, symptoms, personality problems of some patients without dwelling on their large-groups' historical events. This is because individual identity includes investment in large-group identity. I wrote accounts of the psychoanalytic treatment of two individuals, from beginning to termination, in order to illustrate that it would be impossible to understand these individuals' symptoms and personality problems without knowing their ancestors' history (Volkan 2015, 2019).

Shifa Haq describes massive traumas related to large-group identity issues and makes a significant contribution to large-group psychology *in its own right*. Her findings also encourage us to give the necessary attention in a clinical setting to our patient's responses to collective external events. She does not tell us her personal motivations for studying what happened to mourner-survivors in Kashmir. She does however share her discomfort and anxiety as one working in an environment where escape from military surveillance, paramilitary terrorism and other dangers was difficult. I deeply appreciate her courage, her work and her teaching us about the special aspects of mourning processes when loss is related to the sudden disappearance of loved-ones.

NOTE

1. Vamık D. Volkan is an Emeritus Professor of Psychiatry at the University of Virginia and an Emeritus Training and Supervising Analyst at the Washington-Baltimore Psychoanalytic Institute. He is the Emeritus President of the International Dialogue Initiative.

REFERENCES

Alderdice, J. (2010). Off the couch and round the conference table. In: A. Lemma & M. Patrick (eds.), *Contemporary Psychoanalytic Applications*, pp. 15–32. New York: Routledge.

Blum, H. P. (1985). Superego formation, adolescent transformation and the adult neurosis. *Journal of the American Psychoanalytic Association*, *4*: 887–909.

Bowlby, J. (1988). *A Secure Base: Parent-Child Attachment and Healthy Human Development*. New York: Basic Books.

Brenner, I. (2020). *The Handbook of Psychoanalytic Holocaust Studies: International Perspectives*. New York: Routledge.

Elliott, M., Bishop, K., & Stokes, P. (2004). Societal PTSD? Historic shock in Northern Ireland. *Psychotherapy and Politics International*, *2*: 1–16.

Erikson, E. H. (1950). *Childhood and Society*. New York: W. W. Norton.

Erikson, E. H. (1959). *Identity and the Life Cycle*. New York: International Universities Press.

Fornari, F. (1966). *The Psychoanalysis of War*. A. Pfeifer (Trans.). Bloomington, IN: Indiana University Press, 1975.

Freud, S. (1905). *Three Essays on the Theory of Sexuality*. *Standard Edition*, *7*: 123–243. London: Hogarth.

Freud, S. (1933). *Why War? Standard Edition*, vol. 22. London: Hogarth, pp. 197–215.

Glower, E. (1947). *War, Sadism, and Pacifism: Further Essays on Group Psychology and War*. London: Allen & Unwin.

Haynal, A. E. (2005). In the shadow of controversy: Freud and Ferenczi 1925–33. *International Journal of Psychoanalysis*, *86*: 457–466.

Hoffer, P. T. (2010). From elasticity to the confusion of tongues: A historical commentary on the technical dimension of the Freud/Ferenczi controversy. *Psychoanalytic Perspectives*, *7*: 90–103.

Hollander, N. C. (2010). *Uprooted Minds: Surviving the Political Terror in the Americas*. New York: Taylor & Francis.

Jokl, A. M. (1997). *Zwei Fälle zum Thema 'Bewältigung der Vergangenheit'* [Two Cases Referring to the Theme of 'Mastering the Past']. Frankfurt: Jüdischer Verlag.

Kakar, S. (1996). *The Colors of Violence: Cultural Identities, Religion, and Conflict*. Chicago, IL: University of Chicago Press.

Klein, M. (1961). *Narrative of a Child Analysis: The Conduct of the Psychoanalysis of Children as Seen in the Treatment of a Ten-Year-Old Boy*. London: Hogarth, 1975.

Krystal, H. (ed.) (1968). *Massive Psychic Trauma*. New York: International Universities Press.

Laub, D., & Podell, D. (1997). Psychoanalytic listening to historical trauma: The conflict of knowing and the imperative act. *Mind and Human Interaction*, *8*: 245–260.

Mitscherlich, A., & Mitscherlich, M. (1973). *Die Unfähigkeit zu trauern: Grundlagen kollektiven Verhaltens* [The Inability to Mourn: Principals of Collective Behavior]. Munich: Piper.

Moses, R. (1982). The group-self and the Arab-Israeli conflict. *International Review of Psycho-Analysis*, *9*: 55–65.

Mucci, C. (2013). *Beyond Individual and Collective Trauma: Intergenerational Transmission, Psychoanalytic Treatment, and the Dynamics of Forgiveness.* London: Karnac.

Niederland, W. (1968). Clinical observations on the 'survivor syndrome'. *International Journal of Psychoanalysis*, *49*: 313–315.

Opher-Cohn, L., Pfäfflin, J., Sonntag, J. B., Klose, B., & Pogany-Wnendt, P. (eds.) (2000). *Das Ende der Sprachlosigkeit? Auswirkungen traumatischer Holocausterfahrungen über mehrere Generationen* [The End of Speechlessness]

The Effects of Experiencing the Holocaust over Several Generations. Giessen: Psychosozial Verlag.

Rangell, L. (2003). Affects: In an individual and a nation. First Annual Volkan Lecture, November 15, University of Virginia, Charlottesville, VA.

Róheim, G. (1943). *The origin and function of culture.* Nervous and Mental Diseases Monograph, vol. 69. New York.

Šebek, M. (1994). Psychopathology of everyday life in the post-totalitarian society. *Mind and Human Interaction*, *5*: 104–109.

Suistola, J., & Volkan, V. D. (2017). *Religious Knives: Historical and Psychological Dimensions of International Terrorism.* Durham, NC: Pitchstone.

Volkan, V. D. (1997). *Bloodlines: From Ethnic Pride to Ethnic Terrorism.* New York: Farrar, Straus and Giroux.

Volkan, V. D. (2004). *Blind Trust: Large Groups and Their Leaders in Times of Crises and Terror.* Durham, NC: Pitchstone.

Volkan, V. D. (2006). *Killing in the Name of Identity: A Study of Bloody Conflicts.* Durham, NC: Pitchstone.

Volkan, V. D. (2013). *Enemies on the Couch: A Psychopolitical Journey through War and Peace.* Durham, NC: Pitchstone.

Volkan, V. D. (2015). *A Nazi Legacy: A Study of Depositing, Transgenerational Transmission, Dissociation and Remembering through Action.* London: Karnac.

Volkan, V. D. (2019). *A Study of Ghosts in the Human Psyche: Story of a Muslim Armenian.* London: Phoenix.

Volkan, V. D. (2020). *Large-Group Psychology: Racism, Societal Divisions, Narcissistic Leaders, and Who We Are Now. London: Phoenix.*

Volkan, V. D., Ast, G., & Greer, W. F. (2002). *The Third Reich in the Unconscious: Transgenerational Transmission and Its Consequences.* New York: Brunner-Routledge.

Preface

Just as a patient discovers in a long treatment in psychoanalysis how little she knows about herself, the last ten years of engagement with mourning, in the context of disappearances in Kashmir, reveals to me how limited my grasp on the subject of loss and mourning is. The book must therefore begin with a confession and an insight: a writer or a researcher is seldom an expert on the subject she studies; on the contrary, her labor is an admission of how perplexed and unacquainted she is with the subject of exploration. The only relief to be had is in the questions that sustain one's repeated returns. This book is, therefore, an account of my absorption and my limits in understanding the profound interruption called disappearance as it is experienced and elaborated in the lives of mourners in Kashmir. What follows is an exercise in enduring the dark and enduring in the dark—the subject position of mourning.

The book combines reflection on mourning as a subjective capability and a conceptual frame within psychoanalysis. There is, however, another impulse inherent in the project, that is, to see mourning when it is denied, and when it actively seeks to subvert routes to a possible conclusion. From the Freudian moment, one learns that in loss, part of the ego disappears. My enquiry seeks to articulate disappearance, not of the ego only but more significantly and irrevocably, as the exceptional loss of a person through forced abduction or involuntary arrest executed as a method of disciplining, punishing and taking control of the bodies it targets and the community it marks. Beginning in the 1990s, enforced disappearance was used strategically to suppress the resistance movement in Kashmir against Indian rule. In the context of brutal militarization, with 650,000 Indian troops deployed for a population of 12.5 million people in the region, Kashmir remains the most militarized zone in the world with unthinkable human suffering. As in melancholia, where loss is withdrawn from conscious recognition, losses suffered by the Kashmiris in the last three decades of armed response are withdrawn from the Indian consciousness, constituting a melancholic structure at the heart of a collective experience. In going close to loss, to the experience of traumatization and obstructed mourning, this book attempts to sidestep the posture of neutrality in service of an engaged ethical witnessing of the suffering of the other.

The origins of this book lie in the inexplicable, inter-subjective encounters of mourning in psychotherapy with adult patients in New Delhi on the one hand, and the decades-long engagement with mourning in the families of the disappeared persons in Kashmir on the other. In my work as a therapist, two crucial questions emerged: When loss is unacknowledged by the other, what effects does it have on mourning? And, how do we locate the individual in the social suffering produced by a political conflict? While psychoanalytic theory emerges primarily as clinical encounters between a patient and an analyst, it offers a unique perspective on the interaction between social forces and unconscious life—fantasies, identifications and affect—of individuals and their collectives. The book attempts to engage with mourning in the political setting of disappearances in Kashmir where through an irrevocable fate, the one who has disappeared and the ones who mourn for his return are linked by an interminable waiting. The fundamental refrain of the book is an explication of the profound interruption, its nature and scope in the life of the mourning families of the disappeared. In the absence of any evidence of whether the disappeared are dead or alive, the mourners attempt to articulate love as well as justice to counter an extreme social condition marked by militarization and massive trauma. Through their accounts, the mourners shed light on the radical encounters with oppressive forces acting upon them, the complex psychic states not of their own making and a praxis of resistance carried out intrapsychically just as it is carried out socially and politically. Within psychoanalytic literature, mourning and melancholia have been constructed along axes of temporality, that is, how long before one recovers from loss, as well as spatiality, specifically towards making room for new experiences in service of an ever-evolving idiom of the self. The mourning stories included in this book illustrate a unique negotiation between social forces, ideology and subjectivity, questioning prevalent ideas on conclusive mourning and normality.

My own history with mourning is a complicated one. Noticing myself unable to move swiftly from loss to mourning, in relationships I have argued for and defended passionately a different pace and a vast openness to feel the unthinkable agonies of loss. It has surprised me how personal such journeys are and how private these resolves need to be to avoid love's extinction and the futurelessness of the erotic life of a person. When not in a hurry, or forced into submission to normality, a mourner is capable of reconstructing and restoring erosions in history that are not only psychical but also social. In a mourner's suffering, there is a careful tending to memories and affect—a furtive negotiation with constancy and change. If loss is a sinister magic that makes the loved object disappear, to never reappear, mourning is the work of reality, the connecting thread between the life before and the life after. While more and more individuals are diagnosed with clinical conditions such as depression and PTSD, it occurs to me that the predicament of not being able to mourn has become increasingly less characterological and more cultural than previously imagined. Organized on the same principle of *incorporation* that for Freud constitutes a melancholic response to loss, the contemporary moment in history offers an impressive array of alternatives of *consumption* as self-cure or flight from the reality of loss. For me, the figure of the mourner is a curious one. A mourner is ill in that she is unable to participate in the self-cure made possible through the use of denial, forgetting or covering up of the psychic hole produced by loss. On the contrary, the mourner actively frustrates and thwarts the possibilities of erasure of the other in personal and collective memory. For a mourner, coming into existence implies *coming into memory,* to recall the permanent traces of the holy one inside and a return to the self through a relationship of an exceptional longing.

While my interest in studying mourning began with work with adult patients in psychotherapy, the link between the public and the private or the clinical and the political remained a significant lens for viewing unconscious fantasies, affect, defenses and dreams. As a reader- practitioner of psychoanalysis, I became receptive to the tendency in psychoanalysis to delink the individual from the social and the political, turning a blind eye to extrafamilial forces that influence subjectivity and psychological experiences. Similarly, through psychotherapeutic work with religious, ethnic and sexual minorities, sometimes as a therapist and forever as a patient myself, I began to understand the politics of experience that rendered some lives as grievable while certain others were vaporized from social and political consciousness. Whenever a subject languishes to associate, there also exists a lack of association to her life or experience in the social or the political. In this book, I hope to offer a space for reflection and connection with the sorrows of the other whose wound holds a mirror to my own melancholic subject formation. I attempt to imagine mourning as personal *and* political; its aim, a radical reorganization of the self as well as the social; and recovery, not a conclusion but a politics of mourning.

Acknowledgements

To tread on any difficult journey, and the temerity to do so in my case, owes its origin in abundance of loving presence who guided my question-prayers with their spirit. I am grateful to:

Michael O'Loughlin for his encouragement, patience and faith in this project;

Honey Oberoi Vahali, my spirit guide, for her singular devotion to my ever-wavering mind and for her brave friendship in academia as in life;

Parveena Ahangar and Saima Ahangar from the Association of Parents of Disappeared Persons, for initiating me into a network of care and belonging formed over an extraordinary journey of the association in the last three decades in Kashmir. I wish to acknowledge the staff of APDP, in particular, Sabiya for her diligent help in connecting me with members of the association and for her openness to my disciplinary language. I am also grateful to the families of the disappeared persons, the research participants, who hosted a stranger in their inner world. This work is dedicated to their heroic resistance to remember and nourish bonds of love in the face of atrocities;

Vamik Volkan, Lynne Layton, Sverre Varvin, Martha Bragin and Nancy Caro Hollander whose search for a psychoanalytic response to social suffering and social justice continues to inspire me;

Shyam Menon, Alok Bhalla, Nazia Amin, Aneeqa Khalid, Neil Altman Robin Bagai and Anthony Malino for their cheerful support and encouragement to discover my voice;

Kishwar Sherali, Athar Zia, Gowhar Fazili, Shivani Rajput, Bhavneet Kaur, Shobna Sonpar and Akhil Katyal for their intuition, guidance and their writings;

Jayanti Basu, Anurag Mishra and Jhuma Basak, for their engagement and affection during and beyond my doctoral years at the University of Delhi;

Prof. Talat Ahmed, the Vice-chancellor, University of Kashmir for the residency in Kashmir University Hostels, Haba Khatoon and Rabia Basri, Srinagar, a rare opportunity to meet scholars and researchers from remote areas of Kashmir. The pleasant dailiness of our shared time, their generosity and intellect, especially of Sameena Ramzan, bolstered my work and provided a deep sense of sisterhood;

Naseem Shafaie, Nighat Shafi, Iffat Fatima, Bashir Ahmed Nahvi and Masood Hussain for their creative and empathic insights into the collective suffering in Kashmir;

Homes that took care of me in my communicative and non-communicative states in the field and during the writing of this book. I am grateful to Parveena Ahangar, Muzammil Karim, Sagera Kazmi, Ananya Kushwaha, Dana Crider and Judy Crider for hosting me;

Ambreen Murad, Jogin and Diamond Oberoi for their exemplary humanness and faith in collectives;

My patients, who disclose a world of meaning to me even when I am able to give so little in return.

My clinical supervisors, Minnie Dastur, Psychoanalytic Therapy and Research Centre, Mumbai and Pumpi Harel, Israel Psychoanalytic Society, Tel Aviv, for the gift of a thinking heart and for teaching the value of 'here and now'; the Study Group, Delhi Chapter of Indian Psychoanalytic Society for their enlivening presence;

My students and colleagues in the School of Human Studies and the School of Undergraduate Studies, Ambedkar University Delhi, who kept me on my toes to work with rigour and clarity so that we may find articulation of critical, clinical studies in our collective endeavour. I am also thankful to

Krishna Menon, Dean, School of Human Studies, for the gift of leave to complete this aspiration;

Virien Chopra, Nidhi Varma and Mimansa Sharma for reading drafts of the manuscript with utmost care and their invaluable comments;

Kasey Beduhn, at Lexington Books, for crafting this work under her diligent care;

Saima Haq and Mamatha Karollil who helped confront impasses in writing and thinking;

Nidhi Varma, Sabah Siddiqui, Zehra Mehdi, Shraddha Chatterjee, Rashi Kapoor, Urvashi Pawar, Mary Curry, Pallavi Banerjee, Ujjaini Srimani, Ananya Kushwaha and Priya Tiwari- my community of women whose brilliance and candour runs through this work. You know very well that I wouldn't have been able to persist without your fierce and devoted love;

Rakesh Shukla, Niti Dhingra and Aastha Jha for keeping me in good humour and irreverent to the seriousness of life;
Karuna Chandrashekar, for poetic translations of mourning that is our friendship;
Jules, a joyful cat whose cultivated disinterest in academic passions is noetic and grounding;
My parents for reclamation of a faint wish that I might write someday and for waiting patiently;
My sisters Saima, Sama and Sarah, whose creativity far exceeds the world of academics. You teach me what it is to carry someone's heart in one's own;
Lastly, Shubhendu Ghosh for precious illusions to face the tides of time.

Introduction

There is an indiscriminate presence of loss in all lives. Yet we struggle to find words or adequate expressions of what loss means. A gaping void, a memory clot, an eccentric obliquity from the centre of one's existence. A 'me' without 'you'. Betrayed by language, in loss we meet our self, as stranger, exposed to primary vulnerability, begging to make acquaintance with other sides that are now inaccessible. To tell a story from such a place is to recover a resting place, or meaning from a place of arrest, that is loss. To mourn is to dare a fumble and coil in a narrow passage that remains, for the most part, unknown. Mourning, in this sense, is an engagement with loss, its restrictions, its indissolubility, its immutability, with one's strangeness and the stranger's eccentric relatability with her private world. The sad mother, a mother in grief, is the first stranger for the baby who cannot comprehend the culture of privation holding her. Her pain renders her foreign to the baby. To the baby, there are two potential dangers—loss of the mother and loss of a language to revive her. It is a moment of birth, of discovery of an interiority wherein lies future of attachment and longing for an enigmatic, sometimes melancholic other. In returning to the question of mourning, I am returning to the mother. A mother in grief. A slowly disappearing other. To an obsession with language that may connect back to loss made foreign or alien. Yet, it is only the foreign that has the power to elude, to catch hold of our imagination so that we might wish to go closer. The strangeness of someone in pain, or someone's pain, is the object of our concern. Like the imminent kiss in Rene Magritte's 'The Lovers' (1928), we are connected and separated by the sensuous drape, a layer, a skin that makes 'longing' as an experience sharable in one breath and impossible in the next. Perhaps Magritte saw two lovers intertwined in a kiss as also two strangers in recoil. Locked in mutual deciphering of longing, the lovers may discover an irresistible wish, opening and closing at the mouth—to be the other. The kiss, however, exposes the impossibility of becoming the other. A mourner too is a captivated lover, perched on a kiss, in *contact* and *separated* by an enduring sheath, an area of play exposed by life and death. Mourning therefore is an opportunity to glimpse intimacy that grows in confinement of loss as it struggles for a language to make it knowable, to break out of its confines or to speak through them. I see Magritte's subject of two lovers inclusive of any two people, with the dyad casted in shadows by the excess of loss. Mothers, fathers, partners, siblings, children, friends, neighbours and non-human companions—all capable of the pain of separation and the hell of longing. In this book I hope to dwell on the paradoxical relation between the mourner and the lost object; the loss on the outside and the recovery of the one lost on the inside; seeing lovers as estranged from the world and also capable of strange loves. But more significantly, the book seeks to go closer to the loss of a stranger, an other, or the one othered, whose pain can be carefully avoided and denied, whose obsessions to remember, to commit to memory, echoes the pain of my forgetting I no longer wish to understand; and whose mourning continues to trace loss, sometimes as disappearance and recovery, sometimes as fantasy of return, in a psychic terra firma that is both collective and individual.

On 31 October 1908, almost a year after hearing the news of his dear friend Paula Modersohn-Becker's death, a gifted painter and a mother to an eighteen days old child, Rilke (1996) wrote for two haunted nights what is known as 'Requiem for a Friend'. In this difficult piece, Rilke displays a wild contestation with death's authority on the mortality of his beloved friend. He wrote, 'I have my dead and I have let them go and was amazed to see them so contented, so at home in being dead, so unlike their reputation. Only you return; brush past me, loiter, try to knock against something, so that the sound reveals your presence. Oh don't take from me what I am slowly learning. I am sure you have gone astray if you are moved to homesickness for anything in this direction.' The requiem ends on an imploring note, 'Do not return. If you can bear to, stay dead with the dead. The dead have their own tasks. But help me, if you can without distractions, as what is farthest sometimes, helps: in me' (Rilke 1996).

Rilke, like any mourner, is doomed to find himself unable to relinquish the attachment with Paula. With every knock of memory, he imagines Paula, now an inhabitant of the realm of the dead, homesick, tiptoeing surreptitiously into his mind, looking for temporary refuge in memories. The metaphor of homesickness connects Paula's haunting presence and Rilke's dis-ease at life emptied out by the loss. Her 'knocking against something' testifies to her presence within, a secret other bound in the boundless self, an internal universe exposed but only inside. He doesn't think it is *he* who is homesick, who invokes the image of wandering Paula, unhappy among the contented dead.

Perhaps mourning, just like play, is neither inside nor outside, neither only about the subject nor purely about the object. Given the liminality inherent in mourning, what can we say about its essential ambivalence to communicate and not communicate; to be found and to slip away? The answers can only be discovered when we enter as mourners!

Freud, in *Mourning and Melancholia* ([1917] 1971), described a mourner visiting every single one of the memories, each grain of sand in the hourglass, to decathect the object till such a time that the ego is free and uninhibited to love and attach to someone or something *new*. One is able to move on to the extent one is able to 'relinquish' one's ties with the lost object—a necessary step to mourning. One might ask, what is it to relinquish something that doesn't exist on the outside anymore? Or what internal work goes on occurring silently in which one ought to be successful? Lodged permanently inside, the *other within* exists in laments of the mourner. On listening deeply to these laments, Freud speculated the difference or rather a relation between mourning and melancholia. Normal mourning, thought Freud, keeps the mourner in touch with what has been lost; however, in melancholia the object loss is 'withdrawn from consciousness' (Freud [1917] 1971, 245). A melancholic subject is torn between *who* one has lost and *what* has been lost. To interrogate 'what' of loss is a question of cryptic attachment, a speculation about love in its concreteness. It is not merely refusal to mourn but to set up the condition for mourning—a new order of things. Why, or under what circumstances, is the reality of loss withdrawn from a conscious recognition? Would it be a question of psychogenesis or ontological effect of the self (Butler 1997, 169)? What of the contexts in which mourning chooses a melancholic *devotion* as 'adequate to the experience of loss' (Ogden 2000)?

By dwelling in the intimate ties with the lost object, the mourner resists, rehearses and ritualizes the labour of mourning. Through an ambivalent turn following loss, the ego opens itself as a site of grave contestation. On the one hand, there is the possibility to accept the verdict of reality and on another an ascetic turn, clinging to the shadow of the object that exists no more. Barthes (2010, 192), in *Mourning Diary,* writes:

> August 18, 1978
>
> To share the values of the silent dailiness (to manage the cooking, the cleaning, the clothes, the choice and as if the past of objects), this was my (silent) way of conversing with her—And this is, her not being there, how I can still do it.

The verdict of reality, recognition of loss—what for Barthes was losing his mother—does not always inspire a willing renunciation of love and attachment. There may in fact be an intense opposition to it. In such a course, ego turns away from reality towards a hallucinatory fulfilment, a secret nourishment or a heaven-hell of memories, prolonging connection with the lost object. In the economics of pain, a melancholic devotion is far safer than love seeking extinction. The mourner may pronounce the object an ideal, exceptional or unique. Mourning is therefore a unique disappearance of a unique (Derrida 2001). If surviving the loss means to mourn, to commemorate the singularity of the one lost, to not mourn is an attempt to maintain contiguity with the one lost, unbroken and intact. Finding the mother in the dailiness, conversing through cooking or cleaning become ways to both comprehend the inevitability of loss as well as a method of protest against it. Seen in this light, to understand the work of mourning is to appreciate both the current, of surrender to loss, as well as an organized agitation, sometimes a stupor, against it. Somewhere in this exercise, we may uncover neither a simple mourning nor melancholia but an intermediary space, of *profound mourning*.

In Freudian tradition, mourning, or the German *trauer*, carries the affect of grief as well as its outward expression or exhibition. In its very manifestation, for the mourner, the self, like the world, is left impoverished and empty. A loveless self and a loveless world, the image of dejection in loss, undergo intense experiences of debasement, denigration and destitution. The experience of mourning uncovers an underground string of losses. In addition to the excess produced by the loss of the loved one, a mourner experiences circumscription and inhibition to anything new if it suggests *moving on*. At such a juncture, mourning acquires an aesthetic conflict—to be moved, or to move on, is to discover an evocative object, at once, vastly capable of fulfilment or capable of drawing the mourner out than the devotion to the idealized lost object while several other opportunities become missed appointments with the self. This aesthetic conflict—a potential asceticism in a supermarket of human bonds—is an important route to understand the meaning of mourning in someone's life. How would we map the length and breaths of someone's interiority hiding in a relational forest? Could resistance or opposition to mourning be a communication rather than an obstacle to recovery? A communication that in love, like in death, we make ghosts. To love, or to mourn, is to occupy two worlds—the inaccessible present and the attainable ghosts. This book is a look inside the mourner's private experiences of the dark night.

Within the discipline of psychology, recovery from trauma is conceptualized as a progressive freedom from the symptom or coping with traumatic circumstance. There is a distinction between natural, 'normal', and 'pathological' and an understanding that individuals may carry the process of mourning to prolonged, debilitating ends. Although such an understanding has its significance, it fails to contextualize the meaning of loss in the life of the mourner or her community. There may also be prejudicial simplicity in understanding conditions in which certain or specific losses take place. In keeping mourning diaries, in translating loss, there may be a tendency in one to close off from feeling in service of survival, or rationality even. The book is an effort to stay close to the mourner's expressions of loss, their remembrances, as they let in a stranger to the place where the shadow of the object falls, where they fail to mourn. Just as in the experience of loss, the object disappears from the mourner's world, no longer available for cathexis. I try to engage with stories of disappearance in Kashmir, chronicled in the years between 2010–2018, to unearth a complex picture of mourning, that is at once private and collective, exceptional as well as sharable, strange or foreign as well as empathizable or imaginable. In trying to understand mourning, I attempt to think of loss as an experience of disappearance. I wish to make sense of loss, but more crudely and clearly, of disappearance as loss.

In a session with a young woman I had been seeing in therapy, we stumbled upon the difficulty of psychic burials. Like my patient, I too felt that there is no convincing, authoritative understanding of when to conclude loss. As mourners we may in fact carry a need to maintain ties with the lost person as if the dead were alive and amongst us. Tara could not give up on her dead mother, I could not give up on Tara. She wished to go to a remote town and kill herself. She suggested that it felt like willingly entering another kind of life, a world or a sphere her mother had chosen. As she said this she added, 'Don't worry. We are on for our Tuesday session.' I read her wish as bridging of the two worlds—the union with the mother and our ritualized twice-a-week meetings—hoping not to give up on either. I wondered if Tara and I could reach a place in our work on mourning where it would be possible for her mother to visit her, like a memory or a faint smell, instead of Tara having to choose the journey to the other world. Perhaps Tara wanted me to carry for her this feeling: that she could die, like her mother, or that her mother could live amongst us as Tara or as her unassimilable pain in the shape of an *internal foreign body* (Laplanche 1999; Taiana 2014). Most importantly, she wished for me to enter this fantasy as a transitional space, a passage where paradoxical relations such as those between the spirit world and the material world, the pastness and futurity are experienced in simultaneity. Like Tara we are required to embark on a different praxis of mourning, a praxis where we return to memory, affect and belief, the undisciplined instruments, without which we have nowhere to go. Could we uncover other routes to mourning, not necessarily pathological but complex and prickly, in their unfolding? Would it be a juncture of reclamation of continuity, in disembodied, incorporeal experiences as authentic?

In *Beyond the Pleasure Principle*, Freud ([1920] 1955) writes of a vast cultural achievement, an instinctual renunciation, by a baby to let the mother go without protesting. On observing a baby whose absent father had gone to 'the front', Freud became aware of two imaginary scenarios taking hold in the baby's mind. First, the baby in question, at the age of one and a half years with only a handful of words in his vocabulary, developed a liking for throwing toys and objects far from him, far enough to make retrieving them back quite difficult. Through sounds intelligible to those around him, he carried out a play where he would throw a wooden reel attached to a piece of string till it was out of sight, expressing a loud, long drawn-out 'o-o-o-o' suggesting the experience of 'gone' or 'fort' in German, a going away of the object. This was followed by him pulling the reel back, leading to its reappearance with a joyful 'da' or 'there'. Freud related this play with baby's method to express and master the separation experienced by him when the mother left. Freud observed that the disappearance of the reel and the expression of 'gone' is repeated several more times than the happy end of separation through the reappearance or the joyful return of the object. Second, the same boy a year later, began throwing toys in anger exclaiming, 'go to the front', or the fronts where the father had been deployed. Instead of regretting the father's absence, he turned his passive fate into an active position, 'All right then, go away! I don't need you. I am sending you away myself', in a manner to avenge the father's going away (Freud [1920] 1955, 10). In the gesture of mastery, the child tried to repeat the frightening experiences, the separation, to represent the strength of impression left by these events. We are therefore invited to imagine the earliest meaning attributed to the experience of disappearance and return as foundational to connectedness with others, and ourselves, that in the going and coming back our first feelings are born. Love, trust, anger, sadness, longing, hate, mistrust, injustice, surprise, emptiness and wholeness—a shrinking expanding universe within and outside our reach negotiated by contiguity or disappearance of the loved object.

Like a sinister magic trick, disappearance or going away of the loved one must first feel like a shocking turn of body into ether—the way a shiny penny is mysteriously transferred to an irretrievable pocket. A fatal experience of injustice. A 'gone' or 'fort' repeated several times over before the object appears in joyful surprise. To yearn for return, to imagine reunion with the lost object is to work for justice. One meaning of the word 'return' is to go back to a place, a place of beginning; yet another meaning of 'return' is to put or give back. Both the meanings are tied to the act of restoring, making whole, and therefore to justice. It is in disappearance we are left poorer, and it is the search of return that holds the fantasy of wholeness. Return is gain earned in the economics of pain. For the mourner, the fantasy of return to wholeness implies holding contradictory ideas in which there is denial of loss, and its finality, as well as a route to recovery from loss. In listening to mourners we hear an appeal to this sense of wholeness, both lived and imagined. To what end is this fantasy used? How does it affect the future of mourning when it at once denies and describes loss?

While I wish to go closer to the inner world of a mourner, the context in which I would study the cavernous experience of loss is that of disappearances—the act or a fact of someone going missing, leaving them untraceable. In recent years, expressions such as 'ghosting someone' or 'being ghosted' have surfaced to communicate the pain associated with the suddenness of withdrawal of ties and all communication without explaining the reason for going away. The disappearance I wish to understand is not voluntary or staged for veritable escape but rather the abduction or imprisonment brought on secretly by those in power on those who had no forewarning. Rather than ghosting someone, it is 'making ghost' (of a person) that pervades the experience. Such is the experience of more than 8,000 persons who have disappeared without a trace in the last three decades of the armed conflict in Kashmir. Families of the missing person live without any clarity or evidence of their death or life. The missing were picked up either from home, from their neighbourhood, their villages and cities, with or without eyewitnesses. The fact of their disappearance, however, is met with silence and widespread denial. The lack of recognition inherent in official denials is an additional trauma for the grieving mourners who go searching for 'the disappeared' everywhere. Their search takes them to jails and detention camps, in far-offcities, to shrines and unmarked graves, from newspaper offices to courts of law in an impressive reach of a complaint systemically unregistered. Like the boy preoccupied with the stretch of the string attached to the wooden reel, trying to master the 'gone' and 'there', the families of the disappeared take on the work of searching, an affective tracing of those rendered ghostly by a malevolent technique, disciplining and punishing, to construct and reorder mourning in a setting of fear and denial.

Following the catastrophic event of 'going missing' and difficulty in establishing their whereabouts, families turn to memories, their ties with the disappeared loved ones as certain even if an intangible route to connection and kinship even after twenty-five years since disappearance, in some cases. There is a festering wound, of stillness, caused by permanent absence. Also significant to notice is the ongoingness of armed conflict which makes translation of collective wounds into mourning nearly impossible (Galatariotou 2008; Mitscherlich and Mitscherlich 1980). I look at these survivors as mourners, whose stories have a bearing on an understanding of personal and collective mourning that is essentially unending. What is the sense of the ordinary for a mourner when home is rendered unfamiliar? How is the everyday in mourning different from the everyday without it? In the context of disappearance, the work of mourning is interjected by the labour of waiting—the surplus pain. In the intermingling of facts with fiction, the mourners are left culpable, or capable, of using mourning as an outcry against indifference, for letting the private bleed into the public in a unique protest bereft of violence.

To engage with pain is therefore to engage with the system of oppression, conjured deliberately so that the complaint meets an addressee outside of itself—a non-melancholic response in a wide field of melancholia. In the book I hope to present an intricate stylization of pain expressed in stories of mourning of families to uncover a cultural elaboration of disappearance at a historical moment defined by militarization as everyday reality. One particular aspect of mourning in the context of disappearance is the relation between forgetting and fidelity. For the mourner, the loosening of ties associated with mourning drives a wedge not only between the disappeared and the mourner in their fantasized relation but also between the ethic of remembering as it links to justice or bearing witness and an egoistical forgetting or moving on. In listening to the inner lives of the mourners we may go close to the wounds undone by the repetitive picking caused by the events in the ordinary.

It is possible to evaluate the course of mourning as successful or unsuccessful, with or without traumatic loss (Blum 2003; Ogden 2009; Volkan 2007). However, making a case for disappearance will require considering a situation of conundrum in that the forcible abduction of 'the missing' was experienced as traumatic for the survivor and that there is an absence of evidence of her/his death, casting a shadow on the survivor's judgement of whether to grieve for a permanent loss or a painful unending absence. From this perspective, to confirm the death of the loved one is to preclude devoted mourning where there is a possibility of union. To consider disappearance a proof of death brings forth deep conflicts for the mourner. Similar to a melancholic response to loss, the families in a prolonged period of mourning attempt to understand 'what' they have lost and not just 'who' they have lost. The questions before us would then appear to be—how do the survivors of the missing persons comprehend loss and absence, mourning and moving on and the historical trauma of their community? Further, what are the possibilities for collective mourning in a community marked by a shared sense of suffering? How does a 'case' unfold the meaning of a historical 'event' in a symptom or crisis (Erikson 1958, 1978)?

In Search of Return is a book about mourning as a metaphor for attachment. It is a hope and a wish to capture the slowly disappearing traces of those who lived amongst us till very recently, had parents, wife and children, belonged to a community, a neighbourhood, and like us, went about their lives with hopes and dreams clutched effortlessly in their fists. It is a book committed to memory work in the present as opposed to the work of memorializing what must now lie safely in the past. In place of illuminating the psychic cost of trauma perpetuated by years of violent conflict, in a manner of stock-taking that is only possible or necessary in the aftermath of great loss, this book is a decision to perch itself on the fence of the 'here and now', on the literary appeal of 'present continuous' and 'remembering-repeating' as the only methodological standpoint to study mourning that is in its essence non-conclusive. It is an attempt to chronicle the unheard sorrow of those relegated to the margins of storytelling—an other whose foreignness is emphasized deliberately or defensively to avoid contact with pain. Like shamans, in commune with the otherworldly, the mourners in the book speak in their voices, of the hauntings revealed to them, through those who have been rendered ghostly. If a ghost must speak to us, we must open another register or a medium, what Freud called 'memory in feeling' (Freud [1914] 1958), the dance between memory and feelings, and one in the other, that would be the object of our curiosity.

In the end, what can we learn from the recourse to mourning in the context of violence? In many images of mourners, especially those from the context of massive trauma and historical violence, mourners are seen as victims of appalling circumstances, destined to reel under the impact of unrecoverable loss. It is my view that nothing could be far from it! Mourners are not passive actors who make an affective empire of loss, as is commonly believed. On the contrary, they are the instruments and negotiators who carry on an awfully tedious and laborious work of mourning without aid from perpetual observers, without an enchanted audience. To tap into this process is important not only to give a respectful burial to pasts, for private or collective memory, but also for the politics and ethics of remembering and reconciling with probable futures.

This book captures my journey as a researcher and psychotherapist who began meeting, interviewing and observing the mourners of the disappeared persons in Kashmir. Unlike the usual office-based psychotherapeutic practice, these interviews and observations took place in the participants' houses, at the office of the Association of the Parents of the Disappeared Persons, at monthly meetings in Partap Bagh; sometimes shopping and procuring necessities of daily living or through visits to abandoned houses, villages or family picnics when pleasure and playfulness broke our entry into relating on difficult matters. In this decade-long engagement, I learned to offer myself as a figure of transference and the challenges of a real relationship. It was already clear to me that I wanted to be led by the unconscious stream as it emerged between the mourners and me in what they associated or struggled to put into words. Having explored the psychoanalytic method as a patient and a therapist myself, in my interactions I used my feelings as an instrument to enter stories of trauma, gauge both our resilience and work with the anxiety announcing itself to reveal dangers and safety required by the mourners and me. Even though the book presents stories selected for the nuances of personal elaboration of mourning, these stories are representative of many families attached with Association of the Parents of the Disappeared Persons I observed. To preserve the anonymity of the participants, the names of persons and places have been changed or concealed.

As an Indian Muslim my work in Kashmir implied a thorough examination of co-feeling, an experience best described in Persian as 'humdard', or a companion in pain, as someone who enters pain 'like my own'. For the sceptics who use the issue of Kashmir as a litmus test of nationalism, my failure to dissociate from its suffering would produce a warm red. This red, however, says little about my position but more significantly and far more openly the nature of acid spilled at the margins of the state or in the marginal where the self, like a sensitive instrument, reacts expeditiously. This co-feeling however is not based on religion but a subject position reflected in the mourner's fate whose loss, for some reason, cannot be admitted into consciousness. As a non-Kashmiri observer, I have tried to stay close to the affective turns in the stories I gathered, lives that were revealed to me, as faithfully as possible. My interactions with the mourners and people in Kashmir were conducted in Urdu. Where my participants spoke Koshur, I relied on translation by my Kashmiri friend Sagera Kazmi, whose sensitivity to conditions of suffering and love for languages, enabled insightful conversations as they occurred or later in our shared solitude affected by what had transpired in the day through our travels to Srinagar, Pulwama, Kupwara districts in Kashmir area of the state of Jammu and Kashmir. As time passed, the economy of paranoia and terror settled in my body and began to transform me subtly. A day came when a tiny bird sat and sang on the window of my room. It was as if it had never happened; that the bird never came, that it did not sing, and that there was nothing in me that could be moved by beauty of any kind. The melancholic refrain of life in the valley, the everyday reality had shut the window and concealed all possible entry. I struggled to observe the daily strokes of unrepresentable violence in dissociative streaks. Ironically, it was the mourners who let in the everyday and showed me a rigorous method to rework the interplay between aliveness and deadness. 'Sooner or later in life', writes Primo Levi (1996), 'everyone discovers that perfect happiness is unrealizable, but there are few who pause to consider the antithesis: that perfect unhappiness is equally unattainable. The obstacles preventing the realization of both these extreme states are of the same nature: they derive from our human condition, which is supposed to everything infinite. Our ever-sufficient knowledge of the future opposes it: and this is called in the one instance, hope, and in the other, uncertainty of the following day' (17).

While committing to stay close to mourning processes, two obvious reluctances began to get uncovered in my questions and intentional participation. In the last three decades of militarization, stories from Kashmir have been replete with horrors of torture and killing, rapes, assault and a staggering breakdown of institutions. This work, however, is not on torture or extra-judicial killing. The mourners in the study allude to images of the body under torture as an active fantasy concerning the disappeared. Such fantasies underscore an atmosphere of terror exposed through militarization and insurgency as it contributes to the unconscious mechanisms of aggressive drive, moving from passivity into activity (Freud [1915b] 1971). Similarly, while I worked with children of the disappeared, with emotional difficulties organized around issues of separation, hunger for the missing father and childhood depression, the present work focuses on adult survivors. Images of the child appear in the stories included as the missing child or the longing of a child for a father, haunting us with the question: what does childhood in Kashmir look like? Such a study, reflecting on the lives of mourning children might help us imagine the contours of generational processes in a more immediate and penetrating way—something I hope to see emerge from the field.

To state it clearly, the book is humble in its scope. While I hope to show how mourning is being carried out in the families of the disappeared, the book offers to say nothing on the subject of how it should be carried out. I hope that the reader will enter with a sense of freedom from contemplations on what is successful mourning, and how best to help the grieving family, even though the seriousness of such a pursuit cannot be denied. What I hope to do is to stay true to portraits of loss, and absence, transmitted by the life and words of the mourners who have shaped their lives through such devotion. My disciplinary lens is psychoanalytic and psycho-social but it is hoped that the reader will be able to enter the difficult subject of loss and mourning beyond semantic hair-splitting. The chapters in the book are organized in the following manner:

Chapter 1 situates the manner in which mourning has been theorized in psychoanalysis, the debates on successes and failures of mourning and the place of trauma and language in appreciating the complexity inherent in mourning.

Chapter 2 attempts to place disappearance in a historical context to suggest its effects on the body politic with special reference to Kashmir. The chapter delineates disappearance as a torture technique, grounded in the history of repressive regimes of power and negotiations with the state as it informs collective action and mourning.

Chapter 3 foregrounds the voices of the mourners as they articulate mourning in the context of disappearance in Kashmir. The chapter situates the stories as trauma narratives reflecting the slow ingestion of loss through the mourning process carried out privately and socially by the mourners of the disappeared. The stories open a window to a carefully crafted language of mourning, which is at once extremely private and porous so that the affect of mourning ceases the elusiveness of loss.

Chapter 4 reflects on the emerging meaning of disappearance in Kashmiri consciousness. The chapter focuses on the work of artists and poet-writers as they relay the problematic of disappearance in the warp and weft of imaginations on life and death. The chapter turns to their articulation as they address the quandary produced by disappearance in the cultural fabric of Kashmir.

Chapter 5 traces the emerging meaning of mourning, its shape and contours, to offer a possible reworking of existing perspectives. Grounded in the expressions of mourning articulated by the mourners of the disappeared, the chapter seeks to reclaim the radical streak in mourning as well as in psychoanalysis that aligns with the experiences of the subjugated. What does mourning do to politics and how can psychoanalysis contribute to imagining collective suffering? The chapter argues for a re-reading of the unconscious as a political unconscious.

Chapter 1

The Work of Mourning

Anya is a patient in psychotherapy, a decision she made seven years after the death of her sister. One day she began the session with a dream. She said, 'I met a woman who in the dream passes off as me. Or to put it another way in waking life, I pass off as her.' The dream begins with she discovering her sister in a school uniform whom she had lost to a life threatening illness. In the dream she is upset that the sister is leading a life unbeknownst to her. She is left confused and befuddled by this strange occurrence. Later, she finds herself in a house, warming up for a party. There, a maid cautiously approaches the host of the party as though bearing a frightening knowledge. Suddenly the dream is filled with dark dread. The dreamer, as if already aware of a foreboding secret, runs to open the door to a bathroom. As she opens the door, she looks to the ceiling to discover a body hanging. Instead she finds nothing. Without a body to hold or recover, she falls to the ground weeping soundlessly. The death in the tiny bathroom could neither be averted nor could it be found.

On waking up, she called upon loved ones the way one counts all the bills in the wallet after one goes missing. Half-relieved, half eaten by the breakdown in the dream, the day stretched endlessly—the anxiety from the dream bleeding slowly into it. The nervous fight against death began to attach itself to thoughts about the safety of a friend who she invited to come stay with her so that she may secretly watch over her, keep her safe from harm—a mourner's lifelong quest, repeated with newer objects. Relieved to have the friend over, post mid-night she found herself sifting, stirring and baking a soft, sticky, puddle of a fudge before falling in the embrace of a dreamless sleep. The warm oven made the chill of the bathroom disappear. A mourner's mysterious transition between strange stirrings and even stranger comforts. It is not uncommon to see the lost object, sometimes the deceased, return to a dream free of illness or looking younger or healthier. It is often a clue to melancholic attachment to the object as it remains 'unburied', and along with it, the conflicts announced by loss itself. Like the sister from the dream who the dreamer accidently finds in a school uniform, the mourner too lives two lives—one in which the reality of loss is recognizable and the other characterized by the anarchy of attachment, its insistent refusal to 'grow up' or 'grow out of it'.

For the mourner, the knowledge of loss remains a difficult object to represent. In the dream, someone else is recruited to bear the discovery. The figure of the maid approaching the host is an important symbolism of psychic figurability and a silent unconscious labour. It is at once chilling like a murder plot and painful like a tragedy. Someone has died, but the body is absent, which keeps the recognition *hanging*. The dream works up a ploy to out a memory of breakdown that has already happened. While the dreamer comes in contact with the dreaded knowledge of loss or an old breakdown, in place of a body as evidence to loss she finds nothing. The body can now only exist through its disappearance, in hauntings. It is accompanied by a soundless cry. Who does the mourner cry for and whose shape has become irrecoverable? What is the meaning of this encounter in the life of a mourner? What ghosts escape us when we escape our pain? If bathrooms are to be birthrooms, what conditions would enable such journeys?

The dream, I propose, is a method. Of opening doors. Of memory-letting in place of what was once called bloodletting. It is a method to formulate the work of mourning that goes on occurring endlessly in our lives. A mourning that carries holographic messages from the unconscious a mourner knows to read and defend against an unspeakable knowledge of the underworld, or the other life in which nothing is more unreal than the loss itself. It is not a coincidence that the fear of falling asleep leads the dreamer to making a dark, chocolate 'fudge'. To fudge is to *conceal*, to *distort* less than adequately in order to *avoid*—a panacea whose aesthetics Freud repeatedly, heroically, brought to light. It is in this context that I turn to psychoanalysis for a view on pain that is neither 'touchy' or solicitous nor purely academic. The chapter hopes to locate, and sometimes bestow, a complex inner life to the mourner through the lens of power, knowledge and experience such that in the psychic life we find a discussion on trauma, subjectivity and subjection as it occurs in the memory and in the social.

MOURNING AND MELANCHOLIA

For Freud, the loss of a person, a country or an ideology exposes one to the knowledge of our vulnerability to forces of attachment. Mourning is a 'grave departure' from normal attitude towards life (Freud [1917] 1971, 243). In some, it may take melancholic roots, in some others, a profound mourning, likes of which may or may not be healed by time. The distinguishing mental features of melancholia include a profoundly mental dejection, the loss of curiosity in the outside world and the loss of the capacity to love. Freud found that in the lowering of self-regard, there also emerges a strange abundance of self-reproaches, self-revilings and a wish for punishment. With the exception of the disturbance of self-regard, all these traits are present in mourning. To the extent that we recognize the experience of loss and the consequent expression of mourning as normal and inevitable, we may escape its pathologization. But there remains a predilection in us to weigh the mourner's preoccupation with loss and pain as 'too much' or taken 'too far'. Unable to decide the economics of pain between mourning and melancholia, Freud suggests a third position, that of profound mourning, where following loss, one finds an exclusive devotion to the lost object as the most necessary expression of the ego's painful frame of reference which 'leaves nothing over for other purposes and interests' (Freud [1917] 1971, 244).

Faced by loss, it appears, we are forced into a confrontation with reality in which the object no longer exists. An intense impulse in the ego works towards the renunciation of libidinal ties with the object. What makes this demand difficult to perform, according to Freud ([1917] 1971), is when there is loss of a more ideal kind. Loss is ideal in two ways: One, the loss constitutes the object in the image of an idealized object for the mourner; second, the loss is not limited to the loss of the object but also of the meaning of loss itself—who is lost and what is lost must exist as two edges separated by indefinite distance, somehow 'withdrawn from the consciousness'.

The mourner carries out refusals and submissions to the quandary created by 'who' and 'what' one has lost. In melancholic solution, the mourner chooses a state of exile or taking refuge from the requirement of making loss real, imaginable and limited. The mourner may turn away from reality and return to ties with the lost object, now alive in the ego as a shadow, a rupture or a presence carved out of itself. Where there was once the object, there now lives the ego. In mourning, the world without the object is left empty, in melancholia, the ego itself is made empty and impoverished. Freud ([1917] 1971) writes:

> an object cathexis proved to have little power of resistance and was brought to an end. But the free libido was not displaced on to another object; it was withdrawn into the ego. There, however, it was not employed in any specific way, but served to establish an identification of the ego with the abandoned object. Thus the shadow of the object fell upon the ego, and the latter could be judged by a special agency, as though it were an object, the forsaken object. In this way

> an object loss is transformed into an ego-loss and the conflict between the critical activity of the ego and the ego as altered by the identification. (249)

In other words, what seems like the ego's refusal to seek psychic nourishment from a new object is in fact ego's own reworkings, doubling as the one nourishing as well as the one being nourished. The narcissistic identification with the loved object, the turn within for nourishment, makes it possible in melancholia to hold on to attachments with the old despite the appeals of reality. At the time of identification, the ego selects the object and incorporates the object through an oral cannibalistic devouring of it. For Freud, taking flight into the ego 'love escapes extinction' (Freud [1917] 1971, 257) or the subject is the effect of 'power in recoil' (Butler 1997, 6). Yet at the same time, the ego must contend to be a 'foresaken object'—divided between the one with special agency and the one altered by object loss and subsequent identification. The split in the ego, an internal Hamlet, must speak the truth (of loss) about itself to itself (Freud [1917] 1971, 249). While the love for the object takes refuge in narcissistic identification, the hate can be seen in self-tormenting, debasement and sadistic satisfaction experienced by the melancholic. This is how the ego, now a convincing ventriloquist, stages the ambivalent attachment in the working of melancholia in a manner that is both a flight as well as an absorption with the scene of the loss.

The process of laying bare of attachment to the object is long-drawn, carrying the potential of future relations. It is also riddled with questions as to what announces a profound mourning and what reveals a melancholic disposition in persons. It is the ground on which psychic killings and burials are sought or repudiated. Each attempt, every failure, is proximation of the nature of loss and human predicament. Volkan (2007) in '*On Death and Ending*' writes ' . . . a mourner, in a sense, keeps hitting his or her head on a wall, a wall that never opens up to allow the dead person or lost thing to come back' (43). He further writes, 'The physical loss of the person or thing does not parallel the mental "burial" of the object representation of the lost person or thing. In fact, the physical loss (or even a threat of a physical loss) turns the adult mourner's attention to the object representation of what was lost.' (44). As a means to repudiate loss, the mourner may return to a time before the loss occurred. It is a bargain made with reality without giving up life. If there existed an excessive ambivalence when the lost object was alive or present, the mourner may fail to make an enriching selection of identification. One may instead assimilate the object representation 'in toto' into their self-representation (Smith 1975).

While in melancholic response, there appears a wish to preserve the lost object within the fabric of the ego, in another manifestation of complications in mourning, a mourner may choose 'perennial mourning' as the specific route to mourn (Volkan 1981). The mourner does not hope for the return of the lost object since he has not given up the psychological ties with the object. He has no need 'to identify wholly with the representation of the dead and his ego state is such that he does not exhibit the self-hatred and self-reproach that one sees in depression' (Volkan 1981, 90). What is revealed instead is a fantasy of an 'immortal object', preserved tightly to remain alive in the mourner (Schafer 1968). It is in Perennial mourning that memory fails to serve as a 'memorial', a psychic image to return to; it is the mourner who surrenders as a memorial (Pollock 1971; Tahka 1984). The mourner keeps the object representation of the lost loved object within his/her self-representation as a specific, unassimilated 'foreign body' called introject.[1]

Volkan's use of the term introject in place of introjection is interesting to imagine housing the other within the mourner (Volkan 1981). By doing so, the mourner escapes traversing in speech an expression of 'adieu'; on the contrary, the mourner reaches in consciousness Other as a meditation on the indissoluble existence of a bond 'beyond anxiety and stronger than death' (Levinas 1990, 48). It is on the one hand illustrative of psychic pain associated with bargains with reality, and on the other, an explication of how the self comes into being. The other within, the introject, is separate from the mourner's own physical and mental self-representation, its uniqueness preserved within the mourner's self. The struggle between the mourner and the introject is similar to the scavenging carried on by a squirrel for an acorn—one indefinitely poor and perpetually seeking while the desired abundantly prone to being lost in the elusive earth—a psychic investment in losing and finding made intolerable in a thick forest of repetitions. The losing and finding or 'killing' and 'bringing back to life' creates a domain of death symbolism, a preoccupation with obituaries, fallen heroes and patterns of anxiety over what Elizabeth Bishop calls the '*art of losing*', 'not too hard to master/ even though it may look (write it) like disaster' (Bishop 1983; Saima Haq, personal communication).

Like the dream described in the beginning of this chapter announcing a difficult mourning stage, such dreams represent what is typical in melancholic preoccupations. Frozen dreams—with content such as still life, slowness, life and death struggles, psychic overwhelm or loss as illusory—become the backcloth of mourning (Volkan 1981, 2007). In such dreams, the mourner sees herself as looking for evidence of loss or finds the lost person looking younger or healthier. Many times the conflict in the dream remains unresolved and uncertain with the mourner sunk in deep terrors, gasping for air on waking. The absorption with mourning is not limited to internalizing tendencies only; sometimes mourners externalize aspects of introjects through concrete inanimate objects, what Volkan calls 'linking objects' or 'linking phenomena' (Volkan 1972). It is at once an image of the mourner frozen in time as well as aspects of the lost object represented in photographs, personal possession, reminders of significant moments or something the person used routinely. They are also what are called 'last minute objects', that is something at hand when a mourner first learned of the death or saw the dead body and which freeze the moment in which the dead person was regarded as alive. Although chosen unconsciously, the mourner enters a relationship of anxiety, loss and control with these objects, the new object world protected and guarded throughout one's life.

SIDESTEPPING LOSS: INTROJECTION OR INCORPORATION

Freud's theory on mourning and melancholia opened doors to understand an exclusive passion in loss, its pathogenesis and outcomes (Freud [1917] 1971). But in it also lies a theory of the self, a stilt on which the psyche is structured. It is the very structure on which relational constellations are cleaved and the inner world is populated. In Freudian metapsychology, the cannibalistic pleasures in the work of introjection and incorporation, or a more nubile function of internalization, are opportunities for psychic expansions. The term 'introjection' was first conceived by the Hungarian psychoanalyst, Sandor Ferenczi (1980) as 'an extension to the external world of the original autoerotic interests, by including its objects in the ego.' He further adds, 'In principle, man can love only himself. If he loves an object he takes it into his ego . . . I used the term 'introjection' for all such growing onto, and all such including of the loved object in, the ego' (316–317). It is significant to note from Ferenczi's assertion that introjection does not have loss at its kernel as much as the motive of extension of the ego, to find an instinctual force within the subject. The work of introjection is to seek growth and not compensation for the loss of a loved object. Abraham and Torok (1994), following Ferenczi's lead, considered that the extension of autoerotic interests and broadening of the ego by including the object in the ego indicates the *possession* of the object, a rebellion if not a mastery, achieved through the mechanism of incorporation. Offering clarification on the subject of incorporation and its precise function, they suggest that *incorporation implies a loss*. For Abraham and Torok, 'loss acts as a prohibition and, whatever form it may take, constitutes an insurmountable obstacle to introjection. The prohibited object is settled in the ego in order to compensate for the lost pleasure and the failed introjections' (1994, 113). Incorporation may operate through psychic representations, affects, or bodily states, or use any of these modes simultaneously. While introjection is a gradual process, incorporation is magical and instantaneous. By instantaneous and magical what is implied is that the incorporation observes the pleasure principle similar to hallucinatory fulfilments. Abraham and Torok add:

> [F]urthermore, the recuperative magic of incorporation cannot reveal its nature. Unless there is an openly manic crisis, there are good reasons for it to remain concealed. Let us not forget that incorporation is born of a prohibition it sidesteps but does not actually transgress. The ultimate aim of incorporation is to recover, in secret and through magic, an object that, for one reason or another, evades its own function: mediating the introjections of desire. Refusing both the object's and reality's verdict, incorporation is an illegal act; it must hide from view along with the desire of introjection it masks, it must hide even from the ego. Secrecy is imperative for survival. While the introjection of desires puts an end to objectal dependency, incorporation of an object creates or reinforces imaginal ties and hence dependency. Installed in place of the lost object, the incorporated object continues to recall the fact that something else was lost: the desires quelled by repression (1994, 114).

Incorporation sidesteps loss for it is able to discover and inhabit another terrain, forbidden and unseeable, to preserve ties with the lost object. The mourning thus becomes a *cryptic mourning* or of the crypt, where reality undergoes a readjustment. While incorporation simulates reality, it tolerates nothing about it. The fantasy of incorporation is first and foremost a demand for psychic transformation via magic. Magic here is the illusory contract with reality held tenuously by the ego to intercept depositing the loss within its fabric. Abraham and Torok (1994, 127) write, 'So in order not to "swallow" a loss, we fantasize swallowing (or having swallowed) that which has been lost, as if it were some kind of thing. Two interrelated procedures constitute the magic of incorporation: *demetaphorization* (taking literally what is meant figuratively) and *objectification* (pretending that the suffering is not an injury to the subject but a loss sustained by the love object).' The swallowing of the lost object, taking in whole, is a constriction on new choices. If discovery of a new relationship, introjection of a new object, was a communion of two empty mouths, incorporation succeeds by creating imaginary nourishment, a delusive 'cure' for hunger. In the fantasy of incorporation there is a refusal to introject loss. This radical denial of loss erects a secret tomb inside the subject, congealing a clandestine pleasure, like a parallel universe complete in its own right. The mourner, a loyal guardian, protects the lost object from devaluation and attacks. While Freud in 'Mourning and Melancholia' ([1917] 1971) established ambivalence as the founding conflict in melancholia, Abraham and Torok (1994) suggest that it is the 'indisclosable character' of love and a love free of ambivalence that show the traumatic reaction to the loss. The use of counter-investments, in the form of hate or disappointments, stem from the place of a difficult or impossible mourning from where the mourner is unable to return. The lost object, a source of an irreplaceable 'pure love' was lost to the unkind forces of death or separation. This is what makes the melancholics cherish and consume the memories of the lost object—the unadulterated, idealized love is rare and specific to the lost object. The crypt is therefore *manna* for mourner's psychic survival. Where there is a crypt, there is no melancholia. Nonetheless, the safety of the crypt remains exposed to the tectonic forces of the ground it lays hidden in.

FATHER, DON'T YOU SEE I AM BURNING? THE ETHICAL IN LOSS

In his magnum opus, *The Interpretation of Dreams,* Freud ([1899] 1994) writes the dream of the burning child, elucidating the theory of the dream processes. Unlike several other dreams discussed in the book, the dream of the burning child is neither the author's own nor the patient who relays it to Freud. Suffice to say, it's a wandering dream, waiting to be re-dreamt. Unable to learn from the original dreamer about the meaning of the dream, we have instead Freud's female patient who heard the dream in a lecture before affecting the analyst with it. The patient curates the dream from what is relayed, suggesting something about the core of 'cure' she seeks—in this way, she is the dreamer who dreams the dream. In these pages, the great analyst is beguiled by the meaning of the dream. He relays the 'model dream' thus:

> A father had been watching beside his child's sick bed for days and nights on end. After the child had died, he went into the next room to lie down, but left the door open so that he could see from his bedroom into the room in which his child's body was laid out, with tall candles standing around it. An old man had been engaged to keep watch over it, and sat beside the body murmuring prayers. After a few hours' sleep, the father had a dream that his child was standing beside his bed, caught him by the arm and whispered to him reproachfully: Father, don't you see I am burning? He woke up, noticed a bright glare of light from the next room, hurried into it and found that the old watchman had dropped off to sleep and that the wrappings and one of the arms of his beloved child had been burned by the lighted candle that had fallen on them. (Freud [1899] 1994, 509).

The dream for Freud is a wish seeking its fulfilment. To the extent a dream may give the dreamer a chance to stay in the hallucinatory fulfilment, the father is able to keep the child alive as well as overlook the painful reality of death. The dead child acts as though alive; *touches* the father's arm and with his *voice* awakens in the father what lies unknown in him—a call for help and a reproach. Freud speculates that 'I am burning' may relate to the fever experienced by the child in the past illness; the wish to be seen may have been derived from an emotional experience between the child and the father. But more than what keeps the father dreaming, there remains a question—what wakes him up? Freud reaches a conundrum—the dream 'raises no problem of interpretation' (Ibid., 510) and yet as he attempts to penetrate mental processes involved in dreaming, he finds a dark end and leaves the dream *untouched* and proceeds to writing the next discussion, 'The forgetting of Dreams' (Ibid., 512).

Wedged between the two moments, one of death and the other of death yet to be borne by the child seen in the dream as he is still alive, the dream exposes a repertoire of images. He who falls asleep, abandoning the child, killing him once again, and the one who responds to the call of the burning child—are the same father as well as two different fathers. In other words, the father can irretrievably succumb before the appearance of the 'burning question', the reproach, 'don't you see . . .' or rise to help. As a leitmotif of enduring love, the burning arm of the child reaches out to the arm of the father in a moment of profound confusion in which grief in one extends into another. The opacity of the reproach resonates in a new location, now to be heard as, 'Father, don't you see I am burning (in you)'. It is at once a melancholic position, of self-reproach, as well as solidarity with the dead child. For Lacan (1977), it is not the light of the fire falling on the dreamer's shut eyes or the sound of candle falling but the *object voice* of the child that wakes the dreamer—an appeal to the Name of the Father. For Barthes, it is the amorous subject's anxiety associated with a loved object which replies scantily or not in one's language—what the mourner needs is a 'total sonority', to go on talking 'in the void', a place where sound fails to circulate (1978, 167). We are led to consider that when the gaze falters, the voice gains significance. Here, the father too is dead until he responds to the voice of the child lost to the fact of mortality. In this transgression, one of an obscene avoidance of reality, lies the only possibility of an ethical survival for the mourner. It is a politics of response; a covenant disclosed by the appeal or reproach of the one in danger of being forgotten, the one who we lose by sleeping. The father's subjectivity derives its authority from his attachment to the child and his awakening from sleep. To the extent that the purpose of the dream is to prolong sleep, to wake up is to resignify the father's subjectivity as the one who bears witness to the trauma of the child in danger. The plea or the reproach, 'Father, don't you see I am burning', is a transferential moment, an ethical imperative on which rests the future of the commemoration of the unseeable, untranslatable loss or trauma, the only way 'burning' becomes real for the body. It is by seeing and acting that the father is able to *put off* fire, *put off* forgetting. To act becomes a mode of remembering and therefore to care. The inextricable attachment, the arm touching the other's arm, between the mourner—or the father who keeps the child alive—and the one lost is bound by an unavoidable ethical posture. We see the taboo of forgetting in the manner in which the dream wanders from the dreamer's dream, the room of the vigil, to the seminar on dream attended by Freud's female patient who renders it immortal by depositing it in the analyst's mind and he in ours. In a sisyphean manner, the dream goes on moving endlessly, or should we say, is produced repetitively beyond reformative gestures of cure through a 'good' interpretation, asking to consider bearing witness as central to mourning or even as indispensable to loss.

TO FAIL SUCCESSFULLY

As the mourner relinquishes her ties with the lost object, the possibility to love again, to 'cling to life' appear as new potentials (Freud [1917] 1971, 246). Freud in *Mourning and Melancholia* ([1917] 1971), and the psychoanalytic understanding since, asserts that mourning involves that we visit, relive our memories and ties with the lost object in order to decathect from the object that exists no longer. It is suggested that the dead be put to death again. To acquire such a position is considered a 'successful mourning' (Freud [1917] 1971). To mourn successfully implies to have been able to endure the painful task of killing the dead bit by bit, so bearing the guilt of this unconscious murder. The cost of murdering the loved object, abandoning it to the fantasy of refuge in the renewal of attachment to a new object can prove fatal for the mourner. What is at stake is to lose oneself to self-reproach, convincing the mourner of inner fault. The psychic purging associated with mourning can be healing to the extent that it leads to the discovery of an enduring connection with the lost object, a proverbial returning to the surface, from the abyss of loss. Establishing the classical psychoanalytic understanding, Volkan situates the expectations from a successful mourning as when the mourner 'cathects and decathects hundreds of memories of his experience with the one who has died. He examines the dead person's images and his own corresponding self-images, and uses these in a process of introjection-projection. Within a year or two, psychic ties to the representation of the deceased are loosened, and the work of mourning comes to a practical end when the mourner no longer has a compulsive need to cling to the representation of the dead person' (1981, 67). Here too, the image of mourning is a self-limiting capability aimed at the future of involvement with the object world. The conceptualization of mourning, in its successes and failures without disregarding clinical implications of such exactitudes, rests primarily on the anxiety about time in loss—the 'what', the 'who' but also for 'how long'. For instance, in Gertrude's quick remarrying, the fuel running Hamlet's fantasy of revenge is at best a personal response to the question of 'how long' before one chooses again. For Hamlet, the very response of Gertrude is an obfuscation of the question, a scotomization of loss and desired mourning. He is unable to tolerate in Gertrude what he is unable to achieve in himself—a chance at moving on (Shakespeare [1603] 2005).

Situating philosophical debates on the notion of mourning, Derrida (2001) considers mourning as fundamentally impossible. For Derrida, the relation with the dead is an on-going commitment, a responsibility to engage with what or who is both within us, only in us and beyond us. Loss implies to hold the other in their absence with loss not hidden in abeyance but in certainty. For Derrida, there is no friendship outside the crucial paradox of fidelity, that a friend will come to survive the death of another friend. Through this bold and tragic proposition, Derrida asks what would fidelity to the dead look like for the one entrusted with the painful reality to speak of loss, to survive it. The mourner's suffering lies not in loss itself, he suggests. It resides in the task of speaking of the other as dead when the other is still alive, inside. The dead or the lost object does not live as himself, like he once was when he was alive but as himself *in* the mourner or rather inside the mourner. Derrida insists that mourning the loss of someone one loves implies noticing that the loved one cannot return, will not return any more than one can be there for the one lost. Unlike the psychoanalytic exertion to *cling* to life and *adopt* new objects, in Derridian mourning such a 'clinging' is not to be on the side of life, an overcoming or an overlooking, a failure to acknowledge an insurmountable loss. Losing someone is to reach out to a 'non-response' or 'the without- response' (Levinas 1991). Responding to Althusser's death in *The Work of Mourning*, Derrida (2001, 115) writes, 'A whole part of my life, a long, rich and intense stretch of my living self has been interrupted today, comes to an end and thus dies with Louis in order to continue to accompany him, as in the past, but this time without return and into the depths of absolute darkness'. In Derridian mourning, the mourner is marked by the singularity of death. The mourner is destined to speak *of* or *about* the lost object, the dead friend, but not *to* or *with* him. It is a time for a tragic repose to notice absence in the space outside of 'me'. The lost object resides in a different space, shrouded in a kernel from where one cannot leave. Derrida (2001) calls this kernel a place 'far away, inside me'. He writes, 'the most vivid desire and the one, within us, has been most cruelly battered, the most forbidden desire from now on would be to speak, still, to Paul, to hear him and to respond to him. Not just within ourselves (we will continue, I will continue, to do that endlessly) but to speak to him and to hear him, himself, speaking to us. That's the impossible, and we can no longer even take the measure of this wound' (72).

For Derrida (2001), the mourner's body, his mind becomes a place, a new address, for the dead to live within us. But in this knowledge there has to be an admission of the loss. The mourner has to be a witness to what he has lost—to know that one would find the lost object whenever one close's ones eyes but never when one opens them. One is a living memorial of the lost person. The mourner prepares one's own self as an abode for the dead to live as long as the mourner is alive—a complete and finite lease of a mortal friend. Agonizingly, the dead lives there but cannot own his home, like all memorials and crypts. There is deep sorrow in knowing that the non-response shall be the only response from the one who is no longer outside, not inside himself either but only inside the mourner—the traumatic 'excessive clarity' (Derrida 2001, 35).

Many cultural practices and social mores such as memorial services, commemorative gatherings, tributes and obituaries perpetuate the assumption that the dead or the departed are absent. Mourning is an evidence of 'the other's' presence inside us. Derrida (2001) privileges incorporation over introjection and finds it truer to the ethics of mourning than desirable solutions that gesticulate at adaptation. Joan Kirkby (2006) observes that for Derrida, as it emerges from his corpus, when the mourner succeeds normally through the process of introjection, that is acquiring new objects, such a loss is structured through the forgetting of the other. The narcissistic relation through which the other becomes part of oneself forfeits the distinctiveness of the other. If the mourning has to be the mourning of the other as such then it can happen through the use of incorporation—a disobedience to the repudiation of the other's uniqueness. In *Memoires for Paul de Man*, Derrida writes, 'Upon the death of the other, we are given to memory, and thus to interiorization, since the other outside us is nothing. And with the dark light of this nothing, we learn that the other resists the closure of our interiorizing memory . . . Death constitutes and makes manifest the limits of a me and an us who are obliged to harbour something that is greater and other than them; something outside of them within them'(1986, 34–35).

Derrida speaks of mourning as work or labour which one has very little authority to speak to or direct. The dissemination of this quiet work of mourning reveals an inexpressible nature of mourning. The work of mourning, if it is conscious at all, is conscious of the force of time that denounces the new in favour of what Derrida calls a 'unique disappearance of the unique' (2001, 34). Mourning is thus interminable. For Derrida, the work of mourning holds the potential to invert our relation with the notion of success or failure. In order to satisfy the mandate of a responsibility towards the one interiorized, mourning commands that we fail and fail well as a response to loss. In this gesture, one finds a concern for and a politics of mourning. If the other must exist inside us, or can hope to exist only inside as an interiorized image, there can only be dysymmetry in our relating to them, which is marked either by traumatizing, fracturing, wounding excess or hospitality for the other's friendship. In both positions, recovery is deceptively hard. In Derrida's suggestion we glimpse a new articulation of mourning in which to forge ties with the corpse, one begins with the *corpus* (Derrida 2001). As loss implores us to relinquish the painful attachments with the other, the other continues to exude life through what Levinas called 'question-prayer'. The mourner, or the work of mourning, is meaningful to the extent one is given over to think and continue relating to the irreducible singularity of the other's ideas, questions—the corpus. Through these questions the dead leave us like 'rich and powerful heirs, that is both provided for and at a loss' (Derrida 2001). In incorporation Derrida finds hope to reimagine a relation with the otherness of the lost object. However, he is wary of a total incorporation where the other lives like a presence completely foreign to the mourner, illegible and indiscriminate. The dead live on through an on-going conversation in which they no longer respond but inspire fantasies of what would be the final word on the question one poses. While there is predictability in the non-response, what the mourner recovers is the unknown devotion to the oeuvre of the other. The longing to hear back, the commitment to the oeuvre, according to Derrida, is a thinking externalizing memory (*gedachtnis*) that gives us over to writing, thoughts and search (Kirkby 2006). Through an extraordinary leap outside psychoanalytic construction of melancholia, memory work or that of the mourning is not sucked in the quick sand of the past. Rather, Derrida illuminates:

> The memory we are considering here is not essentially oriented toward the past, toward a past present deemed to have really and previously existed. Memory stays with traces, in order to 'preserve' them, but traces of a past that has never been present. Traces which . . . always remain, as it were, to come—come from the future, from the to come. Resurrection . . . does not resuscitate a past which has been present; it engages the future. (Derrida 1986, 55)

MOURNING AND THE WORK OF THE NEGATIVE

Mourning has long been considered a structural excess with its affective propensity elevated to a conscious dwelling in lament, guilt and reproaches. On the one hand is the unqualifiable work of the psyche that responds to loss through mourning or melancholia, enjoy overcoming its depths or give itself over to an impossible mourning; and on the other, there is an externalizing tendency to dedicate oneself to memory work or incorporation that yields eternal presence within the mourner. There is, however, another aspect of the treatment of loss that needs mention, that is, altering the unwanted aspects of reality out or its reversal into its opposite, or in another instance, 'turning round upon the subject's own self' (Freud [1915] 1971).

Freud, in the paper, 'Fetishism' ([1927] 1967), differentiates sharply between the repression of affect and the repression of ideas. Speculating on the theory of sexual difference and its role in fetishism, Freud argues and rejects that the boy scotomizes his perception of the woman's lack of a penis as a response to castration anxiety. On the contrary, observes Freud, that the perception persists and 'a very energetic action has been taken to maintain disavowal' ([1927] 1967, 154). Freud makes a distinction between the use of the two terms 'repression' and 'disavowal'. He argues that patients may fail to take cognizance of a piece of reality without developing psychosis when an important 'unwelcomed' aspect of reality is disavowed by the ego (156). For Freud, repression signified defence against the internal instinctual demands whereas disavowal implies defence against the claims of external reality (Freud [1940] 1991; Zepf 2013). The subject defends against the 'unwelcomed' piece of reality by keeping two currents of mental life, as if existing side by side, such as knowing and not-knowing, hope and dread, and so on. The 'mutually incompatible assertions' can continue to co-exist as the aspects of reality are banished from knowledge (Freud [1927] 1967, 157). Speaking of analysis of two men who as boys 'scotomised' the death of their father, Freud observed that in their imagination the father was still alive while on the other hand they regarded themselves as the dead father's successors. It was as though an alternate imagination was rendered permissible to coexist with what was deadly for the ego. A similar occurrence emerges in the famous case of the Wolfman, who barely experienced pain on receiving the news of his beloved sister's suicide. On the contrary, he experienced continued jealousy towards her even though he now became the sole heir to the family's fortune. He spared himself the pain of mourning for his poet sister but he shed 'hot tears' at the grave of a great poet who had been shot in a duel (Freud [1927] 1967).

The reversal of an instinct into its opposite can lead to change from activity to passivity as well as reversal of its content, for instance, the feeling of love into hate or the erasure of pain itself. Similarly, the pain of loss can be turned round upon the subject's own self, showing how the need to punish turns into self-torture and self-punishment. While there exists in the mourner an aggression towards self or others, destruction without aggression is expressed in a radical withdrawal from objects or a tendency to eliminate the self as the seat of agency. The reality of loss is modified or evaded making it possible to ignore the existence of loss. Andre Green (1999) in '*The Work of the Negative*' revisits the complex mechanism of repressions and related defences to modify or evade reality. He suggests, 'It is more important to start with repression . . . and to look for circumstances in which variations of it appear with which it has complex relations (foreclosure, negation, disavowal etc.). It seemed to me that there was a justification for gathering under the denomination of primary defences these mechanisms which, unlike others, all have a common denominator: the Yes or No treatment of psychic activity falling within its jurisdiction' (12).

For Green (1999), the root meaning of negative is the latent, the opposite of the manifest, and also an active opposition to a positive in order to resist or even to make it disappear. When the powerful reality cannot be defeated, one controls the situation by destroying parts of oneself. The second meaning of negative derives from symmetry that is an ideal devoid of any element of struggle. A more complex aspect of negative derives from the third meaning, which is much more difficult to catch. It refers to the state of a thing that, contrary to its appearances, continues to exist even when the senses can no longer perceive it, not only in the external world but also in the internal world or consciousness. The mind, not being able to absorb everything only retains that part which occupies it in the present. However,'that which is no longer in the mind, existing in a state of virtuality (and yet can be made present in the slightest suggestion), and which is absent, can be called negative (by reference to the presence)'(16). The fourth and last sense of negative is that of 'nothing'. Negative in this sense would imply 'having been so and being no longer', and further, 'having never come into existence'(16-17). In another words, negation or the negative poses a judgement of attribution, the defending of the good and the bad, and a judgment of existence which determines what exists and what does not exist.

In melancholia, the mourner knows neither what she has lost nor who she has lost. The attempts made by the ego to cover up loss is a method of negation. The sense of loss, the ego substitution and what the loss represents—all go on to explicate the work of the negative, the destructivity that delinks the meaning of the loss. This destructive work remains unrecognized from the outside. The mourner cannot know what she is suffering or what has caused this suffering. It is thus possible to speak of one's relation with loss not only through the manifest clinging to the lost object but also a state Larkin (2012, 280) explains as 'a deep blue air that shows Nothing, and is nowhere and is endless'. Green calls it, 'relation of non-relating' or 'desire vanishing in the sand so that it is no longer discernible' (1999, 61). Green emphasizes that the work of the negative makes itself known in the mechanism of incorporation by disengaging with the reality of the actual act of 'eating' yet performing for the psyche that which it forfeits. Further, he suggests that idealization or the ideal is the very type of the work of the negative which sets itself up as a mode of satisfaction when the drive is not satisfied. In place of the reactions following the absence of satisfaction, for instance, unpleasure, frustration, rage at impotence, what we see is the denial of it and the unexpected appearance of a sort of contentment, as if the drive had been entirely, fully satisfied in the manner of an ideal perfection, more satisfying than if it was real because of its deliverance from its dependence on the object. By avoiding the imperfection of the object's response and subsequent wounding, the mourner escapes into the hope and fantasy of satisfaction.

The need to identify with the object, suggests Green, is born out of or a result of having lost the breast to begin with. For the infant, experience of *having* the mother's breast and *being* with the breast are the same. The infant is able to distinguish between the two processes through the tolerable encounters and interruptions with the object. The differentiation between *having* and *being* can occur when there is a loss of *having*. The loss of having incites the infant to search for new objects or displaced objects. Identification works to make up for this loss of *having* as 'a souvenir of the time when *having* and *being* were one' (Ibid., 78). Disavowal, on the other hand, cancels out the feeling of the loss of having. The work of the negative transforms the feeling of loss into having lost nothing, or, having the mother is changed into being the mother. The crisis of human subjectivity articulated by Fromm (1976) as the problem of 'to have or to be' brings back under reflection the severing of the experience at the breast turned into a headless run to incorporating senselessly what does not fulfil. It is both a reversal of the experience of loss as well as turning round upon the self.

Having an object, in Winnicottian terms, is an important development in a baby's life. Speaking of transitional experiences and transitional phenomena, Winnicott (1971) underscores the symbolic meaning of the baby's transition from the nipple to the thumb and to later 'possessions' such as blankets and toys that exist as defence against anxiety, especially of the depressive type. Winnicott observes that, 'sometimes there is no transitional object but the mother herself' (Winnicott 1971, 6). A schizoid patient articulates to Winnicott the meaning of not having as, 'All I have got is what I have not got' (Ibid, 32). To Winnicott the negative was a last-ditch defence against the end of everything, the only positive in nothing. In traumatic losses, the mouth may disappear along with the breast or the mother (Winnicott, 1963a). Like Munch's painting (1893), the scream is trapped in the hollowness of the mouth, in the agony of obliteration or in a stealth of motility to put in the mouth a breast or words that gave meaning to the experience of having or being. As a viewer, one is led to the moment of a disappearing mouth–mother, preserved in the last effort of a humanist painter anxiously attempting to capture a scream from vanishing from the canvas as it does from language.

In 'Analysis Terminable and Interminable', Freud ([1937] 1991) too concerned himself with what he came to see as the loss of plasticity for change. He felt that the force resisting change was more pervasive and immutable.

Eigen (1999a) views it as a significant moment in Freudian writing to imagine a work so silent and more than a sense of guilt and need for punishment. For Freud ([1937] 1991), it is traceable back to the original death instinct of living matter. Eigen writes, 'the fact that many people cling to suffering leads him to imagine a darker desire, wish, drive, or instinct: a pull or even a flight toward death' (1999a, xviii). The experience of pain, like any excitation, requires taming—a psychic barrier to protect, shift and modulate the flow of stimulation. Eigen in his works sees this as an on-off double movement so that aliveness can be toned down to maximum-minimum. He likens it to 'psychic deadness', which is similar to the Kleinian idea of the 'destructive force within' (Klein [1928] 2002). Behind the cloak of psychic deadness is an ego attempting to gain mastery over all too-paralyzing anxieties. The ego's manic defences, in a manner of self-hardening, protect against painful realities. In the portrayal of anti-growth or entropy, one recovers insight into the effort that goes into the cocooning of wishes till the mastery of pain can reach a tolerable limit. Perhaps the wish to be a no-thing is the truest caricature of survival, fragments that hold the whole in abeyance but are not permanently lost.

HAUNTINGS AND THE QUESTION OF REPRESENTATION

Freud ([1919] 1955) in 'The Uncanny' observes that children do not distinguish between living and inanimate objects. Dolls, most often, are live people with whom they attach, excitedly believing that they come to life when attended to in particular ways. Freud found it interesting that for children 'the living doll' represented not a fear but an infantile wish. They are 'at home', friendly or accustomed to the dolls while keeping their strangeness concealed or out of sight. The doll that comes to life effaces the distinction between the imaginary and the real, disclosing a magical solution to dwell in two realms without contradiction except when overwhelmed by anxiety. Freud conceived the uncanny as an experience of ambivalence connecting the repressed material with the moment in the present. The uncanny is at 'once dead but suddenly present', an 'archaic' desire for the dead or defunct things to come alive as a symbol takes over the full functions of the thing it symbolizes, and so on' (244). The uncanny for the most part is something not awaited. It carries the mystical, the allegorical but also the obscure and the inaccessible. It takes on a spectre of something 'foreign' indicating little mastery over archaic anxiety and must return each time, as if of its own accord, in a manner of Dickensian the Ghost of the Christmas Past to remember what one forgets. Things that cannot be represented, that do not speak of their presence, that choose to draw us to the history of their disappearance, estrangement and alienation must return, be heard, understood and imagined as alive and breathing.

Moving from the realm of the visible or concrete to the uncanny implies anxiety. To make meaning in such a realm is to ask questions about the nature of the connection between the liminal and the things 'wholly there'. Because the past knows to bleed into the present, its hauntings and apparitions lurking right behind, the uncanny is an infringement on the conscious mind like an accident. The repressed exiled to exist as disappeared or invisibilized knowledge, marginal in its scope, returns awakened. The history of loss and repression, in the psyche just as in the social, reproduces in simultaneity the dangers of remembering as well as the taboo on forgetting. The uncanny is an opportunity to turn one's gaze to receive the estranged knowledge before it fades again. Like Freud who stared in the looking glass and found a strange, 'thoroughly disliked appearance', terrifying to the eye as well as careful in hiding from recognition the appearance of a double, the uncanny carries an energetic denial of the power of death (Ibid, 9). For Freud, the production of the uncanny, the infantile morbid anxiety therein, is concerned with the function or effect of silence, solitude and darkness. The uncanny, or the unrecognized, illuminates the repressed and more significantly the force resisting it, the force of silence, solitude and the dark.

In surfacing through repression or silence, the uncanny exists as a not-yet-remembered sensation. It manifests as haunting in the story or the room. In the social and in the personal. To be amidst haunting is to turn the sleeves up, to make visible–invisible reversible, to begin seeing the real in the abstract and the concrete as pure speculation. To work with the haunting is to see ghosts as carriers of knowledge; to believe in their strategic disclosures. Avery Gordon in 'Ghostly Matters- Haunting and the Sociological Imagination' writes, 'Haunting is a constituent element of modern social life. It is neither premodern superstition nor individual psychosis; it is a generalizable social phenomenon of great import' (2008, 7). Yet at the same time, as has been illustrated by psychoanalysis, the difficulty lies in the language to explicate how or in what manner someone or something is haunted or possessed, what the possessed possess and how does it change our relation with the world as we know it. When in a socio-historical condition, individuals, ideas and things are banished such that they exist as marginal, excluded, repressed, they take on a ghostly form, and the deliberate force through which they were made to disappear makes itself known in the unconscious of the social and the political. Such hauntings come to the fore when the oppressed knowledge is denied or the loss of the oppressed is treated as imaginary. To turn to haunting is to acknowledge its animation and the material effect it produces. Haunting is therefore the denial of the power of death. Like children who believe in dolls coming alive, speaking and taking on a persona, the disappeared live on for the mourners, who know to listen to the disembodied experiences as integral to the weaving of the past where the ghosts were once alive. If haunting is the language of the disavowed, mourning is its last hope. In mourning one enters as a child to find heimlich in unheimlich, the familiar in the unfamiliarity of death admitting our displacement in the order of the world—something known only to ghosts. This displacement from the order is what makes mourners as well as the ghosts valid social categories and mourning and not being mourned valid registers of experience and engagement. What grants them their validity is the excess through which they announce their presence. The difficulty, however, lies in imagining representations that are discursively constructed. In the social sciences, unlike in psychoanalysis, the visible is an agreeable register of inquiry. To dwell in the absent or to put it more accurately, the absent-present, poses methodological conundrums for the positivist scientific project and our cherished modernity. Or perhaps it is the subject of analysis that produces insight into the limits of the methodological imagination. To study death or disappearance, one enters defenceless and blind such that the only way one comprehends reality of loss is by feeling one's way through the dark. In proposing to study haunting and its function, we are led to an epistemic shift to discover the limits of objective causality in favour of a turn to affect. What was true for Freud and continues to haunt and animate therapeutic work even today is the realization that as a method, psychoanalysis may prove to be far less satisfactory in answering all questions about mental experience. In not being able to make sense of the affective terrain—the unpreparedness of our method—we enter unheimlich or the unfamiliar. Put more radically, the psychoanalytic method is primarily a method of becoming unfamiliar. Restating Freud's faithful determination for the uncanny and the repressed, Gordon suggests, 'The willingness to follow ghosts, neither to memorialize nor to slay, but to follow where they lead, in the present, head turned backwards and forwards at the same time. To be haunted in the name of a will to heal is to allow the ghost to help you imagine what was lost that never even existed, really . . . If you let it, the ghost can lead you toward what has been missing, which is sometimes everything' (2008, 57–58). It is haunting that we are after when we imagine screen memories, the work of the negative, transferences or the introjects of the loved objects. It is hauntings that seize our imagination, the way that nightmares seize the one sleeping. The recognition of the confusion between the wish to know and the prohibitions on knowing leads us to a domain of ghosts and the ghostly. The Freudian dictum to say whatever comes to your mind is a suggestion to notice what avoids being heard or seen, the 'thing behind the thing', the gesture or the effect of the unknown.

TRAUMA AS ANTI-METAPHOR

In 'A Tranquil Star', Primo Levi (2007) stumbles upon the difficulty in the describing life of a star. He notices that a star can be 'very big', 'very far', 'hot', and its weight 'enormous' in a sky 'immensely' immeasurable. As soon as one begins to describe stars, language begins to appear poor, inadequate and laughable as though, observes Levi, one is trying 'to plow with a feather'). He suggests that language, born with us and through us, cannot go beyond its constraints. It is as long-lasting as human life and limited to the registers of senses humans are capable of comprehending. The use of adjectives and superlatives are symptomatic of the fault in the comprehensibility of events or experiences that lay outside shareable knowledge. Levi goes further and formulates a radical proposal—to attempt to eliminate or give up describing with seductive detail what one does not know enough to adequately convey. It is by impoverishing the narrative, the bare skeletal appearance of experience in language, that one can hope to transfer, if at all, the meaning of an event. The life of a star, its convulsive struggle against death in a vastly unknown sky, is a metaphor for trauma or a traumatic event, cataclysmic for the one who goes through it to fade into its incommunicado core. One doesn't know *why* certain effects appear or what causes the unrest in the heart of a star but one hopes to understand *how* trauma ceases imagination in the obligatory symbolization that follows (Segal 1957). What if language were not an empty container devoid of meaning but rather meaning surviving the prison of language? The word trauma itself confesses a peculiar difficulty in naming the complete effects of a catastrophic experience on the mind as well as the body. From bodily injuries, shell shock, exposure to violence or to environmental failures, as an open category trauma is used to connote intense unfathomable experiences.

Just as combustions or explosions in the nucleus of a star continue to take place for millions of years, trauma too pounds and rips at the nucleus of the subject, digesting its effects for a long period of time. It works as a force inimical to speech and understanding even though the changes it produces are strangely observable. There is on the one hand the challenge of the comprehensibility of an overwhelming event for the individual and on the other the difficulty of its transferability onto language or in an interpersonal experience (Barthes 2000). The survivor may not remember anything of the traumatic event or the disturbing effect but may act out the disturbed inner state in displaced situations as belated understanding or understumbling. The survivor 'reproduces it not as a memory but as an action; he repeats it, without, of course, knowing that he is repeating it' (Freud [1914] 1958, 150). Freud thought of these acting-out of the disturbed memories far more difficult for they exist de-linked from the past. He wrote, 'One cannot overcome an enemy who is absent or not within range' (152). Such experiences are brought ashore, into consciousness, like tidal waves of a disturbed sea or allowed to hover around invisibly in somatic experiences like a ghost disconnected from the past. The memory work here is generational work, carried on to future generations to re-member the hauntings in lived experiences.

Exposure to massive trauma overwhelms the ego's capacity to bear the excitations caused by the painful event (Eigen 1999a). The violence of the external world turns the internal fantasy into a punishing reality. In other words, the survivor-adult or child has done nothing wrong but is subjected to attacks, making the infantile annihilatory anxieties and fantasies real (Bragin 2003; Boulanger 2007). Like Levi's star, the ego loses its tolerance in relation to its own aggression as though something flares up in the atomic mechanism, splitting it from within to adapt to destructive impulses and the unsafe external environment (Segal 1964; Levi 2007). Bion suggests that one way in which we move through a threatening experience is by establishing a beta screen against it or a state of not-knowing (Grotstein 2009). The traumatic loss breaks the mind into bits. The experience likens to a loss of the ability to blend dots and colours that may reveal a shape. Each dot or a note of the traumatic event is held in seclusion such that the pontillistic texture of experience is lost to dreaming or metaphorization. The experience is therefore literal, dissociated, part-experienced, compartmentalized knowing through which symptoms are born (Bragin 2003). In a painting titled 'Ethel Scull 36 Times' (1963), Andy Warhol created four rows of nine equal columns, producing 36 images of the model-commissioner, Ethel Scull. With each image secluded from the other images, there is a literalness and fixity in each even as the visual field gets one to participate in considering different images enacting specific moods and tones. In the Bionian sense, the images exist delinked and are unchanged by the act of viewing. The repetition of Ethel's face in the painting creates a sense of serial accidents repeated, for instance, in repetitive dreams.

To experience something traumatic implies a radical change in the structure of experience (Caruth 1995). Caruth suggests that the traumatic event cannot be explained through a distortion of reality, repression of unconscious wishes or the communication of anything vaguely self-evident. Trauma creates a literal return of the event such that the individual fails to possess or inhabit it. The traumatic image remains true and fixed in a way that it resists being historicized. The literality or the non-symbolic nature of the event constitutes an experience of not-knowing or coming alive to the experience. To the extent that trauma de-symbolizes the experience, it is anti-metaphor, an active destruction of representation (Abraham and Torok 1994; Fonagy and Target 1999). The plasticity of words and meaning making, whether in speech or in deed, or the very capacity for figurative representation is destroyed (132). Seen in this way, trauma is therefore not so much a symptom of the unconscious as it is a symptom of history. Caruth writes, 'The traumatized, we might say, carry an impossible history within them, or they become themselves the symptom of a history that they cannot entirely possess' (1995, 5). Seen from this lens, the need to change the passive into an active overcoming of terrifying helplessness, a regression into infantile omnipotence in the survivor's guilt is a mad dash to both possess a moment as well as being possessed by it (Freud 1915). What the survivor suffers is 'too much reality' and the rage at not being changed by it (Oliner 1996; Ogden 2005b). The very inaccessibility of the experience, the opaqueness of literality, discloses the paradigmatic place of truth as well as witnessing in psychoanalysis. On the one hand, trauma is experienced belatedly or only as a crisis of survival itself; on the other, trauma implies a failure of 'witnessing'. To speak to the survivor is to 'take in' the literal, as truth and as an act of witnessing, as an invitation to what we don't know or cannot know yet except through entering the belated as immediate, direct and drive-centred experiences (Bragin 2003, 236).

FROM TRAUMA TO SUFFERING: A PLACE FOR COLLECTIVE

In psychoanalytic literature, trauma and its effect are often linked with the ego's capacity to bear the overwhelm caused by the traumatic event. In Winnicott's vocabulary, the traumatic event breaks into the core, the private sanctum of the self, and violates the 'right not to communicate'. What follows is a frightening experience or fantasy of 'being infinitely exploited', of being eaten or swallowed up and 'being found' or exposed against one's wish (Winnicott 1963a). The experience of being undone impinges on the skin ego and threatens the integrity of the psyche-soma. The more popular usage of the term trauma implies shock and overwhelm but glaringly excludes the experience of the self and the other as they are bound up in the moment of traumatization. Massive trauma, such as the one caused by genocide, natural disasters or industrial accidents, breaks down the cultural, psychological and political assumptions or mechanisms that govern everyday lives (Fassin and Rechtman 2009). Imprinting long-lasting psychic vulnerabilities in the person, in trauma the person's developmental challenges, fixations and resilience deficits are radically exposed (Kris 1956; Khan 1963). Undergoing trauma, however, also redraws spheres of intimate knowing and estrangement from those outside such a knowledge. While a scene of trauma might be ripe with the impossibilities of mourning, there also exists a politics of the social, a fantasy of suffering as expressible where there is an acknowledgement of mutual implication in suffering (Husain 2019; Layton 2009; Hollandar 2017).

In her paper, 'Knowing Terrible Things: Engaging Survivors of Extreme Violence in Treatment', Martha Bragin (2007) suggests that the survivors of trauma suffer a never-ending isolation because of their belief that no one can comprehend their experience. The only others who know what they know are the ones who have died, fellow survivors and the perpetrators. The way out is to connect to the survivor's unconscious aggressive fantasy to convey 'that it is possible to hear, understand and contain violent experiences' (Bragin 2007, 229). This is no easy proposition since for the listener, it implies going against closing-off or *psychic shielding* to avoid exposure to extreme violence and pain. The 'not-me' mode of relating while listening to the survivor widens the distance between the survivor and the listener as one imagines that the survivor endured what one could not have (Winnicott 1971). Thus survivors experience an 'othering' making them increasingly isolated. It is in this regard that for a trauma survivor, the need for the collective is linked with the possibility of recognition and inclusion into humanity by fellow survivors.

Reflecting on the structure of experience in traumatic experiencing, Laub and Auerhahn (1993) suggest that a truthful appraisal of events is defended against if such a knowledge brings affect too violent for the ego's capacity to regulate. Feelings of rage, cynicism, shame and fear are relegated to realm of not-knowing. The phenomenological spectrum of remembering trauma ranges from 'not knowing; fugue states (in which events are re-lived in an altered state of consciousness); retention of the experience as compartmentalized, undigested fragments of perceptions that break into consciousness (with no conscious meaning or relation to oneself); transference phenomena (wherein the traumatic legacy is lived out as one's inevitable fate); its partial, hesitant expression as an overpowering narrative; the experience of compelling, identity-defining and pervasive life themes (both conscious and unconscious); its organization as a witnessed narrative; to its use as a metaphor and vehicle for developmental conflict' (289). It is important to keep in mind that the expressions of forms of knowing are played out in the community life surrounding the survivor. In other words, there cannot be a working through of traumatic reliving outside the purview of the community's resilience. The dissociated, unmourned losses and ahistorical wounds experienced in the individual are brought into the folds of community life for it is in these kinship and binding traditions, a shared cosmos, where bizarre aspects of the experience can be storied. To adapt to such overpowering odds, the individual requires an imagined front of fellow survivors against the vitiating effects of the traumatic event. To the extent that the historical fate of the community comes close to personal history, the subject or the survivor finds deep, empathic resonances with others around. This is not to suggest that survivors of shared catastrophe do not experience ego-shattering and psychic numbing or are able to mitigate such effects. On the contrary, despite terrible psychological metamorphosis, the survivors carry a sense of contiguity even if they lose the continuity of rhythm known to them.

Kai Erikson (1995) suggests that a community profoundly affected is a damaged social organism in almost the same way as a body damaged due to traumatization. As the trauma seeps into community life or its social fabric, waves of shock are felt by members. There is a utopic fervour to recreate the communal bond, seen often in the rehabilitation efforts of volunteers, but also efforts to distance oneself from the contaminating affect. It is as if psychic processes of numbing, fugue states, the pervasive conditions of passivity, fatalism and guilt haunt the community in a manner similar to what goes on occurring in the inner world of its members. Estranged from humanity, the survivor's experience may seek connection with each other, even if the knowledge of what it is like to be altered radically in one's core remains untranslatable. Perhaps it is this experience of falling into pieces which also organizes the members politically and energetically. In societies where there have been no massive upheaval, as rare as they are today, rituals, initiations and confirmations bestow strength and pride in the youth or the new generation (Rosaldo 1989). In situations of massive trauma, rituals and symbols may fail to contain the excess of the shattering produced in the group consciousness. Thinking about the usefulness of generational links in identity formation, and in symbolizing trauma of an individual and a group, Erikson writes:

[T]rue identity depends on the support which the young individual receives from the collective sense of identity characterizing the social groups significant to him: his class, his nation, his culture. Where historical and technological developments (*such as militarization*) severely encroach upon deeply rooted or strongly emerging identities on a large scale, the youth feels endangered, individually and collectively, whereupon it becomes ready to support doctrines offering a total immersion in a synthetic identity (extreme nationalism, racism, or class consciousness) and a collective condemnation of a totally stereotyped enemy of the new identity' (1995, 93).

He adds further, 'every deeply upsetting or uprooting experience brings about a partial regression both to the basic hope for recognition and the basic horror of its failure: the dead, the still-born identity' (95). Younger generations depend on older generations to possess and pass on the integrity of their identity. Failure to achieve possession of such integration in the older generation leave the youth disarmed of its rebellion and hopeful assimilation. Erikson reminds us, 'the key problem of identity, is (as the term connotes) the capacity of the ego to sustain sameness and continuity in the face of changing fate' (95). In other words, it is the ego's capacity to maintain essential patterns in the processes of change that determines the identity formation of a person. While a well-established identity is likely to tolerate radical change, a large scale uprooting can challenge the ways to cope through known by the society. Prolonged uprootedness can lead to negative identities, that is, an identification with debased, rejected self-images and social roles. A prolonged passive acceptance of negative identities rearrange the identification in such a way that generations bear the psychic burden of the self-images proposed to them. Such processes can be seen at work when the persons come to be seen as 'terrorists' or when immigrants and refugees are imagined as inferior or pathological (Vahali 2009; O'Loughlin 2013). There is a danger that the self-uprooting perpetuated through projective identification or survivors' guilt may usher in a 'secondary social disease' (Erikson 1995, 98), casting a shadow of uncertainty on the future of collective healing.

NOTE

1. A rendering of introject or introjection, incorporation and identification is of significance here. For Schafer (1968), identification involves all those psychic processes by which a subject transforms the real or imagined environmental interactions into internal regulations and characteristics. Seen from his lens, introjection and identification are two aspects of internalization. Incorporation denotes a fantasy, a specific wishful primary process ideation. Incorporation is the fantasy to acquire or to possess the other in one's own body. Introjection is the process through which this fantasy is executed or given a form.

Chapter 2

The Disappearing Act

Our first encounter with the drama of escape is enacted most skilfully in the game of hide-and-seek. So long as being on the run or flight is necessary to avoid a life we wish to leave behind, it is in escape we learn to formulate what freedom could look like. The play of hide-and-seek is also a play between two muscle memories—the memory of paralysis, of being found, and the memory of what it is to run. When children hide they know that the game will reach its inevitable end. One would either be caught or be victorious in one's invisibility. The adventure of mastering an escape, to be able to go so far and yet not quite, to be pursued and to be realized by a seeker are functions of the anxiety, an imagination, of an irreversible disappearance when the seeker fails. Whether in burying toy cars in the grainy sand, digging anthills with a twig or looking at decaying body of dead cricket in broad daylight, children attempt to bear testimony to the gaps in the imagination to comprehend the meaning of disappearance. In these innocent preoccupations one finds profound questions of one's relationship with persons, loss and reality. Is it natural to hide or is it a wish to defy nature? Is there a place we reach when we escape? Where are we when we are nowhere to be found? Somewhere? What is the relation between nowhere and somewhere? Are they linked spatially or temporally? How does one talk about it if we are never sought or never found? In this losing and finding, the hide-and-seek, we enact, or are acted upon, the dangers of disappearance in adulthood just as in childhood.

Far from a child's curiosity, in the disappearances enforced by a state agency, the fantasy of hiding or escaping meets its irony, of being held as an irretrievable captive, locked or hidden from a seeker's reach and against one's will. It is a traumatic return of the game 'cops and robbers', or as it is known in south Asian childhoods, the game of 'chor-sipahi', rehearsing the plot of authority, obedience and punishment (Adorno 1950; Asch 1956;

Milgram 1965; Shweder 1991, 1999). More than 8,000 persons have disappeared in Kashmir since the upsurge of armed conflict in 1989 (Amnesty International 2018). The involuntary nature of these disappearances, in the context of militarization imposed by the Indian state, signifies a violation of human rights: to be recognized as a person before law, to be protected against torture and be granted legal defence. Under a pervasive military occupation of the region the disappeared persons are hidden from their families or that their disappearances are denied. It is significant that these disappearances occur in a militarized zone where, with surveillance of the citizenry at its core, 'hiding' of any kind is impossible to carry out. Disappearances in Kashmir were part of the larger policy of repression used by the Indian state including other means such as extra-judicial killings, custodial torture, rape, forced labour and crack downs (Human Rights Watch 2012; Amnesty International 2012; International People's Tribunal on Human Rights and Justice in Indian Administered Kashmir and APDP Report 2009, 2012).

A large number of civilians, students, political activists and militants have disappeared in custody, both during direct central rule as well under elected state governments. In June 2003, the Jammu and Kashmir Government announced that 3,931 persons had disappeared in the state since militancy began in 1990, a figure contrasted with that given by the Association of Parents of Disappeared Persons (APDP), which put the number at more than 8,000. Reflecting on the relation between the invisibility of disappearance, Zia (2019) suggests a reversal into hypervisibility of the disappeared persons in the Kashmiri resistance. She notes, 'The institutionalised violence makes disappearance appear as an aberration of dubious origin, rather than a deliberate punishment. Thus, in times of such violent erasures and unspeakable violence, accessing legal avenues is impossible, and the struggle for memory and memorialization is thwarted as well. However, this does not mean forgetting or that no one remembers or does not strive to' (33).

THE BACKCLOTH OF DISAPPEARANCE IN KASHMIR

Historically, Kashmir as a region has been shaped by Hindu-Brahmanic, Buddhist and Sufi-Islamic confluences. As a political territory, Kashmir requires appreciation of a slowly evolving political consciousness and history, marked as much by its rulers as by people's movements and strivings (Malik 2019). One dominant reading of Kashmiri history is situated and read from the perspective of the end of Dogra rule, the birth of independent India and Pakistan and the rise of the Indian nation-state as it established itself on religious and militarized lines. In the 1930s, what began as a class struggle against an exploitative Dogra rule brought Kashmiri subjects to the forefront of political protests and an assertion of their wish for people's governance. This movement paved the way for Kashmir's articulation of the from Dogra rule to the post-independence negotiations in the sub-continent soon after the British withdrawal from India. During this period, the Government of India Act of 1935 gave provisional autonomy to most provinces of British India and some princely states, enabling Indian National Congress to rule Kashmir for three years before the end of the British rule in 1947.

With the emergence of the Muslim League, Kashmiri Muslims had to imagine aligning their political demands with one of the two competing political representations for their collective future—joining the demand for a separate Muslim state or a democratic independent India. As the Mountbatten Plan executed the two-nation theory, the princely states could join either of the two independent countries or remain autonomous. Ignoring massive protests by the people, the then Dogra ruler Maharaja Hari Singh carried out a massive repression to silence the Quit Kashmir Movement demanding the end of autocratic rule in Kashmir. While the Indian Independence Act of 1947 gave the princely states the right to accede to India or Pakistan, for Kashmir this had special meaning. Malik writes,

> 'From the beginning the National Conference stands remained pro-India India, albeit with the condition that a referendum was to be held and directed by the United Nations resolutions of 1948. The Kashmiri political leader, instrumental in uniting Kashmiri's against oppressive Dogra rule, Sheikh Abdullah, from time to time in his speeches, referred to the special conditions under which his state had joined India and considered accession would be final only after a genuine referendum. The Dogra ruler acceded to India for three matters only, external affairs, defence and communication. The accession was finalised by the Dogra King even though there was a considerable level of contestation from within Kashm'ir' (2019, 34).

There appeared a view that the accession to India was forced upon the Dogra King. Nehru, the first Prime Minister of India, intervened and promised a Plebiscite to the Sheikh and the people of Kashmir. This was, however, followed by military assistance to the King and a war between the Indian tribal militia and the Indian Army in October 1948. The war led to the formation of Pakistan-administered Kashmir and the Line of Control dividing Kashmir into two. The United Nations supported the promise of a referendum in Kashmir as mentioned in the Treaty of Accession. Until the expected plebiscite, Sheikh Abdullah was made the prime minister of the interim government while he continually raised questions demanding Kashmiri people's right for self-determination. The Indian administration looked upon such assertions unfavourably. The far-right opposed Article 370 of the Indian

Constitution enshrining special provisions to Jammu and Kashmir State in the Indian Union and saw Sheikh Abdullah as conspiratorial in joining Pakistan on religious lines. His arrest on 9 August 1953 led to huge protests, with several Kashmiris being killed in police action.

The claims on Kashmiri territory saw the war between Pakistan and India in 1965 leading to a redrawing of territories between the two opponents. This was followed by another war in 1971 that led to the Simla Agreement in 1972 to recognize the Line of Control (LOC) that divides Pakistani and Indian held territories of Kashmir. Over the years, with the Indian control of Jammu and Kashmir, there began a massive Indianization of political and social life on the one hand AND the rise of a path to armed struggle to actualize the people's right to self-determination, on the other. In the context of the rise of a *mazhabi tehreek*, in July 1990, the Parliament of India passed the Armed Forces (Special Powers) Act, granting the armed forces special powers in the 'disturbed' areas to maintain sovereignty of the Indian state and establish its order.

The Armed Forces Special Powers Act (Section 4) [AFSPA] confers special power to, 'any commissioned officer, non-commissioned officer or any other person of equivalent rank who may, in a disturbed area . . . if he is of the opinion that it is necessary to do so for the maintenance of public order, after giving such due warning as he may consider necessary, fire upon or otherwise use force even to the causing of death, against any person who is acting in contravention of any law and order for the time being in force in the disturbed area' (Mehrotra 2009, 68).

Under this Act the armed forces can arrest any person without a warrant who has either committed a cognizable offense or is the subject of suspicion. It enables armed personnel to search any place without a warrant or to destroy any place on account suspecting that such a place is being used by miscreant groups. Any person arrested in these circumstances is supposed to be handed over to the nearest police station. No prosecution or other legal proceeding can be instituted against personnel acting in the exercise of powers conferred by the Act (except by previous sanction of the Central government). The AFSPA has led to countless number of extra-judicial killings and 'fake encounters'. While the Act was meant to be deployed for a short term, it continues to be enforced in the territories of Jammu and Kashmir and the North-Eastern states of Manipur and Nagaland. Even though the Indian Constitution retains that the Act when implemented needs to be reviewed at the end of a six month term, its implementation continues unabated.

The enforcement of the AFSPA has unleashed horrific human rights violations that require a concerted effort to imagine the horrors borne by those it affects. The Act contradicts Article 21 of the Indian Constitution that safeguards the right to life or personal liberty 'except according to procedure established by law'. The meaning of the phrase 'procedure established by law' preserves the encoded justification for the violence that the state apparatus makes a strategic use of through its practices of reason and legal interpretation and treats the violence as 'necessary'. It is significant to note that Section 4 of AFSPA is regarded by legal activists as unconstitutional since it equips personnel at any level of the armed forces to exercise the power to kill anyone based on their 'opinion' and 'perception' of suspicion without theevidence or a due process, leaving many defenceless (OHCHR 2018, 5). Mehrotra writes, 'in depriving citizens of the right to life and liberty, AFSPA is comparable to the Nuremberg Laws of 1936, which allowed for extermination of Jews by the Third Reich' (2009, 70). The use of constitutional legitimacy opens the way for killing through 'procedure established by law', producing what Zia calls 'the killable Kashmiri' and a weaponized democracy (Zia 2019). The license to kill derives from the construction of an identifiable enemy whose body is decontextualized to assert the sovereign power. Striped of affective, bodily and ideological grounding, the killable body is also the unmournable body whose violent death or deadly torture is disavowed. The problem posed by the stripping of the human to bare life returns as the biopolitical fantasy to measure, calculate and capture the other, the enemy or the resistance (Puar 2017). Researching on the reign of terror witnesses in the Punjab and Kashmir area, Mahmood writes, 'At one point in the counter-insurgency in Punjab, so many bodies of "disappeared" Sikhs were being dumped in the state water ways that the governor of neighbouring Rajasthan had to issue a complaint that dead bodies from Punjab were clogging up his canal. In Muzaffarabad, on the Pakistani or "free" side of Kashmir, a blackboard by the banks of the Jhelum River keeps count as Kashmiri bodies float down across the border (when I visited in January 1997, the grim chalk tally there was at 476)' (2000, 72). The looming spectre of the clogged canal is an intractable return of the repressed asking to re-examine the meaning of affectless deaths of othered bodies and tactical memory work in the contexts of violence.

Reduced to a land of contradictory destinies, Kashmir is both a symbol of occupation as well as survival. As Kashmiris struggle to steady their feet in a slurry of gross human rights violations and a wide disappearance of what has come to be articulated as 'normalcy', there emerges an urgency to undertake an analysis of the collective trauma experienced by Kashmiris. In the Indian imagination, embedded in Brahmanical nationhood, the Kashmiri struggle for autonomy, through plebiscite or through emancipatory protests whether peaceful or violent, has come to be viewed as the rise of a virulent Islamic nationalism antithetical to a secular India. On the one hand, there is the heavy hand of nationalism and on the other a rebranding of Islamophobia portrayed in the light of a growing danger to the nation-state (Kakar 1995; Varvin 2012; Shukla 2016; Haq and Siddiqui 2019). In the absence of stable state governance in Kashmir, the rule of law is arbitrarily and forcefully applied through massive militarization. Rashid writes:

'The system operates in ways that punish its unruly subjects by reserving the exclusive right about when the rule of law shall be applied and when it shall be suspended. Over the years, the systematic absence of the rule of law has been documented by local and international human rights groups. Thousands of recorded cases of human rights violation testify to the lack of justice. The cases of Kunan and Poshpor mass rape or the Gaew Kadel massacre remain deliberately not investigated, despite years of activism by local and international organizations. Laws such as the Armed Forces Special Powers Act (AFSPA) and the Public Safety Act (PSA) have been imposed to ensure impunity to the Indian Army. Thus, in the Indian political culture, a Kashmiri signifies as the one who is in a basic relationship with the state sovereignty, the one to whom the rule of law does not apply and the one whose independent political action is misguided or is an act of terrorism' (2019, 5).

More recently, as this book goes to press, the news of the abrogation of Article 370 by the Indian government that granted special status to the state of Jammu and Kashmir was followed by the detention and arrests of Kashmiri leaders across parties and a state-wide curfew along with a complete shut-down of internet services, while a heavy presence of armed forces was deployed in what was already the most militarized area in the world. In addition to the abrogation of Article 370, the abolishing of Article 35A that empowered the state legislation to legislate on the privileges of permanent residents of Kashmir with regards to immovable property, settlement and employment, will bring significant impact on the demography, culture and governance of Jammu and Kashmir. The revocation led to the bifurcation of the state, with Jammu and Kashmir and Laddakh becoming two Union Territories in the Indian state, compromising the discussion on Kashmir's status even further.

The articulation of the Indian nation-state along religious lines represented symbolically as the mythical mother of a united Hindu-nation has produced unambiguous effects. In this imagination, a break from the Indian territory implies the severing of the mother's body and her honour, narrowing the possibility of a dialogue on critical issues concerning citizenship, nationhood and dissent. The lack of allegiance to the image of the nation as the mother, produces a compelling array of the construction of 'the insider' or 'the outsider', the patriot or the traitor, ascribed frequently to religious minorities, in particular, Indian Muslims as well as people from Kashmiri and the North-Eastern states of India. Similarly, the demand for Kashmir's sovereignty, its avowal of an Islamic identity are seen as a deep threat to Hindu nationalism and its Islamophobic kernel (Beshara 2019; Mehdi 2019). Inherent in nation-building is the project of a governmentality that supports 'chosen' narratives of collective pasts, trauma and glory (Volkan 2001). In the dominant narrative, framed within a Hindu patriarchal nationalism, civilian uprising and civil disobedience in Kashmir is seen as anti-national and the views of Indian Muslims on Kashmiri freedom have emerged as a litmus test for patriotism, while they exist as an other to the Hindu Indian.

I wish to focus on the use of disappearance as a specific technique to discipline and punish, relocating narratives of dissent into narratives of mourning. To make someone disappear is to hide permanently, to perform stealth of life, of their living history. When a Kashmiri woman, a mother of a missing person, articulates that 'an animal came and took my baby', she compares the role of the state with the hunt of a predator carnivore from whom the hunted is irretrievable. Here, mourning is interlaced with trauma and victimization. In speaking of disappearance, I wish to return to the articulation of loss as it informs the politics of mourning, remembering and witnessing. A prolonged exposure to armed conflict has meant a massive breakdown of public and private life in Kashmir with psychological aftermaths largely unattended and unaddressed. In recent times, there has been engagement with the exiled Kashmiri Pandits (Kaul 2006; Bhutalia 2002), the impact of terrorism (Kashani et al. 2003) as well as attempts to understand the life-historical perspective on the making of 'militants' or violent activists (Sonpar 2007). I return to the problem posed by the disappearance, a blackhole into which lives have been swallowed, to attempt an articulation of the experience in the everyday for those who survive the missing persons in Kashmir (Das 2006c; Ahmed 2012).

THE DISAPPEARED BODY: INVISIBILITY AS TORTURE

With the advent of 'modern' legal systems and the purported 'humanization' of penal processes, torture as a public spectacle began to disappear. With no public executions or inquisitions, punishments are encoded in strict, explicit, unified penal systems. Paradoxically, as Foucault reminds us, torture did not disappear as much as it was relegated to new locations, such as prisons and detention camps, where punishment is carried outside public witnessing. Foucault in *Discipline and Punish* writes, 'Punishment of a less immediately physical kind, a certain discretion in the art of inflicting pain, a combination of more subtle more subdued sufferings, deprived of their visible display, should not all this be treated as a special case, an incidental effect of deeper changes? . . . The body as the major target of penal repression disappeared' (1977, 8). While the overt form of punishment declined through discontinuation of practices such as the pillory and the public exhibition of prisoners, the meaning and the power of the penal system became increasingly illegible, making punishment the most hidden part of the penal process that coiled the 'body' with the 'crime'. Foucault noted this historical shift in the invisibility of the punishments:

> [I]t leaves the domain of more or else everyday perception and enters that of abstract consciousness, its effectiveness is seen not in its visible intensity; it is the certainty of being punished and not the horrifying spectacle of public punishment that must discourage crime; the exemplary mechanisms of punishment changes its mechanism. As a result justice no longer takes public responsibility for the violence that is bound up with its practice . . . It is ugly to be punishable, but there is no glory in punishing (1977, 9).

With the body reduced to an instrument to curtail pleasure, restrict its mobility and suspend rights, the punishment-body relation constituted a new transaction of pain. One way in which punishment grew distinct from previously held notions occurred in that pain no longer constituted the experience of punishment. It is the certainty of total rights on the body of the punished that established the juridical subject. With the removal of the spectacle of the public execution and the alteration in body-pain matrix, the punishment was no longer a singular event constituting the corporeal bodily experience. Foucault (1977) suggests that it is the body's utilities, docilities, forces and submissions that structured order. In the case of disappearance, the body under subjection is not constituted by the physical pain applied to it, as in torture, rather it is controlled by the knowledge of the body, its location and/ or its erasure from the practices of possession. The overall effect is exercised and transmitted through the position of those who are dominated. Foucault adds, 'if penalty in its most severe forms no longer addresses itself to the body, on what does it lay hold? . . . since it is no longer the body, it must be the soul. The expiation that once rained down upon the body must be replaced by a punishment that acts in depth on the heart, the thoughts, the will, the inclinations' (1977, 29). The soul here is not the soul born in sin and subject to punishment, as is in Christian theology, but one born in the historical reality of the methods of punishment, surveillance and constraint. This 'soul' is the affective ground on which concepts such as the psyche, consciousness, subjectivity, personality have been constructed. The soul is the basic unit on which power exercises mastery over the body. It is instrumental in the political subjection of the body. The soul, in other words, 'is the prison of the body' (30).

In disappearance, the body once snatched from communal life is isolated from history without its claims on life and death. Disappearance procures as well as obscures the evidence of the body in pain. While torture as a technique is built on principles such as precise measurement or calculation, comparison and drawing a hierarchical subjection of pain, disappearance, like death-torture, is aimed not at a sudden blow to life but is the art of maintaining life in pain, a culmination of a thousand deaths against a rigid finality. In disappearance, just as Foucault (1977) sees in torture, the confrontation of pain and the production of 'truth' are intimately tied together through the use of the body. As the confessions of the guilty establish the legitimacy of the torture as well as the surveillance by the state apparatus, it further entangles doubt with punishment for the guilt/y. In several instances, the survivors of the disappeared reported that the subject was 'called' for investigation but never returned home. Rather than seeing punishment purely for its repressive effects, it delivers a complex social and political function. Foucault writes, 'One must not seek a qualitative relation between the crime and its punishment, an equivalent of horror. One must take into account not the past offence, but the future disorder. Things must be so arranged that the malefactor can have neither any desire to repeat his offence, nor any possibility of having imitators. Punishment, then, will be an art of effects . . . A crime without a dynasty does not call for punishment' (1977, 93). It is this particular dynamic that sets the mourners of the disappeared as the dynastic recipients of the technique imprinting them with a deep isolation.

Further, the ritual of punishment for it to be sufficient works through signs, a 'semio-technique' (Foucault 1977, 94), with which punishment becomes instrumental in coding the behaviour of the entire social body. Foucault suggests that there are rules that operate through the work of signs. He suggests what he calls, *the rule of sufficient ideality*, that is, if the motive of the crime relates to the advantages expected from it, then the penalty can be made really effective by establishing the disadvantages expected from it. In other words, it is not merely pain but the pain experienced by the idea of 'pain' that motivates its non-repetition. In other words, the idea of the body in pain is more significant than the use of an actual body. The target of the penalty is therefore not just the one who committed the crime, but equally so the ones who have not. The centrifugal intensification of the effects of the penalty, the *rule of lateral effects*, implies that the condemned is the least important element of the disciplining process. The real objective is to leave a lasting impression on those observing directly or indirectly the unfolding of the punishment. On observing the use of disappearances as a technique, one glimpses the total effect that reverberates through the ones who have not disappeared; they are being held hostage as spectators to disappearances and to an unacknowledged grief. How is one to connect to a mind in pain when the body in pain is rendered absent?

Elaine Scarry (1985) in *The Body in Pain: Making and Unmaking of the World* reflects on the inexpressibility of physical pain and the political-perceptual difficulty that together mark subjectivity as well as the material expressibility of pain. She writes, 'The fact that the very word pain has etymological home in 'poena' or 'punishment' reminds us that even the elementary act of naming this most interior of events entails an immediate mental sommersault out of the body into the external social circumstance that can be pictured as having caused the hurt'(16). The experience of pain reveals a sense of being acted upon by the world or by the body itself. To experience pain is to be powerless, to be objectified. Pain may relate to the weapon and the wound in simultaneity. A weapon creates a perceptual fact—through its shape, structure and force, pain can be vivified. A wound on the other hand may create a bodily certainty, even a psychic for that matter; however, it does not wipe away the perceptual uncertainty of whether the weapon introduced pain into the body or released pain to make it visible. The apprehension of pain, like beauty, is fraught with the challenge of comprehending goodness, strength and generosity of the self as disclosed by the wound with the enthralling size, power and sensuality of the object that is the weapon (Meltzer 2008). To have pain, according to Scarry (1985), is to have certainty but to hear of someone in pain is to have doubt. This unsharability, its resistance to language, also implies the destruction of language. The shattering of language, its incomprehensibility as well as piecing it together, rests upon those who may not necessarily be in pain but attempt to speak on behalf of the one in pain. The act of speaking or acting for someone is foundational to the doctor-patient relationship, or, say, in court rooms to decide compensatory gestures; it is how one hosts the perception of objects or art, controversial journalistic photography notwithstanding. What might be the political consequence of isolation and distancing from the pain of the other? What does certainty or doubt about the suffering experienced by the other signify for the observer? The political consequence of pain's inexpressibility reveals that what is inaccessible in language is also unyielding discursively or politically. Pain therefore discloses perceptual confusion, challenges to empathy and collective action. The imaginative congruence to the experience of the one in pain might get thwarted, obliterating pain's *allowed* contagion. The subject of pain is, at its kernel, a subject of the ethical arrived through the crisis of the sufferer's believability.

A manner is which objectification ensued by pain is rendered tolerable, and therefore less dangerous, occurs by substituting pain with power through the language of agency. In torture, the bodily existence of pain is fictionalized into insignia of power. To explode the body of the one tortured to a total disintegration, for instance, has been codified in expressions such as 'to make the man sing like a girl' or 'to say a line or two' (Scarry 1985). The psychic tendency to distinguish pain's aversiveness as 'me' and 'not me' parallels the political denial of its existence.[1] Though indisputably real and immediate to the sufferer, pain is most likely to be unreal to others, in particular, the torturer. The lack of acknowledgement and recognition perpetuates a second form of negation. In this rejection of experience of the sufferer's pain, the reality of pain is now denied in the social. The psychic wish to split off the pain is doubled by the invisibilization of the body in pain. It is this profound ontological split that creates or perpetuates the forms of the expressibility of pain, contributing to the unreality of the injury or the wound and the inequity of the articulation of what is in the realm of denial. If disclaiming pain is essential for the structuring of power—the way power objectifies and denies claims on bodily integrity—claiming pain is to uncover pain's *intended meaning,* that is, to speak from a place of the unmaking of the world, of the ruptures to the psyche-soma.

THE PASSAGE BETWEEN WEAPON AND WOUND

Wounds are evidence of as well the future of an injury experienced on the body. Wounds, whether psychic or socio-historical, exemplify a silent internal work, a *fleshing out* of a story of hurt and healing. A wound may be a site of afterwardness, a carrier of belated understanding, a way for the past to be recognized. A wound sometimes implies a possession or a place of origin that connects the wounded with the other, irreversibly implicated as 'you leave in me a wound I do not want to replace' (Derrida 1987, 25). For the survivors, the work of mourning entails remembering the wound to an afterwardness to be changed by its contact. In the context of violence, a wound may lack the singularity of one act and may in fact occur as perpetual wounding, requiring an interrogation of the connection between the historical and the everyday. It is no coincidence that in disappearance, one finds another unhealed wound in human history. Amnesty International traces the origin of disappearance to the chief of the German high command Field Marshal, William Keitel, who in 1941 initiated the 'Night and Fog Decree' in Germany's western occupied territories, resulting in secret arrest, deportation to Germany and internment in concentration camps of approximately 7000 individuals (Amnesty International 1981). Besides those found guilty of endangering German security, any person, if suspected, could be secretly transported under the cover of the night. Their whereabouts were not disclosed. Imprisonment under secret or disappearances of persons is violative of the International Humanitarian Law[2] and Human Rights. Estimated to be practiced in about thirty countries, such as India, Bosnia, Iraq, Guatemala, Philippines, Nepal, Tibet under the Chinese occupation, Sri Lanka, Chile, El Salvador, Pakistan and Syria to name a few, the psychosocial effects of disappearances beg for a serious engagement (Justice for Peace Foundation 2012). The obscuring of the disappeared person's body, like a shapeshifting curse, elides the family's memory of the event, forcing the disappeared into the confines of the memory or the mind. As the disappearance fails to acquire the scope of an event, for the families, the experience of losing a member to disappearance is the experience of going crazy (Searles 1965).

In Argentina, during the military government of 1976–83, it is estimated that thirty thousand people between the ages of sixteen and thirty-five disappeared without a trace (Argentine National Commission on the Disappeared 1986). The families of the *desaparecidos* experienced a wounding of their psychosocial sphere, particularly due to the widespread denial of the disappearances and the whereabouts of the disappeared by the Argentinian authorities leading to the postponement of grief (Edelman et al. 2003). One crucial deterrent in healing was an atmosphere of terror, working insidiously and permanently to restrict the victim's own interpretations of the experience. Individuals who witnessed the kidnapping and detention of their loved ones experienced denial as a deliberate orchestration of madness. This sense of 'madness' mirrored the dictatorship; the mourning families denied the existence of the *desaparecidos* yet at the same time felt an internal pressure to consider them dead for their own sanity and continuity. Many children witnessed the abduction of their parents first-hand and lived in the absence of any explanation. The children introjected the parental projections of abduction and violent separation. In some cases, children were told that their parents voluntarily abandoned them or were dead as they became the symptomatic carriers of the secret. It wasn't until the knowledge of disappearances became public, the survivors lived in a situation of powerlessness, isolation and fear of psychic disintegration (Cockburn 2001).

The dictatorial regime also sabotaged several social containers (Arinto 1995). The loss of beloved leaders and public figures who symbolized collective ideals and hope emptied the collective imagination. Their faithlessness in social justice and a credible political system led to 'personal experiences of skepticism, alienation, the loss of collective social values and disillusionment with the authorities' (Edelman et al 2003, 145). It was during this period that the Movement of Mothers of Plaza de Mayo began to organize protests demanding information about the disappeared. The group started as a forceful reaction against the dictatorial tide and mass suffering. Reflection groups offered a linking space to weave the personal and the political wounds in a continuity of experience. The Mothers of Plaza de Mayo Psychological Aid Team helped the families to create an expression of the meaning of trauma and bearing witness to the wound.

A similar psychosocial pattern can be traced in the Cypriot context. When in the 1930s Cyprus's anti-colonial ideas merged with European nationalism, the Greek Cypriots demanded the end of the British colonial rule and union with Greece while the Turkish response to this ideology resulted in the counter-position of *taksim*. The nationalist movement took the flavour of an ethnic conflict. In the early 1950s belief in *Enosis* and *Taksim* led to the creation of secret armed organizations (EOK and TMT). The Greek and Turkish governments and the Cypriot Greek and Turkish leaders agreed to the creation of an independent republic whose integrity be respected by them. In 1963–64, there were bloody combats between the Cypriot Greek and the Turks. Cypriot Turks sought refuge in what became enclaves. The memory work that appeared from 1974 began idealizing a unified past as opposed to a confrontational past. Here one sees an entrenchment and a perpetuation of a dual view of Cyprus and its past. Two external factors cultivated memory distortion. One, the government suppressed information and controlled its dissemination to prevent the communities as well as the world audience from knowing. Two, memory distortion was also affected by the pathological splitting and projection that made the self-other relation as that of pure victim and aggressor. Studying the emergent dynamics between the two groups, Vamik Volkan, a Turkish Cypriot psychoanalyst (1979) described the trans-generational transmission of 'chosen traumas' and 'chosen glory' in Cyprus. Similarly, Galatariotou noted that the coflict 'was used to create a new trans-generational transmission that of belief in union—a union perceived rather as a re-union: for each community came to see itself as a vulnerable child who should and would, as a matter of natural justice be restored to its ideal mother who was longing to be united with the child that had been snatched away from her' (2008, 853).

It was especially in the aftermath of the fighting of 1963–64 that individually and collectively people began to experience what Freud called 'the strange state of mind in which one knows and does not know a thing at the same time' (Breuer and Freud [1895] 1955). Galatariotou suggests, 'In the void between the two, psychological black holes appeared—holes down which facts, lives and memories are thrown and disappeared' (2008, 855). One ost–1974 example from the Greek Cypriot community concerns the uncovering of three mass graves in a Greek Orthodox cemetery by an investigative journalist. It contained the remains of forty-five Cypriot and mainland Greek soldiers, killed and buried. They had been listed as missing. A number of Greek Cypriots knew those who had brought the dead bodies that were buried. Yet in all these years, no one had made the knowledge public. It was as though something known had become unknown. The recognition of painful events had begun to disappear from consciousness though they could be recalled if a person's attention was drawn to it, but to do so was psychically dangerous. By 1964, thirty-eight Greek and 208 Turkish Cypriots had disappeared of whom only twenty-one bodies were recovered. The government played down or denied through silence the disappearances especially of Greek Cypriots (Cassia 2001). In the collective mind, the hushed up disappearance of people came to overlap with the eerie psychic disappearance. There are accounts of Turkish Cypriots who could not notice the rotting dead bodies of the Greeks in the village that lay unburied until the smell of decay reached the insides of the houses now occupied by them, after the Greek Cypriots were forced to leave and run away. Many Greeks who did not become refugees but emerged from the war intact with a home, family and job carried guilt when in contact with the refugees. The feelings varied from compassion and pity to embarrassment, relief and guilt for not having become refugees. They identified with them but also feared their prosperity being snatched away from them (Galatariotou 2008; Loizos 1981). The memories of the missing were kept alive to channel fear and fantasies for the future. The missing were made martyrs, keeping them metaphorically alive and culturally-speaking unburied. In this manner, the recovery of the missing became linked with national recovery and memory. The families too, through their ritualized memorization, contributed to keeping the concern about the missing alive and unforgettable (Cassia 2005).

In Bali, the violence of 1965–1966 led to the loss of 80,000 to 100,000 people over a span of less than six months. Despite its wide-scale repercussions, the violence remains unacknowledged. Several Balinese studies on violence tended to echo official Indonesian histories by circumscribing and distancing the massacres as an extraordinary incidence of a forgotten past. In 1965–66, army officer Suharto had attempted to squash an alleged violent coup attempt claimed to have been planned by the Indonesian Communist Party (PKI) on 30 September 1965. Suharto took control of the Indonesia's military and directed its 'defense' against Left before relieving the first president Sukarno of this duties in 1966. The killing of suspected leftists was justified as a strategic response to wipe out a communist threat to national security. The legitimacy of these actions was supported by western nations for the annihilation of PKI (Robinson 1995; Roosa 2006). Until the fall of Suharto, public debates on the events of 1965–66 were banned, and any interpretation was censored. The New Order led by Suharto imagined communism as a dangerous virus whose contagion was deeply feared and required surveillance, search and termination of those who were 'infected' by it. In her study on the politics of silence in Suharto's regime, Dwyer (2009) suggests that violence can be studied through the production and maintenance of silence through which personal and national memories are reflexibly reduced to singular frames. She opines that contexts of violence not only reveal the practices of silence and repression but also commemorative ones that drown the forgotten and the disavowed. Speaking of disappearances in Bali in the context of the violence of 1965, Dwyer presents the case of Ibu Ari, a young woman who was raped by nationalist paramilitaries while her husband and younger brother were taken away, never to return. During such 'inspections', houses were searched for proof the family's allegiance to communist groups. They searched, in particular, for a hammer and a sickle tattoo that was said to have been drawn by women sympathetic to the communist cause on their vaginas, thighs or lower abdomens. Ibu's rape was thus part of the systematic violence used during this time. One family member of Ibu Ari, as quoted by

Dwyer, stated, 'We knew that she couldn't tell us what happened . . . 'How could we speak of it? Death we could speak of; death was different. Even if we were afraid death was something ordinary but 'inspecting' women, who could speak of it? We were afraid of the words themselves' (2009, 122). The effects of Balinese violence permeated the everyday. The word 'communist' became a weapon to turn people in. Similarly, *jatah*, an Indonesian word meaning an allotment of quota used prior to 1965 to refer to the rations of kerosene, rice, sugar, etcdistributed by the government to each member of the house, was resignified with a ghastly meaning of executions to be served by the state on a particular night (2009, 125). *Pariksa,* the Indonesian work for 'inspection'came to represent state authority, performed by an agent of the state who could enter the private space of one's family home, enact its control and inscribe state authority on a woman's body (Das 2006a). In an atmosphere of terror, the social matrix was transformed to include friends and neighbours as potential informers and collaborators.

Yearning to find the missing bodies of her husband and her brother, Ibu took the help of a spirit medium. Ibu and other widows visited the village graveyard, brought earth to shape into effigies of bodies and wrapped them in white cloth. They called out to the spirits of their missing members to come home and inhabit the effigies. They then cremated the effigies secretly, without the customary acknowledgement by the members of the hamlet in the case of a good death known by the society (Das 2006b). But this too didn't satisfy the yearning and incompleteness brought on by the disappearances. It was during this period that Ibu Ari began experiencing a trance state, bringing the missing brother back safely to the family and the community. Speaking with the dead brother created a counter-memory and a process of memorialization embedded in the psychic that challenged a reign of terror and silence. For the community, Ibu's ability to speak to the dead fostered a link with the dead as they confirm their connection to community life, ritual offerings and kinship. Silence carried a complex cultural and political task, including the arrival of the unexpected in the return of the disappeared (Shaw 2006).

In Kashmir, taking stock of the consequences of three decades of militarization requires accounting for the human-nonhuman casualty, disabilities, orphans and half-widows or the wives of the disappeared persons (Kazi 2010). The effects of militarization have been most significantly borne by women and children. From performing traditional roles to being the new labour force in the unskilled sector, they endure slave wages and stifling poverty for their families. The case of half-widows opens new fissures in issues of the inheritance of property or prospects of remarriage. The precarity that affects them has prompted the of women led organizations to fight for justice and freedom. On 18 August 1990, in the early hours of the morning, a neighbour informed Parveena Ahangar, the mother of 16-year-old Javaid Ahangar, that

Javaid had been taken away by the National Security Guard, one of the many paramilitary forces operated by the Indian government. When hours turned to days, Parveena went searching for Javaid in known detention camps, police stations, torture centres to no avail. The incident unleashed an extraordinary struggle on her part to search not only for her child but also the scattered incidences of disappearances in Kashmir. Parveena Ahangar and the families of the disappeared along with Parvez Imroz, a human rights lawyer, came together to form the Association of Parents of Disappeared Persons (APDP).

Beginning their work in the 1990s APDP has emerged as a space to formulate a fight for justice for the disappeared and the rights of Kashmiris to be protected by law. It is also a platform to articulate their collective disavowed experiences under repression. Over the years, APDP has become a place where the private, amorphous experience of disappearance has been congealed into a collective expression of mourning and appeal for reparative justice. On the 10th of every month the women of the families, the APDP members, gather inside Partaap Park located at the heart of the busy Srinagar bazaar. They hold pictures and banners articulating filial loss as political grief. One member of the APDP articulated their demands as, 'Tell us where our fathers, brothers and sons are. Are they dead or alive? If they are dead tell us what happened to them and how?' They capture and critique the relation between knowledge and power in the working of the state (Ali 2011). For the members, APDP as a collective offers a space to create an alternate interpretation of the meaning of the traumatic event of disappearance against the backdrop of denial and mystification. As a collective, it connects the families to experience the unfinished aspects of mourning and the containment of everyday experiences. Most significantly, the collective helps create a differentiation between the silent work of mourning and silencing by the repressive state. For a mourner survivor, connecting with other families softens the resistance and defending against pain to embrace it in transformative ways. While APDP keeps the formulation of the loss politically and socially alive, by associating with the collective the members give longevity to their internal representation of loss, the continuity of one's ties with the missing loved ones and the structures and institutions governing the social.

THE STATE AND THE MARGIN

The 'state of exception' as a paradigm for governance has seen justification in nationalistic discourse in contemporary politics. Used as a reaction to threats against the government, the problem in defining it in a juridical system resides in that the sovereign prevails over other basic laws by suspending the juridical order itself. The use of the state of exception therefore also contributes in establishing the power of the sovereign even as it blurs the boundary between law and lawlessness. Conceived as 'necessary', Agamben notes, 'the state of exception appears as a threshold of indeterminacy between democracy and absolutism' (2003, 3). The state of exception produces the suspension of fundamental and human rights, installs total state authority, changing citizens into subjects of de facto rule. In the Indian context, 'emergency', 'special powers' or 'martial law' are used as wartime measures to curb 'internal disturbances' or dissent. In the Indian context, Prime Minister Indira Gandhi used 'the emergency' between the year 1975–1977 to allegedly defend the Indian state from internal and external threats, curbing civil liberties, including censorship of press and arresting people arbitrarily.

The complexity of the state of exception lies in the problem of defining it. In other words, does it lie inside the juridical order or outside it? In Agamben's (2003) view, it lies in the zone of indifference where the inside and outside blur into each other. He writes, 'the suspension of the norms does not mean its abolition, and the zone of anomie that it establishes is not (or at least claims to be) unrelated to the juridical order' (23). With the use of the theory of necessity as the foundation for the state of exception, there is a return of the old Latin adage 'necessity has no law', leading to interpretations in two opposing ways—'necessity does not recognize any law' and 'necessity creates its own law' thereby changing the meaning of necessity from authority to acquiescence. The threat to the sovereignty and the fear of annulment by the 'disturbances' caused by resistance give the state of exception its legitimacy. Building on from Carl Schmitt (1922), Agamben (2003) argues that this legitimacy is undecidable in fact and law. There exists a form of dissociation between the two to use the incommensurability to introduce an exceptional situation (Geertz 1983). The state of exception is therefore different from anarchy or chaos—there is an order even as it relinquishes juridical order. The juridical order supports and maintains the state of exception through the work of two fundamental elements—norm and decision. In suspending the norm, the state of exception, in Schmitt's words, 'reveals, in absolute purity, a specific juridical formal element: the decision' (Schmitt 1922, quoted in Agamben 2003). Just as in the normal situation, autonomous decisions are reduced to a least possible occurrence, similarly in the exceptional situation, the norm is annulled. For Agamben , the state of exception is best imagined as 'being outside and yet belonging' (2003, 35). He writes, 'only because the sovereign, who decides on the exception, is, in truth, logically defined in his being by the exception, can he too be defined by the oxymoron *ecstasy-belonging*' (Ibid). Agamben compares the situation of political unrest or anomie with the phenomenology of mourning. In death, anomie implies the collapse of roles, customs and structures. Disorder replaces order and nature replaces culture, underscoring a critical moment in the breakdown of the familiar. The public mourning associated with this state of breakdown reveals a terror of anomie. The state of exception functions as a refuge from such chaos. Law, in this sense, carries within it a fear of chaos that it wishes to write over. Agamben views anomie as funereal, a time where the sovereign as living-law meets its end. There appears an interesting dynamic in the zone of transition—the repressed enact their experience of unrest caused by the sovereign's rule by collapsing order, thus reviving the rule of the sovereign through the state of exception. While for Agamben, the state of exception enables the sovereign to procure and establish law thus claiming fresh authority, Foucault on the other hand imagines its spectres in the routinized use of power in the ordinary and the invisible.

The state of exception is also a decision on citizenship vulnerability.

Veena Das and Debra Poole (2004) in *Anthropology in the Margins of the State* situate the state as a sum total of effects experienced in the everyday negotiations of citizens. Using Agamben's figure of the *homo sacer*, Das (2004) examines the implications of the state of exception, especially in the manner that it may expunge persons from their right to belong. She asserts that the sovereign makes its claim not on territories but on the life and death of persons. *Homo sacer* is an embodiment of *bare life*. According to Agamben, bare implies that it can be taken by anyone without any mediation from the law or without condemnation for homicide. Categories such as 'killable', or more recently, a 'refugee' or a 'terrorist', are produced through a complex legal process carried out by the state to declare them as bare life. The homo sacer is someone legally dead but biologically still alive (Zizek 2007). The presence of the state makes itself felt by the various checkpoints running through its body, its territory. Margins are therefore not the peripheries or the extremities of the nervous system (Taussig 1992). Margins are brought into existence wherever the state exerts its arbitrary claims on what it controls and who it controls. Its ubiquity is demonstrated through military and police checkpoints, through documents such as birth certificates, biometric data or the First Information Report. It is a confirmation of the state's distance as well as its penetrative reach into the everyday. Das writes, '. . . I do not see law as a sign of sovereignty of the state or as an institution through which disciplinary regimes are put into place. Rather, I approach the law here as a sign of a distant but overwhelming power brought into the framework of everyday life by the representation and performance of its rules in modes of rumour, gossip, mockery, and mimetic representation and also as a resource for seeking certain rights, although a resource whose use is fraught with uncertainty and danger' (2004, 226).

The state uses devices of writing to institute forms of governance. The illegibility of the state and its presence are also the route to people's active negotiations and claims or rights in which there is absence, reappearance and maintenance of such mechanisms as well as the critiquing and claiming of rights and power through questions of justice. This is how families of the disappeared persons for instance engage with the state, its laws and the legal system and forms of governmentality. It remains a crucial aspect in their collective strivings and personal mourning. The APDP argue and represent their experience of disappearance through participation in legal reasoning, arguing for and speaking in defence of habeas corpus; they provide First Information Reports or eye witness account to the police; they demand from the Indian state that it ratifies the International Convention for the Protection of All Persons from Enforced Disappearances, adopted by the United Nations General Assembly on 20 December 2006, to bring to justice those responsible for the disappearances (The International Convention for the Protection of All Persons from Enforced Disappearance, December 2008). In an assemblage of solidarity and action, the members of APDP not only visibilize the force of the oppressive state mechanisms but also the gaps in the sovereign articulated in exceptions.

MILITARIZATION, VIOLENCE AND MOURNING

In the last hundred years or so, more than a hundred million people have died in wars fought between nations or between the nation and its people (Hinton and O'Neill 2009). This estimate, however, does not include the casualties of repressive regimes (Hobfall 2003). Globally, militarism has radically defined not only the borderland or the 'disturbed' zones, outnumbering civilian population with military or paramilitary forces that rupture everyday life, it dominates discussions and debates on national security, nationalism, citizenship, and more recently, the weaponization of space. The breakdown of social structures, public institutions and communal life for the ones affected in the militarized zones requires an urgent appreciation of the affective as it challenges the epistemological authority of disciplines (Spezzano 2013; Benajamin 1996). On studying hysteria in women, for instance, Freud and Breuer noted that powerful affect can be banished continually to return in forms resistant to meaningful weaving into the experience (Freud and Breuer [1895] 1955). While in the theory of repression, Freud suggested the banishment of dangerous feelings, in political repression, the dangerous excess is normalized by the deliberate use of violence. A symptom, a hysteric affect or a wandering ghost is a breech of the normalizing contract. The overwhelm of violence and related dissociation in the psyche as well as the social disclose a magnetic nucleus in which the repressed or distorted histories reappear. To the extent something has been made to disappear, it can exist as apparitional or as ambivalence (Nandy 2002, 2003). As armed conflicts and violence wipe and decimate private and public spheres causing traumatic breakdowns of personal stories and social processes or institutions, the disappeared—*decapericidos* or *laapatah*—become the new registers of history-keeping or an other object of history. The erased lurks in the empty spaces crafted by the erasure. Militarization, in this manner, *animates* through death-force what is alive and what has been made ghostly. This animation, or thickening of experience from the ephemeral, reinscribes newer meaning to the surface of objects, structures and stories. Gordon (2008) likens it to opening new doors. Through the literary device of short stories titled 'Open Door', she uncovered the uncanny connection between a lunatic asylum and El Banco detention camp in Argentina where a system called open doors was initiated, such that the doors of the cells remained open while the prisoners in the 'dirty war' (1974-83), like mad persons, remained inside chained to the walls (Gordon 2008; Amnesty International 1980). The slippage between the familiar and the strange is an important component of the total effects of political repression on sense-making. In the Kashmiri context, an interrogation centre run by the Border Security Force from the beginning of the armed conflict in 1989 to 1996, was called PAPA 2, evoking the father's authority and consequences for the minor subject, the slippage in meaning demanding a careful consideration of the lawfulness of authority and the protection of order (Jegenathan 2004). Affectively, militarization makes itself legible as a *state of terror*.

Anuradha Chenoy (2002) in *Militarism and Women in South Asia* situates the context of militarization as 'the use of military to solve political problems. It implies the growing dominance of the military over civilian institutions, with a simultaneous decline in democratic institutions and the freedoms and rights of citizens' (5). However, there is and has been a wider ideological valorization of military values, structural militarization and state mechanisms that impact civil society. Militarism, with militarization as its manifest form, normalizes violence. Freud in *Thoughts for the Times on War and Death* wrote, 'the state has forbidden to the individual the practice of wrong-doing, not because it desires to abolish it, but because it desires to monopolize it, like salt and tobacco' ([1915] 1971, 297). He added:

> The state exacts the utmost degree of obedience and sacrifice from its citizen, but at the same time it treats them like children by an excess of secrecy and censorship upon news and expressions of opinion which leaves the spirits of those whose intellect it thus supresses defenceless against every unfavourable turn of events and every sinister rumour. It absolves itself from the guarantees and treaties by which it was bound to other states and confesses shamelessly to its own rapacity and lust for power, which the private individual has then to sanction in the name of patriotism. (279–280)

In Freud's analysis, to be made into a child or to be controlled by secrecy is significant to the experience of being dominated. On the one hand, the state gains its legitimacy from ideology and ideals of national sovereignty, freedom or rights over land; on the other, it does so by curtailing and binding individuals through their docilities or participation in war for idealized purposes. In an armed conflict or war, there is a reciprocal injuring while the goal is to out-injure the other. In this sense, ideology permits the omission of pain by obscuring its location in the human body to invoke the enemy body. The history of war and the use of modern weaponry are replete with illustration of this mechanism. When thirty thousand Russians and thirteen thousand Germans died at Tannenberg during World War I, it was called the 'Day of Harvesting'. Similarly the Japanese suicide planes during World War II were called 'night blossoms'. The suffering of war brutalities is denied permission to be formulated or represented as pain (Scarry 1985, 66). The omission and redescription of the body's vulnerability is central to the project of militarization. The omission and redescription offer the legitimization of militarization, surveillance, police control and the suspension of rights. These mechanisms are thought to be 'necessary', 'inevitable' or 'collateral effects' for 'safeguarding' or 'protecting' innocent people and national honour. Injury and death are not the by-products of militarization. In the economy of terror, they are the desired outcome. Death symbolism, in this manner, is the consequence as well as the instrument of power and anomie.

The ongoing subjection of people to violence and terror indicates militarization to mean a continual *process* that intersects many power axes of differentiation such as time, gender, religion, culture, race and history through which complex subjectivization takes shape (Enloe 2000; Chenoy 2017; Manchanda 2017). In a persistent practice Muslim men, for instance, are portrayed as 'militants' or 'terrorists' while the women are portrayed as subjugated members to justify military action, a burden shared by white males from developed, peaceful nations of the First World. Here, militarism is exonerated through the appropriation of the feminist emancipatory ideal, covertly legitimizing violence, imperialism and sovereign entitlements (Spivak 1999; Bloom 1998). This divide imbues the discourse of war and violence with the notion of hyper-masculinities, pitched against a devalorized feminine (Peterson 2010). Feminist critics illuminate militarism as a social process that depends on patriarchy and capitalism to sustain military values such as masculine pride, the centrality of violence for survival and sacrifice for honour combined with a dispassionate attitude towards suffering. While identities of men are projected as heroes, martyrs and protectors, the presence of women as actors and as activists is underrepresented. Despite gender traditionalism exposing women and children to the grave uncertainties of existence, they work as agents who take on unfamiliar roles (Manchanda 2001). An exploration of individuals and societies under militarization demands a careful consideration of the nature of victimization, identity constructions and the subjective impact of trauma in the context of ongoing military presence. There is a need to address collective mourning towards an understanding of the symbols and institutions that once held collective life together as repositories of generational continuity (Lifton 1993; Herman and Chomsky 1988). The overwhelming reality of catastrophic destruction demands a reworking of claims as victims and actors to address the integrity of the self (Bauman 1995).

Butler (2003) in *Violence, Mourning, Politics* notes that in violence, the body's vulnerability—the evidence of one's humanness—is exposed to the other acting on it. She suggests, 'Mindfulness of this vulnerability can become the basis of claims for non-military political solutions, just as denial of this vulnerability through a fantasy of mastery (an institutionalized fantasy of mastery) can fuel the instruments of war. We cannot, however, will away this vulnerability. We must attend to it, even abide by it, as we begin to think about what politics might be implied by staying with the thought of corporeal vulnerability itself, a situation in which we can be vanquished or lose others' (18). It is in this manner that a shared understanding of corporeal vulnerability as human, even though it is distributed differentially across the world, may act as a connecting dimension for a politics that introjects mourning as fundamental to acknowledging agency, identity and gender.

NOTE

1. A report published by Association of Parents of Disappeared Persons (APDP) and Jammu and Kashmir Coalition of Civil Society (JKCCS) titled, 'Torture- Indian State's Instrument of Control in Indian Administered Jammu and Kashmir' (2019), builds on human rights documentation on torture in a Kashmir.
2. A major part of international humanitarian law is contained in the four Geneva Conventions of 1949. Nearly every State in the world has agreed to be bound by them. The Conventions have been developed and supplemented by two further agreements including, the Additional Protocols of 1977 relating to the protection of victims of armed conflicts.

Chapter 3

Tracing Back, Moving Forward

The present chapter is a passage into the inner world of mourners, the hollow left by the trauma of disappearance and their quest to know in its darkness, the low hanging cobwebs of memory and the affect of the impossible haunting in the everyday. The stories here exemplify the mourners' ability to give in to the work of mourning, to observe their endurance waver and shape the meaning of trauma as they feel, question and demand to fully comprehend the terrain uncovered by disappearance. From the memory of the day of disappearance, the slow percolation of the mourners' strife to wait in the dark and the incomplete piecing of fragments with no signs of the return of the disappeared, the suffering voiced here covers a vast inner landscape. Like other mourners in Kashmir, the ones discussed here have lived with ambiguous loss of the disappearance for more than twenty years. The expression of mourning found herein carries the imprint of time and the particularity of disorganization unleashed by the trauma of disappearance registered in the profound otherness of their identity as mourners as well the living history of the community. Carried over several interactions and interviews during the last ten years, between 2010 and 2018, the narratives included here have been woven together to organize and assimilate significant moments of illumination, of affect and recall, revealing the mourners' relation with the disappeared and the slow reworking of the impact of the experience in their lives. In this endeavour, my primary role was that of a witness willing to be led on an eerie journey, prepared to endure, even if hesitatingly, the opening of doors to pain largely unmourned (Bollas 1987, 2003; Clifford and Marcuse 1986). During these interactions with the mourners, my function was to stay close to their experience and attend to the shifting feelings and memories, to bear the rawness of loss, its reliving and re-experiencing, sometimes in pastness and other times present between the mourner and me in transferences (Kernberg 1976; Laub 1995). My participation in these stories have been similar to the method articulated by Dori Laub, who in his work with the survivors of the Holocaust, underscored the meaning of witnessing in the lives of persons who have undergone unimaginable events, challenging cognitive and affective versatility in the survivors as well as the one bearing witness to the unfolding of such experiences (Laub 1991a, b; Davidson and Layder 1994; Yin 1984). To the extent that the survivor-mourner of the unprecedented trauma has not had a witness, there is no established relation with a 'Thou' to offer a responsive, empathic involvement. The mourner's experience of not having enough words or enough time to make their story known is really a question and a wish to have a witness for their experience. They appear suspended in speech, thought or time with a pastness nearer than the present that they might be closer to both temporally and spatially. The failure to rely on telling takes the form of the embodiment of trauma or a trauma non-verbalized. It is in this manner that as a listener and a witness, I waited and relied on the slow unfolding of mourning in the lives of the survivors, in action just as in speech, to apprehend the directions they might choose to give shape to the hauntings of loss (Winnicott 1953, 1965, 1971; Giovacchini 1989; Green 2005; Maxey 1999). Sitting with them in city parks, the abandoned homes of childhood or at the kitchen hearth, the stories came haltingly as a reaction to my presence, the one who wished to know, and the day's residue, pricking the bough of memories or feelings beyond control or censorship. Similar to Laub's suggestion, I observed that the experience of disappearance can at best be understood as *an event without a witness*. Not only does the event of disappearance reveal a deceptive psychological structure of trauma, with the particularity associated with a loss rendered unreal to comprehend its meaning, the traumatization of the community at large, affecting immediate members and bystanders, posed a challenge to witnessing (Laub 1991a, b). Laub noted the complexity of witnessing thus, 'It was not only the reality of situation and the lack of responsiveness by the bystanders or the world that accounts for the fact that history was taking place with no witness: it was also the very circumstance of being inside the event that made unthinkable the very notion that a witness could exist, that is, someone could sidestep the coercively totalitarian and dehumanizing frame of reference in which the event was taking place, and provide an independent frame of reference through which the event could be observed' (1991b, 81). Laub compared the secrecy and isolation experienced by survivors of the unthinkable event with the predicament of 'the emperor's new clothes', that a witness, possibly a generation after the survivor, questions as 'the innocent child' to bring into the folds of language and therefore experience. As testimonies or stories bring the event to be experienced belatedly, the listener or the witness contributes to the process by offering oneself to be possessed before the event can be repossessed by the survivor.

The armed conflict in Kashmir gurgitates bloody outcome involving the indiscriminate killing of Kashmiri lives, the use of detention and torture, disappearances and a total crackdown on civic life. With the passage of time, the layers of traumatic experiences open and close to incorporate newer wounds in collective memory to remember and work through the cycle of traumatization. One such moment emerged from the experience of the families of the disappeared. When the abduction of the persons began to unfold, the families gathered against the arbitrary arrest of their loved ones. In most cases, the First Information Report to register the abduction was denied by the police. Some began taking out advertisements in the newspaper with a photo of the missing person. In a similar vein, they began visiting detention camps, prisons, courts and residences of administrators or politicians. These chance encounters enabled the families of the missing persons to learn about each other and that the shared trauma that sealed their collective fate revealed a bigger pattern than a few incidences. During this period, Parveena Ahangar—whose sixteen-year-old son Javaid was abducted in the year 1990—learned about other parents through newspaper advertisements and began contacting them. While curfews and heavy militarization divided the geography of the Valley with severe restrictions on mobility in various towns and districts, Parveena Ahangar travelled to remote areas to connect with parents and families torn by the abduction of their children. She began meeting the affected families in the privacy of her house, creating what was going to become the first opportunity of witnessing for their burning grief. These meetings grew bigger, sometimes including 40–50 people at a time, who she fed and looked after. As their voices converged, they organized protests outside the Srinagar High Court to eventually form the Association of the Parents of the Disappeared Persons (APDP) in 1994.

The processes of connecting with the member families associated with APDP, attending to their everyday issues concerning health, ans social and economic vulnerabilities, the inter-generational transmission of trauma and problems of memorialization, creates a context of belongingness and witnessing. There is a compelling push and pull between the survivors and their joint efforts to nourish and relate with one another as they strive to keep the disappeared alive in their pursuits. Spaces like APDP as shown by Volkan (1981, 2007) are shared 'linking spaces', similar to the 'transitional space' (Winnicott 1971), that performs 'linking' functions for the mourners (Bion 1957). With the disappearance of men in the families, there emerged a loss of the 'paternal' in the psychic lives of the mourners. This lack surfaced and expressed itself as challenges to livelihood, education and marriages in the family—the roles traditionally borne by men in several societies such as in Kashmir (Akhtar and Powell 2004). The APDP has been transformative for mourning the lack produced by the missing fathers by generating an emotional response to the reality of families.

As a shared linking space, APDP offers the possibility of recognition and symbolization of the un-represented trauma of disappearance. As Laub and Auerhahn (1993) note, narratability of trauma is essential to 'translate' to those who lack direct experience or contact with the trauma. Through public mourning, the mothers of the disappeared give form to the pain of disappearance by rendering it immediate and alive to the children who never saw their fathers, members of the families who do not weep, and the members of the Kashmiri community who did not witness disappearance but can imaginatively connect to the pain of the mourners. The mourners turn to activism challenges the tyrannical hold of survivor's guilt while enabling possibilities of solidarity with other survivors. The APDP members stand together with several human rights groups such as FIND (Philippines), KONTRAS (Indonesia), and OPFMD (Sri Lanka) against involuntary disappearances, opening a new politics of mourning which is receptive to the expression and rethinking of a humanitarian crisis that ensued from militarism linking the personal and the political in a continuity of experience. The association has also been instrumental in challenging the hegemony of 'negative identity' processes, resisting the narrative that the disappeared were militants by taking on a militant non-violent struggle against the oppressive order (Butler 2001; Erikson 1964). What a well-integrated identity is likely to tolerate in the face of radical change, in situations of large scale uprooting of societies, identity integration is replaced by the fear of survival. In such scenarios, prolonged uprootedness, historical trauma and institutionalization can lead to negative identities, that is, identification with debased, rejected self-images, and social roles now come to define who one is. These individuals may actively resist the negative identities till such time that they begin to accept them. A prolonged passive acceptance of the negative identities rearranges the identification in such a way that generations bear the psychic burden of the self-images flung at them. Erikson (1964, 98) imagines them to be a 'secondary social disease' that adheres to its own validity like unchangeable truths. The families of the disappeared, in this manner, perform a significant function. That is, they actively and continually resist the narrative of a violent militant self as an obfuscation of their experiential truth and right to life. The families of the disappeared argue, 'Let us meet our children. If they have done something wrong, then punish them but don't take away our rights to see them.' The emphasis on the legal process to establish guilt or innocence of the disappeared and the challenging of the arbitrary arrest and detention create an area outside the projected negative identity, persisting for a re-articulation of Kashmiri identity constituted by a violent history and a spirited non-violence.

The stories that follow hope to enable an entry into the worlds of the mourner-survivors of the disappeared as they bear the cipher of loss. Through a primary connectedness with other mourner-survivors, they articulate expressions of loss and longing in their lives; it is in the broken narratives, fantasies and compulsions that we see a full range of suffering and collapse, the unbridgeable privation and yearning for survival, and most significantly, a wish to tell their story, its horror and the authenticity of experience through repetitious reliving.

A HOUSE WITH NO DOORS

I met Rasool Ahmed on a rainy afternoon in Srinagar in 2011. He chose Jaan Bakery on Boulevard Road for our meeting, a landmark known to locals for its delectable baked goods. I stood soaked in anxiety that first meetings produce, comforted liminally by the smell of warm biscuits each time the bakery door opened for a new customer. As the chill in the air percolated down my cotton kurta, I became aware of a peculiar bodily vulnerability—while waiting I was ruminating on padding myself with layers of woollens to protect myself from the cold, unconsciously needing protection against the porosity of the mind in the context of trauma. In the anxious overarousal, unconscious to the terror running underground, I traversed between imagining the unexpected relief of flight to illness, such as a benign cold, and oral gratifications, of warm cookies and cakes, to make the waiting bearable. Beyond the onslaught of visitors to the bakery, Rasool Ahmed approached me with a purposeful stride and a kind face. We hopped in an auto and on we went through the narrow *galis* of downtown towards his house, noticing bustling bazaars and old houses with crumbling walls and broken windows. On entering the house, I was greeted by Rasool Ahmed's wife, Rafeeqa. In place of a familiar hospitality, they offered to show me a plastic carry bag containing innumerable documents; in it, a photograph of a boy described in Urdu as, 'Junaid Ahmed. Age 13 years, Missing since 1993 from District Pulwama'. She tried to tell me that she did not speak Urdu and gestured towards the photograph to say,

'My son Junaid, my son, *laapata*'. Behind her, a rice cooker worked silently under the shadows of hanging artificial flowers, wreathed around a picture frame of their daughters—Shaheen, who died at age sixteen, and the younger daughter, Husaina, who is now twenty-eight. During our interviews, while Rasool Ahmed narrated the story of Junaid's disappearance, Rafeeqa became a barometer of feelings, sniffing, crying or stifling her pain with the edge of her headscarf. Sitting in the one-bedroom house, our conversations took place in the presence of their daughter, Husaina, whose mourning joined and separated from the father's in a manner of a tributary that charts its own course.

In the year 1993, one day as they sat down to eat, Junaid Ahmed was picked up and taken by the BSF for investigation. He was thirteen years old. Rasool Ahmed, Junaid's father, began with the most impossible knot in the memory, 'They said that Junaid would be home after the investigation'. He insisted on the appeal of the reassurance made to him by the security personnel, their believability and the crushing betrayal over and over again. He recalls, 'Before they came to our house, they went to our neighbour's. The neighbour shielded himself by offering to help them find the militant. They came to our house. One of them put his hand on Junaid's shoulder and tried to take him with them. I tried to stop them. I told them he does not know anything. They demanded that he surrender the gun or he would be given to another party and we would not know where he would be taken. They later reassured me that Junaid would come back in a few hours after the interrogation. I ran to the cantonment to follow my son. I saw it with my own eyes. They said, "Ask him to give us the gun". I pleaded, 'He's so young; what does he know about things such as guns?' He didn't come home for five days. At the police station, they wouldn't write an FIR. After five days, I was called to the cantonment. The chief officer offered me tea. I felt pressed to have it. They then told me that Junaid HAD BEEN in their custody till one night he ran away. I fell to the ground when I heard it. I wept and I wept.'

He continued, 'In my house it was like a *maatam* [mourning]. My village, my neighbours came pouring in. We sat and wept. How could he run away? He was a small little child. He was in seventh grade. My daughter died of grief. My home has been devastated—it cannot be rebuilt.'

I asked Rasool Ahmed whether the officer's story felt like a lie. He said, 'It's a total lie. Everything is a lie. Where would he run to? He was so young. In custody, there is so much security. How could he run? Eight months later, Junaid sent a message through a repair man working on the windowpanes where he was kept. He wrote"I am here in the cantonment, near a college. I am alive. You might have been told that I am dead. Come and meet m"e". When we went there, the BSF personnel asked, Who told you that he's here? He's not here". I tried to convince the messenger to be a witness in the State Human Rights Commission case. But he was terrified and refused to help. He feared he would die or something could happen to his family.'

He recalled, 'We fought a case at SHRC. After four years I had to hear from the judge, "*Kyu nai bhaag sakta. Paer nahi hai, taange nahi hai*?" [Why could he not run? Did he not have feet, did he not have legs to run?]. The court concluded with the story decided by the armymen. The case got dismissed. I did not have money to fight the court case. I left the case where it was. I left it to God. Sometimes I shout and say, 'If he is guilty of something, keep him and punish him. We are okay with it. Just let us visit him where he is'.

Over the course of our conversations, I began sensing two contradictory functions of the memory of the court hearing in Rasool Ahmed's experience. On the one hand, it articulated the dehumanization caused by and deceit in the official denial of the traumatic event that he experienced through the judicial process; on the other, the image of Junaid's escape proliferated a secret world of fantasies in which he was no longer a tortured captive. Which fantasy won the succour of certitude in his mind depended on his internal states. While the judge's humiliating retort revealed a duplicitous fate of Junaid's absence, it also installed his escape as the image of survival posturing for a possibility of return.

'Each day is like *qayamat* [Apocalypse]. They say that all things are moving towards apocalypse. But Apocalypse is right here. Don't you feel *this* is qayamat? They have tortured us so much. There is no limit to *zulm* [cruelty] and now it has exceeded its own limits. When this happened I was 35 years old. I am 60 years old now. When I was much younger, I wanted to pick up a gun and kill them . . . Such injustices . . . It is a shameful situation for the government', he said. For Rasool Ahmed, the mental pain of disappearance was experienced as a catastrophic breakdown. Through the allegorical use of 'qayamat', the Quranic symbolization of Apocalypse, he attempts to give voice to the plunge into darkness, permanently collapsing the realm of familiar. In the apocalyptic imageries in the Quran, such as the dropping of the sun and the moon from the sky, the horrific lightness of mountains flying like cotton or the turning of rivers into cascades of fire, there is an invocation to understand the breakdown as the unimaginable. For Rasool Ahmed, the trauma of disappearance is the loss of a stable orbit or a secure course that governs order and seamlessness of the everyday. *Qayamat* is a metaphor for infinite and absolute devastation, not earthly but other worldly. The use of the Arabic word 'zulm' signifies the particularity of the pain and its origin. To do 'zulm' is to subject someone to cruelty or oppression, to deprive them of their rights or to deny them what is owed to them. 'Zulm' is what differentiates the realm of God from the realm of the human; in the Islamic context, cruelty and injustices are attributed to humans while justice belongs to the divine. To exist in the realm of 'zulm', to be constituted by it, is to be in the dominion of the human, bereft of divine presence; to be struck by 'zulm' is to be made less than human by a human. In Rasool Ahmed's reflection, to diminish the humanity of the other is to effectuate shame in oneself for violating another human, a reparative movement lost in the political sphere, exposing the ones exposed to oppression to further traumatization with shame. After reading through the documents one more time in my presence—with the FIR making-way for court papers, a few more photographs, medical prescriptions—Rasool Ahmed added, 'We have records that the BSF has taken him as a captive. The village gives *shahadat* [testimony] to it. If he is a militant then take him away and punish him.' A stream of tears appeared in the silence that followed.

While Junaid's disappearance is refuted and denied in the official narrative, the community becomes the site of the witnessing of trauma and suffering. To give 'shahadat' is to bear witness or to give testimony to communicate not only the truth but also one's presence such that one's presence counts or matters. The emphasis on witnessing by the community offered an empathic mirroring in the cleft formed by the judicial hearings. 'Shahadat' then operates not through individual truth-claims but the assertion of a collective imagination, a new polity, striving for ideological breakthrough (Erikson 1958). To register the stream of tears in Rasool Ahmed is to bear his testimony; it is to see, transferentially, in a drop of a tear a village of mourners, the organizing principle protecting him from an irreversible fall into madness after the catastrophic breakdown.

Over several interviews as our conversation deepened, we went closer to speaking about Rasool Ahmed's fantasies about Junaid. He painfully returned to the failed attempt at searching for him, the death of the older daughter who passed away two years after Junaid's disappearance, and his inability to sustain work. As he passes through the passage of mourning stretched over three decades, what of Junaid's body? On one such day, I reflected back to Rasool Ahmed, 'More than twenty years have elapsed . . .' He replied, 'Yes, twenty years have gone by. In 1993 they took him. He must be thirty . . . thirty four or thirty five years old now. Who knows where he has been kept. There are many prisons in India. BSF can make him mentally impaired too so that their secrets do not reach their homes . . . These people use things to torture your mind.' Such associations indicated that it was possible to speak of Junaid's body ritualistically as absent from speech and frozen in silence. Rasool Ahmed imagined him as thirty-five-year-old man, the same age as him when Junaid disappeared. It had to be a strange reckoning for the mourning father, something he would not disclose to his family. He imagined Junaid living a secret life, far from home, sometimes in torture and at other times, in benign captivity. The two images resonated with his own state as well. In the context of militarization, his mind is both at risk of dangerous exposure as well as freedom from the images of the body under torture through an active disavowal seeking to cure the mind of oppressive reality. Junaid exists in a state of virtuality, an absence that can be called into presence (Green 1999). To imagine Junaid was to contend with his corporeal vulnerability. To not imagine Junaid was emptying and nullifying of one's own attachment in its dailiness.

One day, as he associated to the stories of prisons and torture, Rasool Ahmed began crying softly. I sensed the pain of imagining torture meted out to an adolescent boy's body and how that thought can vanquish any hope that he may have survived or be alive. I felt sobered by the moment and asked him tenderly, 'Do you think he has a moustache like yours?' and he burst into a spasmodic laughter, unsure and shy but delighted on hearing my odd question. He added, 'Perhaps. Perhaps a grown beard too!'. How does one understand the leaps in Rasool Ahmed's fantasy? From a place of disappearance, or non-representation, to a secret world of presence, of magical recovery? Perhaps the other lives within, embalmed and protected, ready to reveal oneself through the failures of mourning. Thomas Aquinas in Summa Theologica (Supplement to Part 3.80.5) writes, 'For the hair, it seems, is less concerned in the resurrection than other parts of the body'. Hair is less concerned about dying or returning to a new life but with continuing regardless. To a grieving mourner, it is a truer friend than flesh. In Rasool Ahmed's fantasy, hair on Junaid's grown body reveals an insistence to stay in the realm of betweenity, in an area of faith where the other is not lost but lives on in the work of impossible mourning. What routes to mourning can be envisaged when returning to the ego is the only way that 'love escapes extinction' (Freud [1917] 1971, 257)?

During this phase of our work, Rasool Ahmed was able to actively speak about Junaid. He found himself gripped by the suggestion of Junaid developing into a grown man. He said, 'I often think, how will I recognize him?' I asked him instead, 'Do you think he will recognize you?' He felt emboldened and added, 'Yes, I think no matter what, he will recognize us'. In his mourning, Rasool Ahmed wishes to see his son but more significantly he desires to be seen by him, to be recognized for the enduring mourning and sacrifices. He remembers Junaid as brave and clever, someone who would be able to talk to and offer tea to the military men during crackdowns. He replied, 'Can you imagine that? A boy so brave! If he is alive, he must be well amongst those army people in the jail. Nothing wrong could happen to him there. But if he's elsewhere . . .' In Rasool Ahmed's memory, Junaid is preserved as a brave, undeterred boy whose sharpness and friendliness offer itself as material for idealization to the father. His ability to befriend the terrorizing figure of the armed personnel and his ability to survive in a hostile environment are imagined as armour, his shield against the unknown danger (Fazili 2016).

Rasool Ahmed's longing for the missing son finds a route in the dream world. In these dreams, rare as they may be, Rasool Ahmed carries out the conflict of losing and finding, staging and repeating the traumatic devastation of losing Junaid over and over again. He shared, 'He comes in my dreams. In one dream he told me, "I am kept by these people here, come and see me. I am alive". One dream I clearly remember, he came with the army. Then he moved away from them. I asked him, "Junaid, where were you?" He said, Stay quiet, stay very quiet. I will tell you everything. First I need to give you the number of the place where I am kept". I began noting the number anxiously, and before I could write it down, I woke up suddenly in a panic. On waking up, I couldn't recall the number. I could not believe it. I wept for long hours. I have not had any dreams of him since that time. My wife also sees such dreams. Junaid comes and says, "I am alive. I am kept here. I am in trouble." She sees that her son is in her lap or sleeping in his bed. Sometimes he is in the house or has gone to school . . . A child's early life is spent with his mother. Even the *peer-fakirs* [saints-elders] we go to tell us that he is alive but in grave danger. Who knows where he is—a jail or deserted somewhere. There are a lot of jails in this country'.

These dreams offer a link for the mourning family with the trauma of disappearance. These dreams are markers of the underground mourning, its unchanging quality and the wishful mastery of annihilatory anxieties. It is through these dreams that we glimpse the psychic work under way, sometimes frozen at the army quarters, Junaid planning an escape or asking for help; at other times, a fervid longing for his presence in the dailiness of maternal care. In these anxiety dreams, a rescue driven by survivor's guilt, Rasool Ahmed is awakened by overarousal. On not being able to remember the place of captivity or his secret phone number, Rasool Ahmed experiences himself as a helpless, abandoning figure unable to protect his baby. There also exists a diminutive actualization of the wish to be reunited, even if momentarily, despite repeated failures. The imprints of life and death struggle, stuck to the precipice of rescuing Junaid, leaves the situation unresolved (Volkan 1981, 2007; Britton 1998). In it lies not only the internal conflict of one's own survival while the loved one perishes, but also a conflict about forgetting, its perilous strength and its crushing victory. Dori Laub and Nanette Auerhahn suggest that knowing traumatic experiences reveals that 'the individual is stuck with images and affect with which he cannot cope. He may stop such images in their tracks when pursuing his daily life so that they do not interfere. At night, however, in his sleep, they assume a life of their own, appearing in regularly recurring nightmares, which are not only remembered in vivid detail, but affectively colour the day that follows' (1993, 295). In their work with Holocaust survivors, they encountered fantasies of last moments with those from whom they were separated. These thoughts and fantasies obscured and forcibly obliterated the present. The shift to the use of present tense when narrating these memories belies such a mechanism.

A few years after their son's disappearance, Rasool Ahmed's family left the village in pursuit of Junaid. Relocating to Srinagar made visits to detention camps, appealing at the court and support from his brother more accessible. To support the family, he shut down the carpet loom in favour of new work to earn a living, eventually to become an auto driver in Srinagar. The house where Junaid grew up, the house where Junaid was picked up, now remains locked. The state of the house in the village became a recurrent theme in our conversations. There were repeated ruminations about the walls of the house coming down, the inability of the apple and pomegranate trees in the courtyard to bear fruit like they used to and apprehensions about unknown persons trespassing on the property. The old house is also a container of Junaid's belongings such as his clothes, childhood pictures and cherished audio tapes. There are ritual retreats to the abandoned house—a controlled connection and marked avoidance associated with the horror of the sudden amputation of the family structure. The abandoned house, I suspect, in the form of a concrete object external to the self, locked away the unmitigated psychic pain of the loss associated with Junaid's disappearance. As a symbol, it captured the history of familial life before the disappearance, its intactness and ordinariness still thriving unconsciously in the protective foliage of psychic retreat achieved through the exodus (Steiner 1993).

Unconsciously chosen as a linking object, the house knocks at Rasool Ahmed's consciousness. What if he loses the house? The vexing inner demands emerge to get him to repair the walls and the roof, to take a loan, and what of the rent in the city? While his daughter, Husaina, and his wife imagine living in the house once again, a cornucopia of pleasurable memories, Rasool Ahmad is unable to imagine a life there. He reminded me that the house has no doors, the roof is in disrepair, the carpet loom does not work, and concluded a few minutes later, as if looking inwardly, that 'carpets cannot be made because I have no patience left'. The ritualistic retreats between the two houses keep his dread containable and the noises of the mind under check. In their house in Srinagar, hidden under the layer of a pink cotton *dupatta* [scarf] is Junaid's school uniform that comes to life with a strong gush of the evening breeze. Rasool Ahmed tells me that a *peer* blessed the uniform with verses from the Quran. The amulet tied to the buttoned collar protects him from unimaginable terrors. The uniform preserves the beloved child as a cherished thirteen-year-old boy whose body returns in tangible ministrations in the everyday. The ritualistic cleaning of the uniform when it turns dirty creates a space of continuing relatedness with his ghostly presence, giving it a ceremonious form for the family. The uniform is a secret tomb, a source of nourishment for the disappeared body. In this manner, the inexpressible mourning with its clandestine pleasure makes returning to the lost object within the self-possible. For Rasool Ahmed's family, it is in the register of affect, much more than in vivid memories, that a universe of attachments is unearthed. They are now the guardian mourners of a house with no doors—a psychic representation of the traumatic experience.

The image of the house without doors returns in the shape of the auto that Rasool Ahmed drives. A motorized vehicle without doors. It is during the auto rides that he enters a dissociated state in his mind. On some days, he does not remember the way or the name of streets he drives on. On such days, he notices a strange obsessive return to the military men in bunkers and check points. He finds himself driving close to the bunkers and checkpoints to look in the face of military men the face of his son Junaid. Each face that he carefully studies, each face that disappoints is a potential Junaid. He speaks about it as if to seek my confirmation on the absurdity of his impulse, 'What if Junaid is here in Kashmir'. He is madder for it, he concluded. His fantasy is corroborated by a military strategy in prevalent in Kashmir that recruited militants as informers into the Indian military forces. In the fantasy, Junaid appeared dressed in a military uniform. What unravels in the obsessive symptom is a slowly approaching intimacy with the other. In an area of psychic transfigurability, the hated object returns as a potential kin or the disappeared son. In search of his son, Rasool Ahmed recovers infinite possibilities of life and death, an enemy but also a kin, the alterity of the other that orders and ordains ordains him with the responsibility without reciprocity. In coming face-to-face with the other, he recovers an ethical sociality which is contained in the baffling symptom (Levinas 1984).

Rasool Ahmed's daughter, Husaina, is twenty-seven years old. He affectionately refers to her as 'my everything'. He regrets her adamance to not marry. The disappearance of her brother, Junaid, the death of older sister, Shaheen, and parental depression left a deep psychological vulnerability in Husaina. Rasool Ahmed recounted, 'The blanket that you see there, she would pull it over herself and sleep all day. The injustices that she has felt make her angry all the time'. In the minds of the parents Husaina stands for the two children lost to death and disappearance. Rasool Ahmed reflected, 'Shaheen didn't die of a long ailment. She died four years after Junaid's disappearance. We were observing Ramadhan. She felt an acute pain in the head that evening and collapsed. She spread her bedding but Allah couldn't let her rest. Seven thirty in the evening she felt an acute pain and around quarter to eight she was gone. Within fifteen minutes, it was all decided. Just like that. She was gone. She was fourteen or fifteen years old. What do I tell you and how will you listen? We fight everyday but in one sense we are not fighting anymore.' The repetitive losses have caused a deep psychic vulnerability leaving a shared fragility of internal states such that on the one hand there is a struggle to survive and on the other, a psychic entropy (Vahali 2009). Rasool Ahmad unknowingly compares the death of his daughter with the disappearance of his son, Junaid, by reflecting on how 'quickly' within a period of fifteen minutes the fate of Shaheen's life was 'decided'. This stands in sharp contrast with the question that hangs morbidly over Junaid's absence or disappearance. He believes that losing Junaid has thrown the family into a quicksand, testing their ability to resurface. By situating their shared struggle in Junaid's disappearance, the family is attempting to historicize pain, like a seal over other hurts (Volkan 1981). Rasool Ahmed may have been able to defend himself against intense feelings of rage, cynicism, guilt and fear by not knowing them consciously. But it seems as if the work of 'metabolizing' or 'digesting' this intense affect has been passed on to Husaina, who functions as a container of her father's unspeakable dread (Bion 1962; Ogden 2005) or intense catastrophic explosion (Eigen 1999b). These explosions of anger in Husaina are expressed as a 'scream becoming lost in space, so that the scream can go on forever but not be felt or heard. It loses its function as a scream (meant to link the self and the other), congeals, becomes diffuse, becomes a non-scream, a void' (Eigen 1999b, 149).

Husaina was seven years old when Junaid was picked up from home. She was ten when her older sister Shaheen died at the age sixteen. During our first few meetings, I noticed Husaina's cynicism and anger as two significant feelings protecting her from my intrusion into their lives. The years following Shaheen's death, Husaina had her first major depressive episode, something she recalled as a season of 'deep sleep'. She appeared as a repository of endemic childhood memories and a deep yearning for her siblings. Now at age twenty-seven, she works as an assistant physiotherapist to 'mend broken bones and torn ligaments', a work she describes as 'helping people in pain'.

She recounts the memory of Junaid's disappearance in vivid, even if with fixed, faithfulness. 'I remember the day clearly when they took my brother away;I had caught a cold. My mother and I left home and we ran after Junaid. We stood outside the camp screaming and begging "Let me meet my brother, let me meet my son". But nobody opened the gates for us. We sat there the whole day . . . One day after another . . . Hungry and devastated. I asked the guards on duty watching us, "Don't you have a family? Can you not understand our pain?" A guard on duty was moved to tears on seeing our pain. I would not lie to you. He could really feel my pain. He said "Little girl, why do you come here and cry. Your brother is not with us." He cried with me. He gave a chocolate to console me.' The memory of the guard helped Husaina transform helplessness into a semblance of omnipotence that her pain had an effect on the environment. It came to me as an afterthought that perhaps the same moment, the consolatory gesture, obfuscated and estranged the experience of rage and hate that she felt at her victimization.

What appears in Rasool Ahmed's account as an affect of mourning, in Husaina's narrative, the trauma of disappearance is symbolized in the experience of hunger and starvation. She recalls, 'There was no food in the house for ten days . . . Nothing to cook. One day, my mother and I went to a place begging for food. I can not forget that day. My mother held my hand and took me to a *sahib* [a rich man]. We told him that there is nothing to eat in our house; he heard our story and gave some money. With that money, we bought some rice to eat. When my father came back, he asked where we got the money from. We lied that we had some savings. He asked us wherethe money was all these days when we were starving. We were speechless. On the third day, the same sahib came to see us. My father was shocked to learn that we had gone begging. He wept at our state of humiliation. Those ten days are etched in my memory- ten days without food.' The memory of hunger offers an elaboration of how Husaina as a child experienced Junaid's abduction. The ten days of hunger allude to a psychic hole created by the traumatic event, connecting hurt with hunger and humiliation. Emotionally orphaned by the shocked and aggrieved parents, the figure of the beggar offers an affective entry, a narrative cohesiveness, to express an incommunicable state from which spectral prefigurations of disowned neediness and longing find a representation (O'Loughlin 2012). The image of the child-beggar became a crucial unconscious communication between Husaina and me, enabling a glimpse into her inner world, her own liminality.

I noticed her struggle to stitch together different clues to Junaid's abduction. She recalled, 'One day my brother saw the servant of a neighbour doing drugs outside the house. Junaid told him to not do it, that "my sisters live here". He threatened my brother. It was the same boy who framed Junaid. He told the military that Junaid has a gun. After the BSF picked up Junaid, we never saw him again.' When the family received a message from Junaid that a window cleaner delivered, they felt a new ray of hope. She added, 'When my mother and father went looking for him, an officer told them to come later. We were very excited and made all the necessary arrangements. We cooked chicken and carried a *pheran* [a traditional woollen garment] . . .' It was a very cold winter.' The next day, two unknown men, disguised as reporters, appeared at their doorstep. They inquired what the family had learned about Junaid, and vanished. When Rasool Ahmed and Rafeeqa arrived at the detention camp, an officer met them and declared that Junaid is not in the camp. The couple begged helplessly to be reunited with their son. Husaina added, 'The officer cried with us. You see, everyone is not the same. He felt our pain.' Her insistence to recognize empathy in the officer carried a protective function to keep alive a sense of an intact world made of empathic rather than terrifying objects (Alvarez 2012). Husaina's mourning, like for many in Kashmir, unfolded in a context of militarization. On the one hand is the loss introduced by disappearance with a complicated route to mourning; on the other, the reality of loss is interlaced with the experience of over-stimulation, intrusions and terror that ensue from the armed conflict. Her narrative discloses the constant presence of armed men, alluding to a pervasive vulnerability brought on by a radically different social layering that occurs in the contexts of militarization, such that the mind is populated with a mistrust of informers or enemies lurking in the consciousness, suggesting the domestic as undefined and dangerously unprotected. This particular vulnerability keeps returning in Husaina's story. She described encountering 'the same men' again and again in streets, making her wild with fury. During one such encounter, she sat down on the road to stop a military van and climbed inside the vehicle, yelling at the armed men to return her brother to her. On entering the van, she discovered a boy with a black veil and began shouting, 'It is my brother; let me see my brother', only to be left in a wordless stupor by the boy's response, 'I am not the one you are looking for. I am not your brother.' With a mix of shame at being exposed and a fledgling sense of triumph over the old wound, she shared, 'I always go and check the BSF vehicle. Who knows who they have in their van. I keep an eye on it.'

Such moments for Husaina appear to be outside her volition. Like a hypnoid state, she is both in it and also not. She explained, 'When I see *military*men picking up a boy, I don't know what gets inside of me. Something happens and I lose a sense of the present. I cannot tolerate that sight as it were. I feel uncontrollable rage and start quarrelling with the men.' In these moments the moment of Junaid's abduction comes to the brink of the consciousness, waiting to be reworked transferentially. Husaina knows about that experience without knowing it consciously. It is not a case of forgetting as much as it is an attempt to experience it perhaps for the first time. These repetitions occur hoping for an integration of the traumatic loss in the pastness, a psychic burial of the rescue fantasy, so that she may be present to the hidden psychic pain frozen in the mourning.

Over the years Husaina made several visits to the offices and homes of ministers and politicians to have her plea heard. On one such visit, she waited outside the residence of a popular Kashmiri politician, who had on previous occasion demanded that the disappeared be returned to their families. She waited a long time for the minister's arrival. When she was denied a meeting by the guards outside, she flew into a rage to be threatened by the guards they would fire at her. She held the guard's gun and demanded to be shot at. She screamed that she is 'only an effigy', that she 'died many years ago'. Husaina remembered that other complainants, who routinely assembled to get the minister's audience, cried helplessly and begged her to stop. She welled up and added, 'We wait long hours outside the offices and homes of these officers and politicians. They throw our pleas in a dustbin. It is better to ask God, he might give us *our* lost child back. Now we don't knock on any door.' Husaina's search for the brother is intertwined with that of her parents' search for the missing son. In their shared mourning, with Husaina now a young woman, Junaid appears as 'our child' or one of the 'lost children of Kashmir'.

In Husaina's internal world, Junaid is an everlasting thirteen-year-old boy, unchanged by time. While her father Rasool Ahmed imagines Junaid as a grown man, for Husaina, Junaid's face is hazy, best preserved in the few photographs safely preserved in plastic bags. Junaid is eternally a child. Unable to breathe life into a handful of memories, she expressed a greater need for concrete objects as links. She offers herself as the custodian of Junaid's belongings—his music cassettes, his bicycle and clothes, locked away in the village house. But most significantly, unconsciously she offered herself as the only available child to her parents in the aftermath of her brother's disappearance and sister's sudden death—a prepubescent girl a stand-in for the missing son. For the parents, Husaina's body is a site of preoccupations. Her fragility, sickness or depressive episodes circulate endlessly as referents of dread and anxiety. On the one hand, the parents complained of her volatile moods as unmanageable and extreme. On the other hand, she is admired for qualities that she shares with her siblings, enlivening the depressed parents with the mirth of continuity. Husaina idealizes a Tom Sawyer- like cleverness and mischief in Junaid and a goodness of heart and sensitivity like Premchand's Hamid as she remembered Junaid's first gift, a rolling pin, for the mother. The task of mourning for Husaina, the very function of speech, is to transform memory to legend. The task of witnessing for me was to be moved and swayed. She liked telling me about the ways she is like her brother and how delightful it is to find these qualities in herself. It certainly is a source of delight and nourishment for the parents. However, the fluctuations between these two poles of personality appeared unmodulated and worrisome. Standing in for Junaid and her sister Shaheen, Husaina carries a boyish charm and a cavalier disregard for her feminine body in a complex synthesis.

Between her parents and her heroic interventions with armed personnel in the streets, there is a differentiated, co-emergent response to disappearance and the site of action they have unconsciously chosen. While the parents participate in monthly sit-ins and demonstrations, Husaina finds herself increasingly cut off from the collective imagination of concerted protests. Compared to her parents, Husaina's mourning takes on a solitary route. As she walks into scenes of conflict between young Kashmiri boys and armed military personnel when they are dragged out of their houses into the streets, she intervenes and intercedes on behalf of the boys. It is an attempt at once of courage and helplessness reorganized or reordered into 'doing' when the internal trauma is stoked in a repetitive reliving. The very repetition of trauma, its resurgence in the psychic, becomes a site of activism. The fantasy of rescue recreates a context of survival for Husaina as well as the boys she shields, becoming a propitious link between personal trauma and political action as it radiates into the social (Foucault and Miscowiec 1986; Gampel 2000; Vahali 2009; Chatterjee 2018; Zia 2019). She refers to these moments as a 'spectacle' of life and death. There is an inter-generational link in the mourning of Rasool Ahmed and Husaina. For Rasool Ahmed, the loss of the security of the domestic world is represented in the image of 'house with no doors'. For Husaina, mourning takes her compulsively to the outside as though to 'create' a spectacle of a spectacular pain.

During the second year of my visit to the family, Husiana took me to show the house in the village where Junaid was picked up, the bunker where she and her mother protested to see Junaid, the courtyard where the rose bush and the pomegranate tree planted by Shaheen stand tall and green, 'unable to bear fruits since she died', where Rasool Ahmed's loom stands dusty and still. In place of windows and doors, there were plastic sheets nailed to the wooden frame to give it a temporary fix. Husaina remarked that a few years ago, thieves enter the house but they found *nothing inside*, a mental representation of their internal world. I asked Husaina what it is like to live in the city, away from this house. She replied, 'When we decided to leave this house, my mother told her sister, "I want to live where not even a crow could come for us". Who knew we would have to see such a time. This house has lost two children to an unknown abyss.'

During my interaction with Husaina and Rasool Ahmed, the motif of death and disappearance appeared interchangeably. Over a period of time, Husaina was able to articulate two distinct fantasies about her sister Shaheen's death. On the one hand, the ritual of burial and mourning for her death by the family and community made the death real and augmented natural mourning. She experiences a thriving life force in the plants sown in the courtyard by Shaheen. The pomegranate tree and the rose bush are used to memorialize Shaheen and grant a future to mourning. On the one hand, the flowering of rose and the pomegranate tree is experienced as a testament to and a legacy of Shaheen's unforgettable life, the family's bountiful history and place in nature; it stands as their claim or attachment, their rootedness in the context of painful exodus and alienation caused by the mutative experience of the brother's disappearance. On the other hand, Husaina experiences Shaheen and Junaid as though they disappeared to be united again with the family one day. She alluded to the fantasy of rebirth as an eminent source of pleasure and comfort. The two facets, the reality of disappearance and that of death, could exist in her side by side, like a split within, without betraying the other. The pull of the fantasy of reunion 'energetically' disavowed the reality of death or disappearance (Freud [1927] 1967). The keeping of two contradictory states, a facilitation made by the splitting of the ego, re-appears in the image of the aggressor, implying a deep chasm in the self and the other. The image of the police or militarymen, in Husaina and Rasool Ahmed's world is a complex one. In Husaina and Rasool Ahmed's experience, the uniformed men carried out the brutal abduction of Junaid leading to the disappearance. However, the same men are seen crying for their loss, expressing their shared helplessness and utter inability to help. For Rasool Ahmed and Husaina, it lays bare a site of deep conflict to carry the fractured image of the other, sometimes as irreconcilable, and at other times, as a tolerable version of humanity. When their loss touches the military guards and officers, they introject a penetrable and a potentially vulnerable aggressor. They are able to host the aggressor's humanity, an affective link with the noted object, but there is little room for the expression of their own anger, hate and helplessness. In one way, they enter what Ferenczi (1949) called the 'terrorism of suffering' where the self is recruited to return, through projection, the goodness or kindness of the armed soldiers. The psychic necessity does not stop here. The image of the weeping military personnel becomes exponentially detoxifying for the traumatic encounter. Exposed to this strange knowledge, the affective vulnerability of the terrifying object prepares Husaina to be unafraid of them in her adult life while it makes Rasool Ahmed imagine Junaid in the cast of the young armymen present all around. It marks their mourning in a manner that is distinct, unfinished and open.

Rasool Ahmed was one of the first parents who, along with Parveena Ahangar, started what were then small, informal meetings at Parveena's house in which the families of the disappeared persons came together to form APDP. Parveena's house became a place to contain and hold each other through the breakdown and reflect on the ways to find their lost loved ones. In the last three decades, Rafeeqa and Rasool Ahmed have remained motivated mourner-survivors and activists in the monthly sit-ins at Partap Park. Between the couple, there is a shared understanding that Rafeeqa must participate in all protests even if his work keeps him occupied. At a monthly sit-in in Partap Park, when I saw him sitting with Junaid's photograph, I inquired about Rafeeqa's absence. He shared that she was needed to attend to the house in the village, so he came to the protest. He sat there embodying a sombre silence. The countless days of sit-ins, visits to the court and interviews with journalists leave him in doubt and despair. The fantasy of reunion and the ethic of mourning triumph over the sense of failure. In these moments, Rasool Ahmed reminds himself that to keep Junaid alive, the inner crypt, is the sole purpose of this struggle. He suggests, 'Everything except this pain and longing is a distraction'. In a monthly sit-ins organized by APDP, Parveena Ahangar shared the idea of creating a commemorative memorial building for the disappeared persons. Rasool Ahmad recalled his hesitation and said, 'The children should come back and that's what the association needs to work towards'. In his view, a memorial would fade out but 'who can forget this poison', of the trauma of disappearance, in which life force is mixed with the death work of destruction (Bragin 2003; Eigen 1999a, b; Kakar 2008; Krippner and McIntyre 2003). Is it possible that cultures of violence produce subjectivities that undergo such mutations that life and death live intertwined and undifferentiated where a poison may come to support future actions? (Bollas 1999).

COMB GENTLY

I first met Sameena at a primary school in Lolab Valley during a reflective immersion with primary school educators. The school offered free education to students in a context marked by poverty, deprivation and unemployment that ensuedfrom the near-total shutdown of work opportunities and public safety. Built to address structural inequality in the access to education, the school appeared like a field hospital, caring for the wounded whose childhood was taking shape under heavy militarization. At the school, however, the dis-remembered grief came drifting into classrooms in the form of the children's failure to cope. The teachers worked with such excesses and symbolic emptiness most intuitively and cogently. Reflecting on the effects of militarization and exposure to trauma, a teacher remembered a student whose mother, a half widow, impressed upon her the need for psychological work with the parents. She wondered if I would like to meet such mothers. I agreed. Of the three mothers I met, Sameena looked the youngest and most disturbed. Extremely anxious in her demeanour, it felt as if she might run out of the room any second. She looked everywhere but towards me. Anxious and overwhelmed, she looked trapped, and I began to feel like an executioner.

On several occasions, Sameena's daughter, Amna, fainted in the school. The teachers found out that Amna had had a few fainting spells at home as well, sometimes followed by a nose bleed. Unable to understand what the fainting meant and what brought it on, Amna's teacher felt concerned for her. While medical investigations ruled out epileptic seizures, the fainting continued to occur periodically. I attempted to speak to Sameena about her daughter as a way to understand their world. I wondered how the experience of disappearance shaped their experience. Sameena articulated worries about Amna as, 'a peculiar condition that needs attention'. She explained, 'I have to take her to doctors . . . If I grab her forcibly or comb her hair unthinkingly, her nose might start to bleed or she might faint. The doctors say that there could have been an injury inside . . . somewhere . . . but it's not obvious where. Some days ago, when she was coming back, someone pulled her hair and she fainted. Her nose started to bleed profusely. The driver had to stop the bus and make her lie flat on the road and put cold water on her head . . . I comb her hair gently. She can not take it'. In describing the injury 'inside', 'somewhere', Sameena laid out anxieties about the daughter, whether something terribly wrong happened to her, so terrible that it carried no name. Her daughter's condition served as a condensed 'dream image', a metaphoric allusion to the silent bleeding in their shared wound, awaiting a gentle grooming of the damaged self so that it may heal. At the same time, the troubling image of the comb and the hair spoke to me about Sameena's unconscious ambivalence towards what might happen should she and I enter a tangled, unruly inner world. If we must go 'inside' or 'somewhere', into the thick of things or sore surfaces, we must remember to comb gently and carefully.

Sameena's husband, Abdul Hameed, disappeared in the year 2000. In our conversations, Sameena vacillates between the use of the word 'disappearance' and 'death' to make meaning of her husband's absence. In the absence of an eyewitness account and the FIR about the circumstances of Abdul Hameed's disappearance, Sameena resolved the looming ambiguity by switching to the appeal of the certainty of death over the incomprehensibility of his absence. The slippage in the language however, between disappearance and death, kept the psychic conflict alive and unburied.

'It has been eleven years since my husband *died.* He held a clerical job in a government office. It was the month of Ramadhan. He went to work and did not come back. We were together for three years. We have two children. On the night of the disappearance, I thought that his work has detained him. I told my in-laws that he has not returned. They thought that perhaps his work was keeping him away. We knew nothing. No one knew who had taken him. Had we known, we could have looked for him . . .' Sameena spoke, wiping her tears. A sense of helplessness and guilt keep returning to Sameena when she revisits the loss. She articulated it as a personal failure to have not acted on time, to have not known about the danger Abdul was in and now to have survived while he slipped through the cracks. She adds, 'A few days later we received the news that he was *taken*. When we went to the cantonment area to inquire, they denied everything. Somebody said perhaps he was killed. He never left like this before. I was carrying a child and he made sure that he returned in the evening. When he did not come home that evening, I asked my father-in-law, "Where must he be?" He said "He's not a big officer or a commissioner who will come home so frequently. After all he's just an employee." I consoled myself.' After a dissociated reprieve, she returned to the story, 'My son was two years old and my daughter was born ten days after my husband's disappearance'.

'When I realized that he is missing I was swallowed by shock. I felt I should die as well. I was pregnant.' The abrogated death wish came haltingly in clipped sentences. To live was to suffer. She thought she stayed alive for the unborn child. The enormity of what had happened manifested in a psychotic break. She recalled, 'I lost my mind. I kept looking for him everywhere. My daughter was born the very next day. I walked into the canal and sat down in water. What can I tell you about my state in those days . . . I was out of control. The realization that he is dead was devastating. My family came searching for me and took me home.'

As an analyst to her own experience, Sameena made a demand on me as a listener, suggesting that to understand the meaning of disappearance as loss is to first lose one's mind, to tip over the edge of cohesion or sanity. As though whatever else it might become, without the imagination of what it means to lose one's mind, the story cannot move forward. She shared in fragments her running on the streets, going from neighbour to neighbour, day and night, in a state of madness. She tried to explain madness as not belonging in one's body or in one's mind. She did not remember her pregnancy, the dangers of miscarriage or those to her own health. She walked for hours, sitting occasionally on the streets to cry and recover—a repetitive cycle of despair- stopping only to ask those she met if they had seen Abdul. Sameena's immersing of her body in the canal stood as a metaphor for a self-caving in, an unparalleled breakdown in a profound disorientation in life. In what she relayed, it was difficult to imagine the moment of childbirth—was it before she immersed herself in the canal or after? Perhaps what was bursting forth from the confusion was a melancholic fugue. The canal provided a halt in movement, a fantasy of near-complete weightlessness, a dissociation from the pregnancy—a perceptual approximation of belonging nowhere. To the extent that to wait is to be in attendance of someone, to commit to the stability of one's observance or to be fixed in space and time, to be weightless is to become without wait, to openly abandon or even disregard all orientation in the world. The extraordinary circumstances of Abdul's disappearance are signified by Sameena's catastrophic pain. The image of the woman with a protruding belly wandering the streets returns as a vivid image of Lal Ded, the saint poet of Kashmir, who having lost her mind, and in particular, feminine shame, walked naked as a testament of the singularity of devotion to the sacred. In folklores, her protruding belly covered her shame, making her immune to the onlookers. Sameena's absorption in pain transmits a powerful stroke of the mythical into the present, digging its claws in the receptive unconscious of the culture to claim a container for privation.

Paving her way through silences, she added, 'When my daughter was born, I did not give her milk for thirteen days. I thought that she has brought this [disappearance] upon us. Then my mother and my aunt told me to not do something so abhorring in the eyes of Allah. I melted a little. They told me that if I do not take care of the baby then my in-laws will also not care for my children. After the birthing of the baby, I did not stay a single night inside. When it snowed, I was out looking for my husband. I would walk the same path he took to search for him. My sister-in-law would come to get me home. They said that I am first Allah's responsibility and then theirs. When I fell sick, they slowly began to turn away. After his disappearance, they [the in-laws] started disgracing me, devaluing me. I have no worth because I do not have a husband next to me. We only saw three years together . . . (long pause).'

Sameena's refusal to feed the infant, a complete turning away from the maternal function, is an expression approximating the loss. She found herself unable to be a mother to the new-born child whom she considered evil and ill-fated for her. At the time of her marriage, Sameena was twelve years old. At fifteen, she was the mother of two, and a half widow. Overwhelmed by the shocking loss, the new-born's dependence on her felt muted. Her attention returned to the baby only as a persecuting presence from whom she felt emotionally detached. The inability to return to maternal ministrations raised questions about the baby's survival. She found it painful to feed or hold the baby, suggesting a complete withdrawal from social and moral expectations as voiced by her kin. Sameena's experience raises significant questions. What place does the mother's love have in conditions of historical trauma or a traumatizing social formation brought on by violence? Can it be free from the internalized devaluation of female genealogies (Benjamin 1988; Butler 1990; Das 1990; Scheper-Hughes 1993). The restoration of maternal love is made possible by a community of women healers—mothers, aunts, sisters and neighbours—who try to revive the dead breasts from the claims of melancholy. Through their invocation of religion, with Allah as a mother, they argue for Sameena's maternal duty to protect forms of continuity, meaning and order. Her grief, a total apathy, is seen as a crisis of faith—a state far dangerous than grief. As much as it is a response of a grieving mother, Sameena's indifference towards her new-born child is also a social production. In the absence of any record keeping of disappearances and deaths in the context of the massive loss of lives, birth too runs the risk of occurring unrecorded and unregistered. In Sameena's memory, we see that just as Abdul's disappearance had been left unexamined, the birth of a child was rendered profoundly unremarkable.

On being asked what made her feel that Abdul Hameed would not come back, she replied, 'Many things made me feel that. I was pregnant and my father warned me that he will burn the house down if I keep on doing this forever. Then one day, I saw someone much younger losing her husband. She lived in our neighbourhood. When her husband was martyred, I thought that if something like this could happen to her, it could happen to me. If being so young she could come to terms with her fate then I should make peace with my destiny. Seeing her gave me strength—that it is possible to live. My father also told me that "you are not the only woman with whom such things are happening." I stopped crying in front of my children because I could see that they were getting badly affected. They can sense my condition. My son, Ajaz, hardly speaks. He does not eat.'

Sameena's mourning flows into the vast stream of mourners who are witnesses to the indiscriminate violence metted out during this time. It changes the meaning of personal guilt, self-blame and loss into collective witnessing. It creates a possibility of freeing the isolated frames of mourning to a movement of shared experiencing, a collective trauma. As she returns to think about her children, Sameena can sense the emotional abandonment experienced by them. She is more connected to the inchoate pain experienced by the two children—of a missing father and an irretrievable mother. Her son's silence, his refusal to eat, and her own tendency to fall ill have found a permanent expression in their lives. The unconscious identification with maternal deadness, what Green (1986) called 'the dead mother', may rule the emotional economy of the child. He noted, 'The transformation in the psychical life, at the moment of the mother's sudden bereavement when she has become abruptly detached from her infant is experienced by the child as a catastrophe; because, without any warning signal, love has been lost at one blow' (150).

When her son, Ajaz, and the daughter, Amna, ask Sameena about the father's return, her answer is an inevitable 'tomorrow'. This necessity of 'tomorrow', the empty consolation, has deep implications for the children of the 'missing' persons negotiating the ambiguity of loss. Not having known their fathers, the children embark on a 'father-search' (Volkan 2007). At one level, it is a way to establish a connection with the father they could not get to know; on another level, it is a cry to end the maternal preoccupation with loss. There is an unconscious feeling of anger or guilt associated with abandonment as well as a failure of internalization of the healthy aspects of the parents (Green 1986; Abraham and Torok 1994; Kumar and Sen 2018).

With no source of income, Sameena now lives with her parents. She has three younger sisters and a brother who studies in the district college. With her father as a daily wager and the only earning member of the family, money is difficult to come by. She negotiates a deep sense of guilt 'for adding to the burden'. She shared, 'My youngest sister in-law got married recently. She was married on the condition that her husband would live with the in-laws. I could not live with another man in the house. My in-laws deny me any rights on the house. My children will not be given anything. They ask me to remarry and leave the children with them.' Sameena's hopelessness latched on to me. I was impressed by the entrapment she lived in. She had lost a husband, a home, and may lose her children too. It gave me an insight into the affective field of her two children whose anxious-withdrawn states had worried the school teachers. The children, in a way, reproduced Sameena's two important self-states, announcing how they experienced their environment.

After our initial conversation in the school, I began meeting Sameena in her house in the neighbouring village. I walked across green meadows and herds of cattle grazing near clusters of houses. On my first visit, as I asked for directions to her house, a villager asked me whether I mean to visit 'the one whose husband is missing?' He accompanied me while telling those we crossed that we were going to Sameena's, the one whose husband is 'laapatah' or missing. It was evident how the event marked her everyday. On arriving I greeted her. Sameena was visibly exhausted. She complained that her fever was back along with a pounding headache. She added, 'The memories keep me sad. Three days I am alright and then in bed the whole time.' She began crying softly, 'I feel I am lying in my grave'. It now began to appear to me that the confusion between Abdul's death or disappearance was in fact a projection of her own inner states. Abdul had disappeared; it was she who had died! She continued, 'I was a little more than twelve years old when I got married . . . And about fifteen when he disappeared. I am twenty six now. It has been eleven years . . . Before he disappeared they [the husband and his family] used to *measure* me—they nurtured me like a small child watched over by her family as she grows up'. As though adrift on a secret terrain,

Sameena returned to whisper to me, 'He used to keep me like the cream on milk . . . with such care and caution'. I joined her in the warm glow of tenderness; I had a vivid image of a lover or a mother, blowing gently on the layer of cream, protecting it from spilling or splitting, a profoundly delicate gesture to preserve what is more precious than milk. Sameena's traumatic legacy is a longing for the recognition of a relationship; it is an amorous devotion that she struggles to access and articulate to herself as well as to her children. To the extent that she was able to recall and share the pleasure of being loved, she returned transformed by the memory. The memory also helped her to access a wish to care for her children by hosting and becoming alive to a caring introject of Abdul. It strengthened Sameena's self-worth and motivation while revealing a dependence on, or bondage to, a very specific psychic representation. In rediscovering the memory of being held with 'care and caution', Sameena could feel the longing of her children, who were now eleven and thirteen, approximately the same age as she at the time of Abdul's disappearance. The memory also offered itself as a resistance to the systematically produced and internalized misogyny in which the identity of a half widow remains entrenched. In the context of poverty, deprivation and ambiguity on her status as a widow, issues concerning property rights, remarriage and employment remain unresolved for Sameena. A few years later, when the father-in-law sold a landholding to the army, the village *panchayat* suggested that Sameena be given a share in the money. But the family did not do so. Unlike her sisters, she is unable to work and make money. When she is physically able to, she collects wood from the jungle and sells it in the local market.

When Sameena's daughter, Amna, was eight years old, she fell ill with jaundice. Sameena had not noticed how dangerously it escalated while Amna continued going to the school. Terrified of losing the last link to the missing son, Abdul's mother (Sameena's mother-in-law) picked up her granddaughter from the bus stop and refused to let her return to her mother. The event proved catastrophic for Sameena. She was forced to face her dissociative disconnect and consequent neglect. This was, however, not the first occasion when Sameena's mother-in-law tried to 'steal' her child. When little Amna was five, the mother-in-law took the girl to the jungle with her and hid there for hours. Sameena's family looked for the missing child everywhere. They later traced the child back to her grandmother's scheme. Keeping Amna in her custody, the grandmother stopped sending her to school. When the teacher noticed her long absence, she inquired about it from Amna's brother. The school teachers learned that Amna was locked in the grandmother's house and the grandmother refused to let anyone meet her, including her mother, Sameena. The situation reached its climax in a battle for custody which was later resolved by the community members supporting that Amna be returned to Sameena. For the mother-in-law, giving up her granddaughter, the living link to the missing Abdul, proved unbearable. She continued to 'make a scene' at the bus stop, accusing Sameena's family of 'snatching my child away from me'. The image of abduction, hiding, 'locking up' and 'snatching' returned the unassimilable experience of Abdul's disappearance as alive in the traumatic repetitions, in the image of the possessive grandmother just as in Sameena's wandering (Volkan 1981; Laub and Auerhahn 1993). By establishing itself in the theatre of inter-subjective enactments, the baby becomes a site of transferential reworking. The experience of loss returns as the fear of dispossession, in Abdul's mother and Sameena, each standing in for a nameless saboteur or a hideous oppressor. But more significantly, the event of the disappearance has become a condition, revealing a traumatic quality in the fear of loss itself. Though the enactment keeps an affective hold on the traumatic moment to relive it compulsively over and over again till further assimilation, it prevents it from slipping back into its proper chronological place in the past (Erikson 1995).

Moving unconsciously from memories to a palpable threat in the room, I asked Sameena whether she sees her mother-in-law as radically altered by Abdul's disappearance, unconsciously abrogating the irreversibility of loss by stealing the child. She showed interest in my comment. I told her that it seems that they both are trying to sum their pain as bigger than the other, a kind of competitive victimhood, by claiming authority over the child. Sameena voiced, 'My mother-in-law says, "what pain do you have? I have lost my child, my son. You cannot measure up to my loss".' I asked her what she thought of her mother-in-law's lament, to which she said, 'She has lived a huge part of her life. She's old whereas I am just a bud yet to bloom; I have my whole life in front of me. She's old . . . she would die. On whose mercy will I survive? How will I look after my children?' How does Sameena survive the onslaught of guilt, terror and grief reinjected by the figure of her mother-in-law? Her associations took her to several memories of Abdul's difficulties with the mother. He was 'forced' to go deep into the forest to gather wood, and was often beaten by the parents for defiance. On one occasion, the mother dragged him down the staircase for not waking up on time to go work. For Sameena, these memories ward off the persecutory anxiety injected by Abdul's mother. Seeing her as a 'bad mother' helps her maintain the internal cohesion for survival. She compared the mother to a mad dog, a terrifying image compared to her self-image of a precarious bud. This differentiation enabled Sameena to view herself as worthy and innocent in an ambit of scarce self-affirming voices around her. Instead of the dominant feeling of 'social refuse', to me she was able to advocate for a more empathetic picture of her melancholic state and withdrawal from maternal care. The presence of her mother and the sisters offered a surrogate community, sometimes egging her on to share more or elaborating stories as witnesses to Sameena and her children's experiences (Laub 2017). When beseeched by intense pain, Sameena left conversations mid-sentence to make tea or fetch things from another room, in a manner to regulate affect. In such moments, her sister or her mother offered a continuity of narrative, filling the gaps or making observations about experiences that overwhelmed Sameena's ego capacities or swallowed her whole, absenting her from the scene. It was evident that while Sameena withdrew in depression, her family offered themselves as surrogate figures, story tellers, to her and to the two children.

Sameena connects to the father hunger in her children but the stories she offers to them were too few and flaky. It was in the third year of their marriage that Abdul disappeared. I sensed that alongside feelings of love and longing, there is an unconscious anger and hate at being *eternalized* as a young bride. She expressed her envy at women her age or younger marrying or living happily with their families. Stricken with a melancholic fervour, Sameena's only hope is Abdul's return. She expressed confusion about whether she still waits for Abdul's return or it is a veritable make-believe tale invented for the children. There is a disconnect with how the children make sense of the father's absence. There is a paucity of stories about Abdul; the possibility of real affective contact for the children to know and learn about their father remains truncated. It is not merely the internalization of the father that helps address emotional need or void but also the mother's conscious and unconscious expectations and fantasies towards the father that form the internal representation of the father in the child (Herzog 1982; Marks and Lovestone 1995).

As we began speaking of Sameena's yearning for Abdul, Sameena repeatedly brought a sense of disenfranchisement back in the space of the domestic. Leaving Abdul's house cut her off from access to everyday objects, revealing another extremely pivotal aspect to mourning. In the absence of these objects of belonging, she is unable to establish inter-generational memory, attachment and custodianship (Gibson and Carden 2018). She shares, 'I had some of his photographs but his mother stole them from me. She grew insecure—she thought I might lose them or use them to do something to the family . . . like black magic. She would come, with some excuse or the other, and take his photographs. Over a period of time she locked all his clothes and other things. (long pause) . . . I have wanted to show his photograph to *peer sahab* [a Sufi healer] but she will not let any photograph remain with me. It is not her right to keep them with her'. In a plea for recognition as a custodian of melancholy objects, Sameena articulates a mourner's journey through the changing relationship between the objects of the disappeared and the disappearing objects. The relevance of photographs, for her, carry an unconscious acceptance of the futurelessness of the memory while mediating with the permanence of loss. She has a unique purpose for these pictures—they are not only symbolic of mourning, or rather 'locked up' mourning, but a medium for prospective mourning. Through the figure of the Sufi healer, she expresses a wish to link Abdul's otherwise inaccessible body to an accessible mourning. In the absence of the material-corporeal link, the psychic too has been left unformed. In other words, Sameena's mourning is bereft of objects, a transition, to mark the passage between the nothingness produced by separation and the meaning inherent in playing and reality (Winnicott 1971). In the absence of an alive connection to possessions or belongings to externalize her mourning, Sameena takes her 'body in a grave', or a body as grave, a primary object suspended and animated by an attachment to its ailments and complaints. The intensity of grief memorializes Abdul in her body. She describes several failed attempts to access the missing Abdul as trails of 'going from peer to peer', in a manner similar to patients passing through one therapist after another, trying to articulate her suffering 'written on a special page on which no other writing is tolerated' (Freud [1915] 1971).

'Some of them [the peers] said that he will come back, then there were some who said he has died. They would take a lot of money from me. Some gave me a specific date. I waited . . . He never appeared. All they wanted was the money', she said. At this point I asked her if she says the same things to her children that the peers said to her. As though now conscious of the connection between her disappointments and those of her children she replied, 'Yes, I too dodge my daughter . . . She is growing up . . . She senses things. She keeps thinking. If I will tell her that her father's never coming back, she will not be able to tolerate the sadness.' Unlike the daily objects whose wear and tear carry the marks of time, in not being able to carry a photograph in one's hands or to hold to one's chest, safeguarding the melancholy objects of signification, and in the failure of hopeful divination by revered peers, the bodily memory of Abdul remains frozen. The impossibility of mourning for Sameena's family is fused with the lack of opportunities for personal memorialization. The cultural formulations that ordinarily preserve the flow between life and death, the spirit world and the corporeal, have weakened her belief in a sympathetic cosmos. Instead, she finds a castigating universe, deeply disillusioning and bereft of magic.

Symptoms such as chronic fatigue, headaches and emotional withdrawal seemingly released Sameena from domestic obligations. More acutely, I heard her describe her body in a torturous relation characterized by deteriorating intactness of the body-self. Even though Sameena did not make any direct references to Abdul's body through fantasies about his health, captivity or body in pain, I sensed that such fantasies existed in de-symbolized forms in the way that she felt colonized by her pain, a kind of metonymic overload that compounds suffering. Through her illness Sameena embodies a wounded storyteller whose dread and cry would be attended to by the family or she would reel under the uselessness of suffering (Frank 1995). The image of her lying in the grave is a significant symbolization of the internal drama; to the extent that her pain goes unwitnessed, her experiences are unburied, 'unmarked' and unmemorialized similar to the hauntings revealed by several discoveries of unmarked graves, carrying the horrors of unrecorded killings and deaths in Kashmir.

Sameena's journey as a widow to a disappeared person is rife with several challenges. To not know the verdict of reality on the finality of death, to be devoted to endless waiting for the return of the one disappeared and to survive without the acknowledgement of widowhood define the complexity of psychic vulnerabilities associated with mourning. In the context of disappearances, the emergence of a new social category, of the 'half widow', points towards a singular, most notable kind of displacement or dispossession, lacking stable markers of identity for women who traditionally, or ambivalently, associate security in society through the institution of marriage. The figure of a half widow speaks to us from a place of liminality—she is the subject and the object of mourning, the lamenting and the lamented at the same time. Her status as 'half' widow points towards proximity to the disappeared husband; she cannot be adequately acknowledged for sacrifices made to the community such as might be possible for war widows. 'Half', in this regard, poses a semantic rupture when in fact it labours an excess of affect and purpose in keeping mourning ceaseless.

Sameena's loss, in her own rendering, is heightened by the abandonment by the husband's family. To the extent that no social space is guaranteed for her mourning, her body becomes a site of a dramatic proclamation of melancholia. She not only embodies personal loss but also enacts the community's expectations to keep alive, or permanently present, the disappeared husband. While the symbolism of political widows, as carriers of social memory, is extended beyond personal mourning to include political formulations or public voice to situate the loss of fallen heroes, in the context of the official denial of disappearances, mourning offers a way for the psychic incorporation of the male body into her body to abate the erasure of the disappeared through forgetting (Ramphele 1996). It is through the work of memory, which is mourning, that Sameena lays claim on a tender and cautious Abdul, who in his boyhood stood precariously between home and a nation under siege. By doing so, she resignifies the masculinity of Kashmiri men contemptuously paraded in images of terrifying masculinities, such as terrorists, militants and jihadis. She renders Abdul imaginable, grievable and human. Her mourning becomes a haunting of a future that was.

THREE DAYS IN THE RIVER

Through labyrinthine streets of the downtown area of Srinagar, connecting houses with sleepy shops and old buildings converted into military posts, covered in meters and meters of concertina wire like dead, exposed nerves. Behind a naked wall of sandbags, two soldiers observed the streets unblinkingly under the scorching sun-the landmark Aasa, a mother whose son Ajeet disappeared in 1999, had chosen for our meeting. As I anxiously confronted the daunting presence of security forces in the neighbourhood, I was struck by the irony of the affective field of Aasa's everyday—a woman who lost her son to disappearance in a surveillance state where nothing goes unnoticed. With my consciousness returning to the figure of the two soldiersand with the appearance of sweat lines on my face, I found myself thinking whether underneath the bulky combat boots, their feet were wet with sweat. At an unformulated level, the thought carried an admission of my own terror, the cold feet, at another, an encounter with a trauma story. Aware of my idiosyncratic response to the field of study, I was able to appreciate how in such moments, especially in context of surveillance, I could defend my body—dissociate and disappear—or rid myself of the vulnerability by projecting vulnerability on the one before me. These moments also brought out a profound isolation—I could lose my own humanity, deadening myself under terror, or lose it by doubting the other's humanity. A connection with the aggressor was the only redeemable strand that protected a shared humanity. A little later, I could return to myself as my own bodily vulnerability, the prickly heat and the mounting thirst announced their appearance. In the most elemental manner, the corporeal vulnerability made me susceptible *and* receptive to terror. It signalled a dehumanizing tendency of militarization. Noticing young men standing outside a small shop, drinking churned yogurt known as *lassi,* I began to inhabit my body again. I gulped down water, aware all the time that from a window slit covered with dusty netting, CRPF soldiers were watching me. This setting of my interactions with Aasa was as important as her private inner world.

A dark and narrow staircase, sandwiched between tall iron gates, led me to Aasa's home. Inside, a miniature Indian tricolour, the only Indian flag I had seen in any Kashmiri house, stood poised on a small television set. Hung on the wall behind the television, was a big picture frame carrying Ajeet's image, which dwarfed the neatly arranged kitchen vessels, the television and the flag. A big window, the only source of ventilation in the tiny one room house, opened to the banks of the muddy Jhelum, asserting a miraculous freedom from the check posts and the guards stationed outside the building in which Aasa lived. If the entry into the neighbourhood dominated my sensorium, speaking to Aasa was no simple feat. It was evident that she felt unsafe and unsure about my presence in her house. Our initial interactions felt cryptic and perched on precipitous interruptions. Although Aasa had consented to meet, I wondered how safe she felt emotionally talking to me about Ajeet's disappearance. The inescapable military surveillance outside created an ambit of traumatic reliving for Aasa. I too began to develop a somatic response, a claustrophobic reaction to the small house—a signal anxiety that was to inform me about Aasa's inner world and my own preparedness for it. Needless to say, there were no guardrails in our encounter (Layton 2006). Slowly, as time passed, the window overlooking the river became a raft to carry us safely into the stream of consciousness where the terror and the sublime rocked gently.

On being asked what she remembers of the day Ajeet disappeared, she said, 'He was young then—He would have been earning by now . . . In the evening, he went out for evening classes. He was usually backon time, but when he did not return, I became worried. It is a big loss for us. It is the loss of a life but a material loss too. I don't know where they have taken him, where they have kept him. Where have I not looked for him? Delhi, Jammu and Amritsar [prisons]. Except Bombay, I have looked for him everywhere. The day I went looking for him, that evening there was a crackdown in the Rawalpora area. I asked people whether they have seen my boy. It was winter. Everyone was indoors. Those days, crack-downs were organized; the boys were marched outside. Some were held and taken away. They were beaten like hell. People were petrified. Who could I ask about him? Everyone was worried. They would simply say that they haven't seen such a boy.' Ajeet has been missing since 1999.

As she began to open up, Aasa discovered a string of memories, of curfews, crackdowns and extra-judicial killings by the Indian security forces. She added, 'The situation had got worst . . . I would go looking for the task force . . . The police did not register my complaint. When nobody heard my plea, *I just sat silently*. To the other parents whose children disappeared, they said, that "your child is with militants" but my son cannot be with militants. Why would he be?' As a Kashmiri Sikh, Aasa saw herself outside, but not disconnected from, the wave of *tehreek* or the movement for freedom in Kashmir. Struck by the shock of the disappearance of her son, Aasa sees her loss as illogical and meaningless. She doesn't see Ajeet as a martyr identified with a cause but as an unintentional casualty. On not being able to find Ajeet, she claims she sat 'silently'. She explained that for her to sit silently implied mournful repose and withdrawal; but also an acknowledgement of and a turn to that which is not silent within. I took that her emphasis on sitting silent lacked an insistence on apathetic posturing. On the contrary, she seemed to claim silence as an active search for 'ekanta' or seclusion. As a Kashmiri Sikh woman, a minority community integral to the land and ethos of Kashmir, she actively resists divisive rhetoric and denounces the blaming of Kashmiri Muslims. For her, the experience of indifference at the hands of the police and security forces led to a shocking discovery of duplicitous practices, where instead of recording incidences of disappearances, the blame fell on the ones missing. The experience of repeated failure in lodging a complaint with the police and their apathy proved vital for imagining a shared kinship with other parents whose children were also reported missing by them.

Our conversations were full of reminiscence about the village life where she grew up, married and bore two children before the exodus to Srinagar. In its essence, her narration stitched together the fragments of shifting political currents in Kashmiri history. She remembered raising her sons by herself with a sense of pride. There was pleasure in owing one's own house, cattle and a piece of land that the family shared with the in-laws. In the 90s as the tide of change grew bigger, the affect in her stories also grew darker. Aasa recounted witnessing an unprecedented reign of terror and innumerable losses. She shared, 'I lived alone during the time when militants thronged the village. One evening when my children were asleep, I was chopping vegetables to sun-dry the next day. Two militants asked me to open the door. They needed to sleep before they could go further. I lied to them that I am alone at home and cannot open the door. They yelled and left. We used to see them come and go. They were everywhere, all the time. My village was located on a mountain. There was a narrow canal at the bottom of the mountain which was an easy escape for them. If you killed somebody and threw their bodies in the canal, no one would get to know'. It occurred to me that the proximity to the checkposts and barricades littered in the downtown area carried an eerie continuity of terror. She continued, 'In my village, right inside the garden of the*gurudwara* [Sikh temple] many militants were shot dead. They were people known to us. One child identified as a militant was the only son of a mother. Though he was a militant we grieved for him. He had never harmed us. Our houses had no boundaries . . . Everything was out in the open. When they came to a sardar's house to take refuge at night, nobody was harmed. I cannot lie. That is why I feel it is not the militants who would have done something wrong with my son'. Aasa's associations are a palimpsest of memories. Her articulation kept on forging complex connections beyond a private mourning. While Ajeet's disappearance led her to connect to other families where there had been a disappearance, she continued to register and carry the collective wounding she had experienced in the Sikh community. In the year 2000, a year after Ajeet's disappearance, a violent event shook the Kashmiri district of Anantnag, later to be known as the Chattisinghpura massacre. On returning from evening prayers in two local gurudwaras, thirty-five Sikh men were lined up against the temple wall and brutally shot. The killings were attributed to a Pakistan-based outfit, Lashkar-e-Taiba. The incident remained shrouded in mystery, only to be used as evidence of the ethnic cleansing of Kashmiri Sikhs by majority Muslims, invoking the spectral remains of Kashmiri pundits, whose mass migration remains an open wound in the Kashmiri imagination.[1] Aasa views the victimization of Kashmiri Sikhs and Muslims interconnected as the 'subjugation of the innocent' or them as minor subjects in the national discourse (Kumar 2013).

One afternoon, as Aasa and I sat shelling peas and cleaning spinach in her kitchen, she began revisiting the memoriesagain: ‘I used to cry all the way while searching for him [Ajeet]. You know, I have borne a lot of hardship—no one can tolerate such times. My husband is paraplegic; the shock of my son’s disappearance really shook him. I used to go to all the police stations on my own. If someone suggested that I go to Sanwara Thana, I would go there. If someone said there was a *peer* [Sufi healer] who could predict Ajeet’s whereabouts by seeing his clothes, I would try and go. I would go to so many police stations and wait. One day, the Deputy Superintendent of Police asked me to go back but I had no place to live. There was a waiting hall made of wood. Everyone there had a loved one missing. I had no utensils so I could not cook. One day I got a place to sit. I would cry all night long. A person from the local press asked what is wrong with me. He felt sorry and gave me a stove . . . It was filled with oil. I could cook then . . . I got a pot and a heater as well. Then someone got me two plates, glasses and cups’. Shocked and homeless, Aasa lived on the streets outside the police headquarters for weeks only to return to the hospital where her husband had been taken after falling ill. She concluded, ‘I had different vessels to cook rice and vegetables but what could I eat in a state of devastation?’

‘My eldest son, Ajeet, is a year and a half older to my second son, Anik. Ajeet was born in 1983. He would have been ready to marry by now. My niece who is one month older has four days left for her wedding. She is an engineer. They were the same age. When I went to see the Deputy Commissioner to find out about my file [Ajeet’s case], I could tell that he wanted to get rid of me. There are a lot of cases [of disappearances]. The Deputy Commissioner approved my ration card and declared, ‘Your son wasn’t eighteen years old when he went missing. Neither was he earning anything. He was of no value’.[2] I told him, ‘If that is the case then he would be of age by now’. The Commissioner’s statement that her disappeared son was of ‘no value’ lodged in Aasa as an experience of humiliation and retraumatization. The manifest indifference towards the disappeared, the denial of liberties and rights and a deliberate disavowal of their corporeal reality renders the disappeared as a ghostly presence, seen by one and rendered unseen by the other. There also emerges a spectre of militarized, patriarchal capitalism attributing value to citizenry based on notions of productivity. In the bureaucratic system of signification, where the loss of children is considered worthless, insignificant and of ‘no value’, Aasa sees children, in profoundly clear terms, as victims of the law, which is complicit in the routinization of and indifference towards agonies borne by children (Scheper-Hughes 1993). This is further compounded by the disenfranchisement delivered by denying compensatory mechanisms making such losses ungrievable. The ‘unworthiness’ of Ajeet’s loss is further accentuated by police records in which he is fixed in the image of a ‘vagabond’ who carried ‘a history of running away from home’, such that the responsibility for

Ajeet's disappearance is displaced onto the parents to have not supervised or reared him well. In her response to the officer, Aasa attempted to rework the traumatic, even if implicit, misogyny against her asserted in the context ofmilitaristic impunity that systematically uses guilt, blame and disavowal of the survivors' reality. By claiming Ajeet's body as an ageing, growing body—its relativity in time such that it is continually present and alive- she resignifies the category of the 'disappeared' as perpetually unstable, provisionary and free.

In Aasa's views, the denial of the right to a remedy or reparation by the government has a direct relation with economic and psychological vulnerability. Living below the poverty line, with two dependent family members and no reliable source of income, she is perennially on the brink of homelessness. The last job where she worked as a temporary attendant at a school, paid her 3000 rupees (less than 43 dollars) a month. Losing the job produced a new onslaught of helplessness and impotence. She shared that when she approaches the office of social workers, lawyers and police now, she no longer asks help with finding Ajeet. Instead, she asks for help to support the education of her younger son, Anik. When she failed to find work in a college, she begged the teachers to coach Anik for competitive exams. A teacher agreed to teach him for free. In Aasa's world, dealing with psychological and economic vulnerability is a daily struggle to accept the dependence on others' generosity and her own worthiness to receive it. She recalls being helped by a woman who found her weeping by the road and in turn disclosed the tragic disappearance of her own husband. The woman had been forced to remarry and let go of her children. Aasa and she developed a bond. The woman continued to offer her food supplies for a year. Similarly, a man helped her stay in a house that belonged to Kashmiri pundits until she found another place. For Aasa, surviving daily atrocities has meant a preoccupation with appearances and the strategic use of persuasion to avoid experiences of shame and humiliation. The agitated anxiety of being able to run the household frequently triumphs over a warm and affectionate sense of being. One such day, as she returned from the market, she took out a dozen soap and detergent bars from two bulky plastic bags. She seemed upset and cross. As she began to empty her bags, she said, 'I bought soap for 170 rupees and vegetable for 20. How I will get milk, I don't know . . . How we will manage for the rest of the week? We had no soap . . . I thought it is ok to go hungry but to go somewhere we need to look clean'. I saw the choice between soap and food as part of the same struggle—a struggle against dehumanization, a denial of the rightful chance at dignity of life. The choice of soap over food prevented Aasa and her family from a permanent slide towards a trepid transmutation into vermin, perhaps an experience of dehumanization that has already occurred (Winnicott 1974). The sense of ethical disengagement with disenfranchised persons sometimes shows itself in an ostensibly neurotic preoccupation with the morality of orderliness, including cleanliness, as a form of unconscious protest against erasure, against being perceived as a source of nuisance and, in its most oppressive form, a source of nausea (Guru 2009).

Over a period of time, mourning for Aasa has moved from desperate travels to prisons, hoping to find Ajeet, to visits to gurudwaras where she searches for him in the internal, melancholic confines. Unlike the legal route that has brought repetitive failure and hopelessness, the turn to communion with the mystic offers Aasa an identification with and incorporation into the other. This journey, however, has been a difficult exploration, often laced with terrible disappointments and disenchantments, not only with the worldly but also with the divine. She shared that an unplanned visit to the Golden temple led to her losing a job. 'I went to the temple in the winters for ten days. There was heavy snow and the roads were blocked.' As though trying to work out why going to the temple felt so important to her, she began telling me a legend, 'Inside the Golden Temple, there is a *baer* tree [old jujube tree]. Under that tree, whatever you wish for comes true. It is called "dukh bhanjini" or the eradicator of suffering. Once, there was a girl called Rajani. Her father asked her, "Tell me by whose grace do you exist?" Rajani replied, "I live on my god's mercy and because of him I exist." The father was upset and married her to a leper. She obeyed the father wholeheartedly. She took great care of her husband. She dragged her husband on a cart to take him to the Golden Temple and right under that *baer* tree, she made him rest. Do you know there is a pond there? A pond with water as clean as elixir. Anyone who bathes there gets healed magically. A black crow bathed in that water and was transformed into a white bird. Rajani's husband saw it happening and dipped his feet in it. When she returned she could not recognize her husband. It is said that all those who suffer or despair, must go to the tree to pray, give alms, and bathe in the water. I went there last year and the year before that. My husband is still the same, there's no improvement.' Slowly I was able to appreciate the manner in which the turn to religion was offering a method to Aasa's family. The trauma of Ajeet's disappearance that reduced them to a less-than-human condition did not arouse triumph of hate and vengeance, even though such feelings or fantasies could be denied as both useful and necessary for survivors to acknowledge and process. On the contrary, she immersed herself into the slow tilling of the self through suffering. Unable to cure her husband's illness, the magic of the holy tree and the water waned. The transformation of the crow in the story into a white bird, however, stood out in our conversation as an extremely private communication of Aasa's mourning. In wishing a cure for the ill body of her husband and access to the missing body of Ajeet, Aasa's turn to Sikh mysticism, and to the Guru, stood as a search for the body's sovereignty. By turning to the praxis of absorption through selfless action and devoted surrender, Aasa claimed a shared power with the divine. In the Sikh mystical tradition, to surrender the I/mind is to be a gurmukh or 'facing the Guru', in distinction to manmukh or 'facing the ego'. The transformation of the crow into a white bird is not so much an ascetic denial of the body, an eradication of suffering, or an ascendance to a higher mind/self, but a reawakening of bodily possibilities as it relates to self-overcoming in non-dualistic forms. It is a communion with radical noetic possibilities (Bhogal 2012). The contour of mourning, its shifts and turns, as is signalled by the transformation in the bird—black and now also white—and in Aasa who is restless and also still, speaks to us about an incalculable outcome of traumatic 'knowing'– a deathless reconditioning.

Contrary to faith in transcendence, Aasa's turn to religion is not an urgent surrendering of the melancholic position. Instead, she is increasingly able to abandon a sense of autonomy over loss and connect to a deeper sadness. She shares, 'Even now, when I sit in gurudwara, Ajeet's face comes to me', and 'I remember how sharpminded he was, so good at studies. I remember him helping me in household chores. I remember him cooking for me, milking the cow and helping with the household chores.' In these memories, Ajeet comes alive as a caring companion, a daughter-like son. In these memories Ajeet is much younger, younger than sixteen, the ominous age when he disappeared. In several other fantasies and dreams, Ajeet appears 'walking with a school bag', 'sometimes in a pheran' with 'hardly any beard' and she wakes up crying. 'Sometimes I look for him inside trucks thinking maybe he's there, with someone. Sometimes I see someone resembling him. When I go closer, I see it is not him and I walk away. (long pause) I was sixteen when I got married. I had Ajeet three years later. I didn't have milk to feed him. He was fed cow's milk. When Ajeet disappeared, my breasts started pouring milk. When a child is in pain, the mother's chest heaves with pain. God knows what trouble he might have been in. I don't know whether he was saved or killed…'. The sudden reappearance of milk in Aasa's breast magically revived the infant imagined in mortal danger to life-like in a state of devouring hunger. Aasa too glimpsed a danger—of being swallowed by the unconscious wish to meet the infant's need and the guilt at not being able to do so (Winnicott 1956). The experience of disappearance traumatically recreated, and simultaneously denied, the experience of the mother's bodily separation from the baby. Though no longer physically joined, Aasa's mourning reproduced milk as a method to relate through contiguity, a connection in the mind and body, enlivening the erotic—the life-giving force—in the knot of loss. The maternal lament, her preoccupation with loss, 'pours' out of her breasts, revealing mourning as a form of memory (mammary) secretions, a somatic underworld unchained in loss. This heightened sensitivity, Aasa's revived maternal preoccupation, what Winnicott called 'almost an illness', is a deep longing to make up for 'the missed boat at the earliest stage' of motherhood (Winnicott 1956, 302). She found herself identifying with the vulnerability and complete dependency of the child, whose body was brought to life, as in the negative hallucinations, like a ghost baby at the heaving breasts of the mother. The figure of the lactating mother stood out like the weeping Pieta.

The wish to feed Ajeet returns in the scene of everyday domesticity as a medium of inexpressable mourning. Aasa shared that she feels Ajeet's continual presence in the liminal, when she is least conscious. One such day, absorbed in a hypnoid state, while rolling out *rotis* [bread], she called out to the missing son, 'Ajeet roti kha le' ['Ajeet, come have food!']. This maternal call was answered by the younger son, Anik, who responded, 'Aaya Maa' ['Coming Mother!']. For Aasa, such moments make mysterious reliving, however impossible to capture in language, real and nourishing even if they are only disclosed in 'magical' enactments. For Anik, the younger son, responding to his mother's call yearning for the missing son does not bring about depletion in the self. He becomes the keeper of a '*secretly perpetuated topography*' (Abraham and Torok 1994). One glimpses a communication between two mourners, each invested in hosting Ajeet, not through the vehicle of memory but through an immediate hallucinatory fulfilment, immutable in reality. Through such enactments, the magical work of incorporation returns as constitutive of mourning. She recovers in secret an object refused in reality. In her imaginal ties, she is able to sidestep the pain of the permanent loss of Ajeet.

In my interactions, Aasa expressed that she blames herself for bringing the children to Srinagar to seek treatment for her husband. She bemoaned, 'A lot of Sikhs went missing [a reference to disappearances in Punjab and Kashmir], but they were older men . . .' In recalling the disappearance of Sikh men, Aasa connects the dots between incidences of enforced disappearances in Punjab and Kashmir. The Punjab Documentation and Advocacy Project has investigated 8,256 cases of disappearances and illegal cremations carried out as part of counter-insurgency operations between 1983 and 1995 under the Punjab Disturbed Area Act, 1983, the Terrorist and Disruptive Activities (Prevention) Act, otherwise known as TADA and the Prevention of Terrorism Act (POTA), which gave power to security forces to act with immunity and impunity (Dhonthi 2019). Aasa's sense of persecution was further accentuated by seeing herself and her family outside the Kashmiri struggle for sovereignty. She added, 'I ask myself why it had to happen to us when we haven't done anything. It feels like a sham. I felt suspicious when they took my son . . . I thought they might have killed him and buried him somewhere. I went mad. But now I sit silently. What has happened has happened. What can I do now? It was part of my destiny.' In several interactions, Aasa kept the memory of the 1984 Sikh massacre alive, reminding me that the Sikh community has seen 'terrible times', the rise of ethno-nationalism and violence against minority groups in India. The fantasy that Ajeet might have been killed and secretly buried has its roots in the collective memory of the massacre in which thousands of Sikhs were lynched, burned and killed.

In search of freedom from the states of persecution and anxiety, Aasa's turn to religious and communal life offered an opportunity to overcome alienation. By reclaiming ties with gurus and mystics, Aasa's unrepresented pathos found a place in worldly suffering. To the extent that all suffering is a test of endurance, Aasa searched to find other meanings of the tragic loss. She expressed this as, 'God is testing me to see how much I endure. First we plant a sapling, then we tend to it with care. We water it and prune it. Only then the plant matures into a fruit bearing tree. Can I get all the fruits without taking care of my tree? Can that happen?' Seeped in religious symbolism, an imagery of salvation, Aasa saw her absorption into pain—the bottomless fall into melancholia—as a point of conflict. She shared that she experiences her mind as a site of blaring disquiet. If the longing for the disappeared child is a ceaseless suffering, she struggles to formulate *how* to suffer. She spoke of selfless devotion and service at the temple, cleaning floors, cooking and attending to the devotees as a rhythm that sustains her. When she would not show up at the temple, women devotees asked after her and encouraged her to attend prayers. They insisted on the benefits of *seva* [service] and encouraged Aasa to become regular at the temple. Aasa remembered a woman devotee telling her, 'Once you hold his hand, you are never to let go'. The articulation 'never let go' fermented Aasa's hunger for a connection with Ajeet. The parallel between yearning for the mystic and the child that eluded her maternal love became a combined pursuit. Aasa shared, 'I used to feel depressed and ill all the time. I had no hope, no energy in my body. I cried all day'. This changed significantly, when during a visit to the Golden Temple, the most significant place in the Sikh religion, she saw a vision of the first Sikh Guru, Guru Nanak. Knowing the personal significance of such a vision for a devotee, I did not ask Aasa about what she saw. She also held the experience as both open and private. During our interactions, however, she narrated several stories of Nanak's life, miracles and genius with marvel and care. A story that had special affective significance for Aasa concerned Nanak's three days in the river. Nanak, who began his day with a ritual bath in the river, disappeared for three days with his clothes lying by the riverside. While his friends and family searched and grew afraid that he had drowned, far from danger, Nanak, who had found God, sat in the womb of the river in a divine trance chanting what is known as the first root mantra after his enlightenment. Just as people gave up hope of ever seeing him, Nanak returned from the river bed, changed and the same. The story has a deep bearing on Aasa's mourning. As she tuned into the image of the mystic in the river, in the immensity of his absorption with the divine, Aasa also recovered the disappeared son in an unknown realm, where he grows secretly and infinitely like the mystic himself, unflattened by the loss, and deathless. The story kept alive the possibility of the protection of the river-womb and hope of return. The three days in the river is an allegory of losing and finding, a moment of awakening and discovery, or a meeting ground for the unseeable. In the image of the clothes lying next to the river, one glimpses Aasa's own disappearance. While she sits embodied in melancholic stillness, she is immersed in an underground union. The 'three days in the river' is an expression of the transformation of 'useless suffering', a chaos of alienation, into an assimilable moral pain carrying a private mourning, its use and a radical purpose (Haq 2020; Seeman 2008).

As a response to Ajeet's irretrievable absence, she now prays that he has a 'turn of heart' or an internal resolve to return home from the vanishing river. When I first heard her articulate it, the fantasy that Ajeet will experience a 'turn of heart', I was led to think that it corroborated the unconscious guilt and pain she experienced at being abandoned by the son; that perhaps this guilt colluded with the dynamic of 'victim-blaming' demonstrated by the police who manipulated the facts to make Ajeet appear as a vagabond or a runaway. As years went by, Aasa surrendered the impulse to search for Ajeet in different prisons. It was much later in my interaction with her, through a growing appreciation of Aasa's private language, I began to hear that the 'turn' that she spoke of was embedded in mysticism. Aasa was articulating the reality of all beings—a willing return to the oceanic womb—conceived by the first Guru in the hymns. In Guru Nanank's hymn concerning the stages of human life, the four stages symbolize the four watches of the night. In the beginning, the first stage, the person residing in the womb remembers the Name and enjoys the complete union/merger with the Name or truth. In the second stage, one is born only to forget the Name, the primal union or the natural meditation on truth. In the third watch, the individual through wealth, vanity and addiction goes on living in ignorance, to eventually die without knowing the gift of primal union. In the fourth watch of the night, the soul—the reaper of meditation and rightful action—'harvests the field' (Guru Granth Sahib 74–75; Bhogal 2012, 870). The wound of disappearance carried a deeper terror for Aasa. What if Ajeet forgets the oceanic womb, the original home in Aasa, a place of their mutual belonging? The terror, to not be able to make it home, felt like fear of psychosis or death even. To imagine the 'turn of heart' in Ajeet therefore implied a wish that he may remember what he has forgotten by the traumatic bodily separation, that is, the oceanic womb of the mother. To lose recognition of the Name implied an endless drifting into nothing from which the oceanic reunion is irrecoverable. The 'turn of heart' is therefore a provocation for Ajeet to choose remembering and for Aasa to not be unremembered. The scatter produced by the unthinkable loss is dreamt by the image of the mystic, the temple and the community of devotees (Ogden 2001). The mystic Guru stood as a symbol of limitless protection, an intimate companion and an affirming source in an unstable world (Vahali 2009). Amongst the women devotees too, the vision of the Guru granted Aasa a special status and standing. The women told Aasa, 'It is his *hukam* [Divine Will]. He has ordained it—It is a deed to be done wholeheartedly'. Marked by surrender, to be guided by *hukam* is to host a radical shift in subjectivity wherein the claims of sovereignty are not individual but collective. To be led by it implied a sovereignty of the body to defend its existence, to belong with, rather than rule over, implicating the self in a sphere of responsibility and action, *seva* (service) and *sangath* (community). Once turned away from the ego-self, *hukam* speaks to and leads to a collective of the true, a place of sovereignty not exclusively owned but as the birth-right of all beings. It therefore worked to implore Aasa's melancholic rigidity, a preoccupation with ego-self to join, through suffering, an 'innerconnected immanence' in an effortless becoming (Bhogal 2012, 864). At the temple, she is recognized as a symbol of survival and mourning. Over a period of time, her son, Anik, is also recognized with affection by community members who call him 'wakeel sahab' (Sir lawyer) replenishing the narcissistic needs for the family's continuity.

The unbearable futility of mourning in the context of disappearance proved significant in Aasa's undulating rhythms between loss and recovery. In the language of religion and mysticism, the traumatic rupture is given a new opportunity, a stage to rework the nameless dreads. Through myths and stories transmitted in the temple, as a trauma survivor, Aasa not only made new linkages with the personal but could also seek assimilation into enduring cultural memory that offered a healing possibility to make meaning of the unrepresentable loss. She asserted, 'He is the one who shows colours and devoids us of colours. He wipes the tears and gives them too. We won't live eternally . . . Even our gurus did not live forever.' I saw Aasa reclaiming the ambiguity deposited by Ajeet's disappearance to extend a possibility of transformational self-work such that her unremitting pain and loneliness began to co-exist with warmth, generosity and eloquence. In our final interview, while reflecting on the dilemma of the memorialization of the disappeared through a dedicated memorial and the unearthing of unmarked graves in Kashmir that some speculate is an evidence of death of the ones missing, she cried, 'It is a sin—they are disappeared persons; they are not dead!' She recounted yet another story of Nanak's life, who on observing the priests in Haridwar offering water to the sun god and the ancestors, reoriented the ritual with a childlike play. Imitating the gesture of the priests, Nanak attempted the impossible feat of sending water to the fields in Punjab, in a way to reason with the baffled priests on the emptiness of rituals. For Aasa, there is no substitute for justice, no memorialization outside the truth and no scope of departure from witnessing the survivors' suffering. She is a mystic-sceptic, suspicious of the politicization of memorialization practices if they fail to reach the elusive, here the disappeared, and the tortured mourners who miss them and live out a continually disappearing fragment of lived history.

NOTES

1. More recently, in 2017, an investigation led by Retd Lt Gen KS Gill, suggests the involvement of the Indian Army in the massacre. The report was submitted to the Home Ministry of then NDA government (Sikh News Express 2017).

2. Aasa, here, is referring to SRO 43, an exercise of power conferred by Section 124 of the Constitution of Jammu and Kashmir. It enables the compassionate appointment of a person who is a family member of a government employee who died as a result of militancy- related activity but was not involved in any such activity or a civilian who died as a result of militancy related activity but was not involved in the militant activity and whose total income of the family does not exceed Rs 3,500 per month as assessed by the Revenue Officer not below the rank of an Assistant Commissioner. In some cases, when compassionate appointment is not possible, the family is given a compensation of four lakh rupees.

Chapter 4

Bearing Witness, Imagining Disappearance

In 'The Location of Culture', reflecting on the anxiety of our times, anxiety fatally connected to survival in the present, Homi Bhabha writes,

> The beyond is neither a new horizon nor leaving behind of the past . . . Beginning and ending may be the sustaining myths of the middle years; but in the fin de siècle, we find ourselves in the *transit*, where space and time cross to produce complex figures of difference and identity, past and present, inside and outside, inclusion and exclusion . . . These in-between spaces provide the terrain for elaborating strategies of self-hood—singular or communal—that initiate new signs of identity and innovative sites, of collaboration and contestation, in the act of defining the idea of society itself (1994, 1–2).

The allusion to the in-between as a propitious site for the emergence of the unknown, not as sublimation but as play, offers *experience* as neither an account of inner psychic reality nor does it concern itself exclusively with external reality. In a stroke profoundly similar, Winnicott (1967), in his paper, 'The Location of Cultural Experience', reflects on the birth of hitherto unknown symbols and objects in the interstices, the in-between or the third, similar to the interplay of edges between two curtains where 'beyond' peeks reluctantly. Winnicott writes that the object that peeks 'is the symbol of the baby and the mother (or part of the mother). This mother can be located. It is at the place in space and time where and when the mother is in the *transition* from being (in the baby's mind) merged in with the infant and alternatively being experienced as an object to be perceived rather than conceived of. The use of an object symbolizes the union of now two separate things, baby and mother, at the point in time and space of the initiation of their separateness' (Winnicott 1967, 96–97). The symbols and objects produced to be used, similar to what Bhabha calls ‘elaborating strategies of selfhood’ (see above), offer a personal continuity of existence against the ‘repetition of unthinkable anxiety’ (Winnicott 1967, 97). For Winnicott, culture is a common pool of humanity, from which ‘we may all draw if we have somewhere to put what we find’ (ibid 99). Seen in these terms, culture appears like the mind, a space and temporal orientation, to place and draw out, to create or to find, objects and mental representations that have shared meaning. One may ask what symbols and representations might appear in cultures ravaged by violence and repetitious unthinkable anxiety? What of the cultures where the space ‘to put and draw later’ has been replaced by loss and disappearance and haunting absences? What forms does psychic representation take and how do we make meaning of uncontainable messages? What modes does an artist make available to speak of suffering? Remembering the significance of Picasso’s ‘Guernica’ or Goya’s series of prints titled ‘The Disaster of War’ and Nilima Sheikh’s large scrolls, ‘Each Night Put Kashmir in your Dreams’, we turn to the wakeful artist, her empathic inwardness to dream the undreamt in the symptomatic aspects of traumatic moments in Kashmiri history.

Exposed to excessive pain, the mind-body duality ceases to host the certainty of painful experience, exposing the limit of language to situate it. For the one observing and attending to the other’s pain, the only certainty is to ‘have doubt’, for such an experience is fraugt with primary unsharability, a problem of transference of pain (Scarry 1985). Pain here is neither denied nor recognized. For a person or a community undergoing massive trauma, survival is an exercise in taking up this very challenge, of recognition, to risk the other’s limit to comprehend one’s experience while attempting to represent one’s experiences still unthought. Consider for instance, the confusion, horror and sadness I experienced when a Kashmiri woman in the village of Kupwara showed me a framed picture of the bleeding, bloating body of her dead husband, who had been killed along with others by Security Forces in an encounter with those involved in pro-freedom activities. She smiled proudly as she showed me the picture. The bleeding, bloating of the body suggests the frozenness of the image, in my mind just as in the photograph, trapped in-between a continuous traumatic reliving. The picture was an invitation to understand the significance of the ‘good death’ of a martyr, sometimes articulated as the highest form of death. Under conditions of upheavals, there appears a resignification of meaning, expressed through a complex play of affect, images and symbols that govern ruptures and the continuity of identity processes. Mahmood notes, ‘While part of the intent of such exhibition is to provoke continuing anger, there is no doubt that torture pictures are mostly received as inspiration by Sikh and Kashmiri audiences; see, they exclaim, what we are capable of overcoming! See how nothing stops us! Christ on the cross, after all, provokes both sorrow and joy—and is the continuing inspiration for some Latin American resistance movements through the image of Cristo guerrillero' (2000, 77).

Through the use of photographs, memorabilia and art, people listen to and produce private inflections in mourning stories to preserve and ascribe meaning to the individual struggles and collective survival. Lifton, in his work on the Holocaust and Hiroshima bombing, began to see that 'whatever it is that the survivor knows, that knowledge is bound up with the dialectics between life and death, with "dying" and being "reborn" . . . A survivor [should be viewed] as one who has come into contact with death in some bodily or psychic fashion and has himself remained alive' (1969, 40). It is through art, symbolizing the threat of extinction, that the survivor-artist can cease to be immobilized by the survivor's guilt, death imprint and the psychic numbing that ensues from what feels like 'the end'. It is in this manner that 'survivor art' imagines the death encounter, a moment of mutation and the movement beyond. Survivor art, according to Lifton (1973), has the task of expressing, symbolizing, and representing how in the face of or the threat of extinction, one imagines human continuity. Unlike Hegel (1993), who considered art an impulse to exalt the inner and outer world into spiritual consciousness or spiritual freedom for the artist, in the context of violence and mass destruction, the spiritual struggle is perhaps a spirited struggle against disintegration and annihilation. The struggle is therefore not only to make the experience explicit within and without, but to recover *forms* of representation that can contain the breakdown of experience.

For Lifton, the artist is a 'prophet of forms' especially when forms are in radical disarray. He sees the artist as someone who suggests patterns of reordering, even if in the process he may seem to contribute further to the disarray. Here the artist is devoted to the illuminate in 'exquisite details' the experience of desymbolization (Lifton 1983, 40). The Survivor art attempts to give artists and the community a chance to master end-of-the-world imagery while ascribing a place in an aesthetic cultural history as well as moral imagination. The subject of survivor art includes reflection on bodily damage, the breakdown of cities and structures, philosophical perils and the insufficiency of traditional symbols. For this reason, I do not differentiate between survivor art and what is known as resistance art. The aesthetic force—the subject of the art and its aim—that the two forms carry are deeply linked. The subject of survival, with annihilation as mutative, recur along with an active resistance against the experience of oppression and indignation demanding attention towards the creation of forms and metaphors which communicates transformation along with the continuation of destruction and survival (Dea 2012; Kabir 2009). Such an impulse is illustrated in the works of Kashmiri artists and poets as they bear witness to collective trauma and the subjectivity of passive bystanders.

Masood Hussain, a Kashmiri artist, articulates the challenges in sustaining artistic expression as a graphic designer and in his work in advertising and watercolour painting experienced as the situation in Kashmir grew worse in the 1990s. In an interview, he shared the incomprehensibility of the changing landscape in Kashmir, with 'sudden eruptions' of the feeling of panic. In an interview he recollected, 'Houses were set ablaze till such a day when the entire valley was engulfed'. His earlier work focused on watercolour landscapes. However, during the surge of conflict, as long curfews and violence sent artists and painters into their living rooms, there appeared a growing dissatisfaction with known forms of expression. In the days to come, he saw his advertising agency and the surrounding neighbourhood gutted, destroying several design records and paintings. Under such cataclysmic circumstances, with curfews lasting hours and days, Masood Hussain started painting from home. Trained at the JJ School of Art, Mumbai, and faculty at the Institute of Music and Fine Arts, Srinagar, Hussain began afresh to imagine his experience of Kashmir under siege as an artist afflicted by the suffering surrounding him. His turn to the use of mixed media and relief work came out of the dissatisfaction with the flatness of canvas. The use of relief work enabled him to incorporate traditional art forms such as papier mache and lattice work prevalent in Kashmiri architecture to carve faces, hands and persons, not only in colours but in living, breathing form, peeking from windows in moments of shock and mourning or in the privacy of prayer.

During the peak of the turmoil, Masood Husain painted a series of works titled 'Transparent Strokes'. This series reflectes the many tragedies engulfing Kashmir, through works, such as 'Thou Knoweth My Misery', or 'Exodus' and 'Those who Disappeared'. The subject of these paintings includes the migration of Kashmiri pundits, disappearances and the changing meaning of cultural symbols. Hussain found himself drawn to the ruins of broken and burnt houses and began reclaiming broken structures such as windows with lattice frames. He incorporated the lattice windows in his art, mounting them on canvas in mixed media, giving a visual home to the broken pieces of history such that art produced a form of witnessing by a bystander looking inwards. This is perhaps most clear in a painting titled 'Submission' (1995). In a similar manner, one finds Hussain recording the violent history of Kashmir by representing moments in time, the memory of critical events offering an eyewitness account in imagery. For instance, in a work titled 'Stampede' (2004), Hussain painted the scattered footwear of the crowd that had gathered for the funeral procession of Mirwaiz Maulavi Farooq, a chief preacher, who was shot dead in his house on 21 May 1990. The mob was scattered by police gun shots near Islamia College, killing seventy-two people. The painting is a memory, of the collective, captured by Husain's actual witnessing of the site laced with scattered shoes as he retraced the street where the awful events transpired. The deluge of unclaimed shoes and slippers coloured in blue appear like a river, with a red epicentre, a volcanic blood stream, around which nothing is discernible.

Within Kashmiri contemporary art, Masood Hussain elaborates on the theme of absence and continuity. His two paintings on disappearances occur at a gap of seven years, giving us a glimpse of the artist's internal resolve and absorption with the psychic conundrum posed by the phenomenon. In the painting titled 'Those Who Disappeared' (2004), a painted relief work, an empty frame hangs while the picture of the person appears stolen. The frame carries a silhouette standing in relation with a demonic shadow outside it. Hussain alludes to the loss of the body by creating a cascade of empty frames from where the images of the disappeared have vanished. In the painting titled 'Look Behind the Canvas' (2011), he memorializes Mogul Massi, the mother who died waiting for the return of her missing son, along with two generations of mourners—a half widow, a sister of the disappeared, and a child who never saw her father. Compared to the earlier painting titled 'Those Who Disappeared', made in 2004, we see the subject of the painting shift from the one who disappeared to the subject of waiting carried out ceaselessly by the mourning women and children. The paintings moved from the shock of disappearance towards inter-generational mourning. While in the painting 'Those Who Disappeared' (2004), the frames are shown as vacant, in the painting 'Look Behind the Canvas' (2011), the mourning wife, a 'half-widow', is seen clutching the photograph of the missing husband as her child looks on. The passage of time is represented by a broken watch and a white dove's ascent, carrying a computer chip in place of a sacred thread or an amulet. At the bottom of the frame, there is a collage of newspaper headlines, 'Mogli's mission continues after death . . . 2000 shutdown . . . curfew stopped life . . . 98 persons killed since June'11', creating a chaotic excess of the deteriorating political situation in the valley.

In conversation with me, reflecting on the creative impulse behind the painting, Hussain explained, 'Instead of putting a sheaf of grain in the dove's mouth, I put a computer chip to suggest development, advancement . . . The young woman wants to get away from what has happened in Kashmir. The broken watch symbolizes the twenty two years of life that I have lost. Out of the sheer frustration, I tore the painting and left a needle . . . I don't think that the *condition* in Kashmir will get better . . . We say, "*Humare zakhmo ko kaun seeega?*" [Who will stitch our wounds?] . . . It is an open wound. I will stitch it when times change'. He thinks of the tearing of the canvas as the 'conclusion' of this work, a final act of destruction preserved in what the canvas cannot bear but failingly allows.

The pervasive motif of hope and survival and the piecing together of history translating the concrete world into memory work makes Masood Hussain's work a poignant vehicle of the generational mourning in Kashmir.

His contemplative engagement with art forms such as pepier mache, lattice work and weaving as well as the use of traditional symbols are interpreted on the canvas in vivid imagination. The turn to mixed media and relief, a visible layering of the mind, as an offshoot of a gnawing dissatisfaction with other technique proved to be a creative subterfuge to reach an aesthetic experience of traumatic rupture (Haq 2015). There is a recurring portrayal of prayer performances and shrines, restored as sites of the reawakening of the mystical in the face of human limit, during a time that saw a targeted destruction of the sacred realms of communal life.

While testimonies as first person narrativization of a memory, like eyewitness accounts, have been accepted as a relevant literary form in contexts of unprecedented events or history, in poetry too there may exist a testimonial form, a device through which the poet seeks to construct a memory of events for the bystander-reader. The poet's wish to commit a traumatic event to memory against the effects of forgetting is completed when the reader's unconscious volition hosts a reciprocal remembering, even if at first it feels as though one is infected by an experience alien to oneself or as the other's suffering. Such poems invoke a close proximity with the actual event, the arising conflict and affective incommensurability, confounding the poet or the protagonist's reality. The poem may invite a doubling of latent purpose as a testimony and as a literary artefact. By doing so, it may preserve a radical uncertainty—the intention as well as the outcome for the reader are coded against easy translation. In this manner, the bystander-reader comes to witness the catastrophe, its pictorial construction, the decisive moment of shift as something occurring both inside and outside. In the context of disappearances in Kashmir, the Kashmiri poet, Naseem Shafaie, exemplifies such witnessing most notably in two collections of poems, *Open Windows* (1999) and *Neither Shadow Nor Reflection* (2017).

In a poem titled *Baakh* ('The Wail' 1999), Naseem Shafaie gives voice to maternal lamentation, sometimes in the figure a woman or as a city ravaged by the disappearance of her children. The poem begins with the story of a queen who awaits the return of princes, her sons, who have not returned home. The reader is denied a sense of time except through the grains of rice growing cold in a plate. The actual period of waiting is kept hidden. The poem begins thus:

'A'
Once upon a time there was a queen
At the end of the day she would wait,
With the doors thrown open,
For her little princes to come home.
A little hesitant, a bit afraid,

She'd ask her neighbours, women like her,
'Are your children out still?
My own have quite forgotten their home!
God knows where they have stayed,
The grains of rice grow cold in the plate.'
'B'
She is the one to whom someone said something one day,
And her doors and windows were shut.
But in the dead of night, the ocean broke its bounds,
And the neighbours heard a long unending wail.
'Do not die on me, you are so young!
Do not die, your nails but barely henna-tipped!'
(Translated from Kashmiri by Indu Kilam, *Open Windows* 1999)

In the poem, the queen addresses her apprehension to other mothers, calling out for an empathic resonance with her difficulty. It is a call to the womb of the reader to connect to the concern for lost children, their safety and the yearning for union. 'Women like her' is suggestive of Kashmiri mothers, mothers in wait, the expectant mothers, in the house, outside the school gates, at the bus stops, at the detention camps and police stations who *know* the dithering swings of anxious watch for the return of children. The queen inquires about other children and confesses a deeper condemnation—that her princes have forgotten her. As the poem progresses, as readers we witness a catastrophic shift in the queen. Through suggestion of 'someone' saying 'something' and 'one day', the reader is called to lend her imagination to recover what the poet cannot utter. The reader's task is to ask what made the searching mother recede to the confinement. What caused the doors to be shut tight? Through the use of words such as 'dead', 'night', 'ocean' and 'unending wail', the reader is taken on a melancholic tide, without an addressee to inquire what caused the mother to fall to pieces. In her wail, the reader turns to endless search as being more benign than the confirmation of death. Towards the end, the poem reveals the nature of maternal yearning, collapsing the return of little boys—the princes—into the return of young grooms yet to celebrate a bashful youth culminating in wedding celebrations.

In the poem titled, 'The Return' (1999), Naseem Shafaie returns to the disorientation in time as a poignant device to imagine the trauma of disappearance. The first verse openly and daringly acknowledges that 'years' have passed in waiting. The poem adamantly keeps the experience of the ambiguity of loss alive. Time is offered as a riddle, a fort-da, between the mother and the son, between childhood and youth, without the negation of a darker battle between life and death undisclosed in disappearance. The poem unfolds as follows:

Years have passed since,
yet it seems as if it was only
yesterday when you hid under
the mounds of earth, under
the grave-yard stones—a still body
hidden from my sight.
Why did you hide?
Why did you hide?
Did they not tell you there?
Did you not hear the path near the wide
road, in the small by-lane the old chinar
with its frightening shadows and evil spirits,
that would follow you in your child fantasies,
have long since left for far off unknown places.
Now there is no danger, no fright, no wait for
endless nights to return home.
Come back to me without fear or fright.
Return home once again like a child
come home for my wait for you is
unbearable. Come for I pine for you. I
will call out for you and sing wedding songs
for thee. Come back my dear O! I would
give my life for you.
(Translated from Kashmiri by Indu Kilam, *Open Windows* 1999)

The pictorial construction of the home, the streets and the familiar trees in the neighbourhood are brought to bear on the dialectic of erasure and timeless evenness. The symbolism of melancholia is abound in the mother's reminiscence. The disorientation expressed by the protagonist mother is not perceivable through any radical shifts in the inner or outer realm. On the contrary, it operates through the sameness of the everyday, the seamless flow characterized in waiting for the return of the missing child. The game of hide and seek is shown to have entered a grim playground of life and death, expressed in the imagery of 'mound of earth' near a 'grave-yard stone'. The tone of the lament is soft, with the mother and the imagined child whispering, confiding and speaking about their ominous fears, the 'evil spirits' and 'frightening shadows' lurking around the Chinar tree. The mother's reassuring voice is convinced that the spirits have left the streets and neighbourhood is safe for the child's return. The 'evil spirit' is disambiguated to suggest militarism in the region as the shadow forces snatching and scaring the skinless, defenceless body of a child. In the lament, the mother is seen reasoning with the child's terror, convincing him that the old fears are no longer founded in the reality of danger, promising her presence as safety against future harm. The trope of the 'withdrawn child' emerges in the poem confounding the 'evil spirit' with the failure of the maternal environment. Waiting, as an experience, is expressed through the mother's unfulfilled yearning, the savage severing of the union between the mother and the child. Here, the laments carry the ring of wedding songs, the oedipal passions wrung dry of erotic connections.

In depicting the mother as a figure in mourning, Shafaie articulates the loss of the mothers of the disappeared as an intimate other whose homes have been destroyed or whose children have been lost to incalculable devastation. In Shafaie's poetry, the myth of the savagely protective 'maternal instinct' competes with the equally powerful forces of a devouring state (Scheper-Hughes 1993). The evocative image of the wandering mother of the 'pained city' leaves the threshold of the domestic, becoming the protector or the custodian of the children, the city and history. Representing the experience of the conflict that violently forced Kashmiri women into the public sphere to protect their families, particularly men, Naseem Shafaie records the transition and transformation in Kashmiri women's agency and subjectivity (Scheper-Hughes 1993, 354; Rashid 2011).

To wait, in the way that it has come to be known in the lives of women mourners, in Winnicottian terms, is 'to be ill', to grow into a condition of heightened sensitivity, a desired identification with the baby that is more than a symbiotic or homeostatic relation (Winnicott 1956; Mahler 1954). The tenor of maternal lament, in the lived experiences and portrayals originating in artistic works, point towards the 'maternal' as a formidable psychic representation, open for identificatory and actualizing tendencies within survivors, especially in the context of disappearance. Here, the state of waiting, an expression of maternal preoccupation, is an achievement of maternal love. In his paper 'Primary Maternal Preoccupation', Winnicott suggests complex and varying expressions of the mother's concern for the baby, in a kaleidoscope of symptomatic embodiment (Winnicott 2012). To begin with, maternal preoccupation can seem like a psychiatric illness, a commitment to a dissociative break comparable to schizoid withdrawal and fugue. For Winnicott, the mother's ability to reach this state of illness is a sign of positivity, an inner unconscious instrumentality, to go closer to the baby's fear for its survival. While maternal lament, in the context of infant death or historical trauma, especially in the context of disappearance, has been seen as affect fantastique capable of cementing, articulating and mobilizing political action—the erotic life of protest fuelled not by or as lover but as mother (Scheper-Hughes 1993; Hollander 2010), I see maternal lament as fruitful psycho-socio-political praxis for its origination in 'illness', remitting preoccupation with the life of an infant against the backdrop of unrelenting impingement. In place of the 'flight into sanity', the mother in wait, through a melancholic return, attempts to claim the baby in danger of disappearance from the mind, as in corporeal reality, to the exclusion of other interests and aims. In his work on early mother-infant relation, Winnicott considered that the state of maternal preoccupation, while appearing dangerously close to psychosis, recedes and the mother recovers, repressing the memory of her mental torment in service of their joint survival. The mother-mourners, or persons ‘devoted’ to the disappeared, carry the state of preoccupation without the possibility of ordinary ‘repression’. On the contrary, the manifestation of trauma associated with ‘repressive’ circumstances, or in regimes of oppression, lies in exposing the unbearable states previously worked through in benign forms. Playing imaginatively with this maternal quest to keep alive the disappeared child in every breath, the Colombian artist, Oscar Muñoz, in a series of ten steel discs photo serigraphs titled ‘Aliento’, or breath, involves the viewer to breathe life into the disappeared (Graham 2012). As the viewers breathe on the surface of the disc, the photograph of the disappeared persons, as though warmed by the other’s wish to find them, appears momentarily on the surface. This life-giving gesture, a fort-da of losing and finding, imitates the mother’s longing to keep alive or bring back the disappeared by offering a reflexive participation in wish for return. The mirror-like discs, resembling breasts at one level, make the image of the disappeared visible as the viewer’s internal body participates with cardiopulmonary resuscitation of the viewer breathing on the disc. The viewer is at once the mother for whom the image of the disappeared reappears as though by magic, and to the extent one is born through the mother’s intuitive seeing, the viewer is also a child at the mother’s breast. With each blow of the breath, and repetitive enactments from one disc to another, the maternal fixation is visibilized as primordial ‘illness’ or preoccupation, returning us to the state of illness as the epigenesis of psychological and political resistance to forgetting—a refusal to repress the search under a climate of repression. The act of breathing life into the photographs reveals another aspect of the grief held by the mourning mothers. For the mother, contact with the disappeared is a bodily contact and the mourning, a dwelling in the psyche within the body (Winnicott 2016).

Besides maternal lament for the disappeared body, its unavailability for conclusive mourning, the lament for the disappeared reappears in the children of the disappeared in what James Herzog (2001) calls ‘father hunger’. He writes, ‘Absent nutritive experience with the actual father, restitutive fantasies and overwhelming hunger are likely to become prominent features’ for children who lose their fathers to emotional and enduring absences due to disappearance (21–22). Without a father to identify and integrate paternal functions in service of aggression, bodily motility and aliveness, the opportunity for the consolidation of the masculine sense of self for future drive and fantasies is severely challenged. Herzog (2001) enters the child’s internal state through

Goethe's poem 'Erlkönig', the story of a little boy haunted by a monster, the elf king or Erlking. Herzog notes that the Danish etymology of the word suggests an old or menacing woman as the root. In the poem, the boy begs his father to save him from the menacing apparitions and hauntings of the monster. The father, unable to comprehend the monster, fails to perceive the little boy's terror and plea for help. The boy dies in his father's arms, slain by Erlking. The death of the little boy is symbolic of childhood depression and the frightening symbiotic relation with the mothering figure when the father's absence threatens a nutritive triadic relation with its hopes and promises of mutuality and the identification of a vital recognition (Wolman 2004).

In the emerging cinematic representation—as seen in films such as *Tahaan* directed by Santosh Sivan (2008), *Haider* directed by Vishal Bhardwaj (2014), *Hamid* directed by Aijaz Khan (2018), *No Fathers in Kashmir* directed by Ashvin Kumar (2019), *Where Have You Hidden My New Moon Crescent* (2013) and *The Dear Disappeared* (2018) by the Kashmiri documentary film maker Iffat Fatima—there appears a deep hunger and search for the father to address the developmental needs of the child frustrated by the missing father. These films portray struggles of the abandoned child, deprived of the father's presence, who undertakes a search for the link with the father which is expressed as an unbridled curiosity for the person of the father to attach, connect and know. In the externalization of the search for the father, there is a wish to be found worthy of attachment and to be known by the father. The circumstances of disappearance, the violent condition of abduction, produce extreme distress and helplessness in the survivor children. While the memory of the disappearance might be consciously-available trauma, marking the everyday of the family with psycho-social vulnerability, the meaning of father's absence appears as beta screen, or raw sense impressions, unready for mentalization into introjectable forms. While in the film *Haider*, Haider, the male protagonist, tries to make sense of the father's abduction in early adulthood, films such as *Tahaan, Hamid* and *No Fathers in Kashmir*, portray the challenges for younger children for whom the father is an absence-presence, available in fleeting memory traces, the secret obsession of the psychically dead mother or the search for linking objects such as a donkey who goes missing in the valley, an unfinished boat that the child wants to resuscitate, or a chance encounter with the father's shoes against which the girl wishes to measure her development and belongingness in the father's body.

Because the father is both real and imaginary, the place of a father post the traumatic loss is all the more significant (Akhtar 2005). The objects of fascination, the last minute objects, represent the father wrapped up in the moment of loss, experienced repeatedly by externalizing rather than internalizing tendencies (Volkan 1981, 2014, 2018). The relevance of these linking objects lie in creating the possibility of losing and finding by engaging the mourning child to bring the experience of loss into the frame of endurance. There is an illusion of control and choice, that is, while the reality of loss is postponed, the mourner may continue to have internal ties and may struggle to come to terms with it. To the extent that adult carers allow for the linking objects to be used in the service of attachment and mourning rhythms, the paradoxical meaning of the linking object can prove to be useful—the object is both created and was waiting to be found (Winnicott 1971). In the representation of the predicament of children and grieving mothers or wives, there is the suggestion of an emergent historical moment, ushering a change from passive by-standing to active witnessing, indicating 'a healing process at many levels—personal, interpersonal, community, inter-community, and, sometimes, between humans and the natural and built environments. To move toward engaged witness is to reclaim history and to look for one's place in it; it is to look forward into the future for one's own role in creating it' (Watkins and Shulman 2008, 76).

In the Kashmiri context, the link between the human and non-human environment is a significant aspect of cultural life. One the one hand is the usefulness of concrete objects for the mourners, and on the other hand lies the ubiquitous presence of the mystical relation governing a psychic realm of body-to-body relation, not excluding a persistent reference to the soul as a seat of experience. The disappearance of a father's body, now available in its disembodied form for the child, acquires imaginative prominence both in the hunger for attachment as well as in the hauntings brought to the shores of the mind in dreams, transferences and substitutions in relationships.

Just as artistic endeavours enable the possibility of re-membering the dissociated experiences, attempting to articulate the colonizing tendencies of helplessness and terror produced by trauma (Lifton 1969), the human and non-human environment such as shrines, mosques, lakes and mountains offer themselves as empathic restorative spaces or symbols (Waheed 2019; Altman 2015; Siddiqui 2016). As the shrines and mosques began to be targeted during the political turmoil, the symbols that offered a generational continuity and life to the community's sense of belongingness, Kashmiris experienced it as an attack on human dignity and their cultural freedom. In the Indian imagination, the inclusive mystic tradition of Kashmir was underplayed in favour of a rise of a virulent Islamic force, damaging the Kashmiri narrative of a syncretic living. The pervasive militarization contributed to the functions and role of mosques and shrines, especially in catastrophic moments of violence. They became spaces to record and bear witness to the collective suffering, mark deaths and offer prayers in times of grave uncertainties. They served as a place for an empathic confrontation with a frightening reality. The mourners of the disappeared persons attest to making fruitless visits to detention camps and prisons, and a poignant turn to the venerated Sufi shrines for succour and relief.

The philosophical underpinnings of Sufi-Islamic roots, a soul-body dualism, influence the Kashmiri imagination of the intangible, non-corporeal experiences in dreams, clairvoyant intuitions and the uncanny. Many mourners of the disappeared reported dreams in which the disappeared appeared before them desperately seeking to be helped. On further exploration of what the dreams mean for them, they shared that they believed that the missing use dreams to communicate their states and feelings—meeting them or losing them was experienced as real. The 'meeting' here implied a contact between souls, the organizing principle for the body, freer than the physical entity. Not only do these dreams point towards a wish fulfilment for the mourner to help deal with the painful separation, it is as though dreams are experienced as an intuitive space, a mysterious portal through which the missing persons escape the surveillance state that keeps them hidden under shadows. Dreams thus become the stage for *political theatre,* enacting themes of loss and psychological breakdown as well as formulations of protest, escape and freedom (Dwyer 2009; Peer 2012).

Within the Islamic religious-cultural framework, following a loss, a period of three days is considered necessary for mourning. Resumption of life post this period is considered normal. To bear the loss with restraint or *sabr* and accept the will of god is considered essential for the mourner's relation with the lost person as well as one's faith in the Divine (Yasien-Esmael and Rubin 2005). Acceptance of death implies a reaffirmation of the spirit world. The grave is, therefore, not seen as an enduring place of continuity, or a 'second home'. While death entails the end of corporeal materiality, it does not demand a permanent relinquishing of ties by those who survive. Offering prayers for the one who is gone, giving alms or *sadaqa* to the needy, or naming a child after the dead are a few ways through which cultural continuity and mourning are achieved. In a conversation, a gravestone maker, working near the famous Sufi shrine of Maqdoom Sahab, Srinagar, observed that in Islamic philosophy, the process of mourning for the dead involves a gradual decrease in preoccupation with the grave, and a gradual giving up of the ritual return to the deceased who lies buried. He shared, 'There is no body there anymore. The dead goes to another world. Tending and caring of the grave inhibits the mourner's acceptance of this knowledge. The mourner thinks that "here lies my beloved", but it is not true. A grave should be left, should be left alone for weeds and plants to take over. It is a reminder that the beauty and display of human civilization ends as a barren stretch'. It is in this manner that the disappearances have ruptured the warp and weft of cultural wisdom. The wounding of the link between the human and the divine propels the mourner's claims on the body of the disappeared. They seek to correct not only the political but also the spiritual order of things (Zia and Bhat 2019).

A devoted mourning, with the fantasy of incorporation at its helm, is the realm of magic, a way to immerse in not-knowing. The mourner and the *object within* live incommunicado—separate but not disconnected (Winnicott 1963b). The ritualistic return to memories or the belongings of the lost person lies in the area of object-relating. Mourning is thus an immersion not in comprehending separation but holding the union in a third area. Between love and loss, one swings in the rhythm of creative living—of aloneness. Eigen (2007) articulates this as, 'a certain moment, central or primary, that is blessedly un-agnostic, possibly touched by the language of mysticism, the peace that passeth understanding' (417). A mourner's connection with the lost object is not formulated around body functioning but on body experiences—the difference between orgiastic satisfaction and ego-relatedness for survival such that continuity gives place to contiguity (Winnicott 1971). Within the Sufi-Islamic tradition, the mourning of families of the disappeared persons make claims to contiguity by engaging with what is *batin*, that is hidden or latent, over what is *zahir*, or manifest. It carries the possibility of imagining a complex subject-object relating enshrined not in the tangible or corporeal but rather in the manifestations of the mystical in the ordinary, with culture as a container for the undreamt dreams. Such psychic work, of re-establishing a sense of connection, of an organic relationship with human and non-human elements in the immediate as well as the imagined world, is necessary for the Kashmiri collective to reach symbolic integrity, cohesion and generational mourning.

Chapter 5

The Shape of Mourning

In the novel *Anatomy of a Disappearance*, Hisham Matar sees ritual returns of his disappeared father in the everyday as a permeating truth of his consciousness. From the slippery experience of the disappearance, emerges a litany of questions—When did the disappearance occur? Who took him? What became of him? While these questions remained unanswered, they are replaced by a perpetual sense of absence. He writes, 'There are times when my father's absence is as heavy as a child sitting on my chest. Other times I can barely recall the exact features of his face and must bring out the photographs I keep in the old envelop in the drawer of my bedside table. There has not been a day since his sudden and mysterious vanishing that I have not been searching for him, looking in the most unlikely places. Everything and everyone has become an evocation, a possibility of resemblance. Perhaps this is what is meant by that brief and now almost archaic word: elegy' (Matar 2011, 1). The story revolves around Nuri, a fourteen-year-old boy, searching to piece together the moments that led to his father's disappearance, mirroring Matar's own mourning for his father whose disappearance was carried out by the Libyan authorities in the 1990s. In the heaviness of the presence sitting on the chest, there is an awareness of a *shape* disambiguated from a blank interiority. It is the shape of mourning. A presence heavier than a shadow and clear as a dream. In place of the object—the missing father—there exists a grieving child. An absence present in the excess of heaviness. The shadowy image of the child, the vanishing features of the father's face leading to the ritual return to the photographs, call into memory the states of possession in the dispossessed. The fantasy of return for the mourner, the one who traces an elegy in surviving the other, is an encounter with the strange proposition to be satisfied with resemblance rather than recovery or a search over discovery. Freud imagined that in loss, the mourner visits every single memory till such a day that she is free from the attachment to the lost object. Free to seek a new object, to love again. In case of disappearance, the lost person guides and eludes the mourner searching for the traces of the disappeared in all likely and unlikely crevices of personal as well as social memory. While the disappeared may not transition from the terrain of absence to presence, the decision to search, the posture of waiting, reveals the mourning possibilities. The psychic terrain or the inner labyrinth of the mourner searching for the disappeared discloses an intractable loved object and the mourner as a living memorial. As the search of the mourners of the disappeared acquired a new obsession to reclaim their bodies, in their search they discovered social black holes, resisting representation of loss: prisons, detention camps, unmarked graves which functioned as flashpoints of an impossible return. I asked what would be the register for an exploration of the experience of disappearance? How do we piece together the traumatic loss, the horrors of making someone absent or gone in the story of the persons in pursuit of their return? What does survival imply in such contexts? It is in the register of mourning, the total effect of loss—the unique interruption—on the mind and body of the surviving mourner, that serves to throw light on the experience of disappearance in the lives of mourners.

The *shape* of mourning, or the shape incorporated in the mourning, is discoverable in the dark shadow cast by the lost object. The forsaken ego fends for its survival from a narcissistic identification such that the ego is the object, the mourner is the disappeared person (Freud [1917] 1971, [1914] 1958). The mourners of the disappeared are in the dark in two specific ways: one, that they do not know what happened to the disappeared person; two, caught in the melancholic predicament, they live in the shadow of the loss. What possible method, or ways of seeing, can be conjured to adapt to the darkness in melancholia, to trace its muted terrain? Freud, in a statement to Lau Andreas Salome, imagined that perhaps we might be better able to find our way in the dark if instead of illumination, we throw *a beam of intense darkness* to make what is an indiscernible begin to glow. In Bionian imagination too, to contact the obscure realm of the mind, the brilliant, knowledgeable light stood little chance. Bion, following Freud, suggested that we 'bring to bear a diminution of the 'light'—a penetrating beam of darkness; a reciprocal of the searchlight' (Bion 1990, 20). Through their mourning, mourners of the disappeared in Kashmir bear such a diminution that we may learn to recover the disappeared as a percolating shape in the individual and the collective memory. As we have been able to witness in the stories presented, it is not only the disappeared who stand out in the darkness but also the edifice of militarization in which mourning is transmitted from the individual to the collective, to be contained sometimes as symptom, sometimes as phantom. Unlike death, a situation of the clarity of loss's finality, in ambiguous loss such as a disappearance, the work of mourning involves the search for the lost object inside as well as the search for the one lost in the outside. This brings mourning in contact with the state machinery that may perpetuate further traumatization when loss is denied or rendered unmourned. Cassia (2005) suggests that the state appropriates 'an interrupted mourning process, or more precisely inserted itself in the mourning process' and fabricate 'a simulacrum of mourning into a discourse of resistance' (81).

To the extent that mourning in the case of disappearances is a response to the context of militarization, the mourners are also victims of massive trauma and state repression. The uncontainability of the traumatic loss due to disappearance and the widespread exposure to violence have a deep impact on the survivors' intersubjective worlds. On studying the Argentinian experience of military rule, Antonious Robben (1995) noted the ways in which victims and perpetrators induce specific emotional responses, what he calls 'ethnographic seduction' which may lead anthropologists 'astray from an intended course' (83,86). Robben preserves seduction as false leads that disarm critical detachment, falsely announcing itself as though one has accomplished something profound. The suggestion is similar to George Devereux's idea of 'ethnographic repression', where the researcher represses the cultural experiences in the field that correspond to unconscious desires and wishes through the use of omission, soft-pedalling, ambiguous description or a rearrangement of material (George Devereux 1967, 42,45). These notions, seduction and repression, point towards an intersubjective field, what in psychoanalytic framework we have come to heed as a realm of transference–counter transference, enactments and projective identification (Klein 1946; Kernberg 1967; Altman 1995; Ogden 1989, 2001). Such phenomena are especially tenable for reception when one enters the realm of the mourner-survivors' in-communicado core. My own view tilts towards a willing readiness to be disarmed by the affective charge of what is urgent in the mourner to project and exile from within in search of a host in the other. Where mourning has been left interrupted, there must appear an opportunity for reworking, a possibility of re-telling. Just as an elegy depends on the reader to be alive to the affect surrounding loss, the work of mourning depends on an intersubjective field to carry the process of remembering (Rose 1997; Scheper-Hughes 1995; Benjamin 2017).

It is through enactments in which I became the missing person who abandoned and forgot or transferences of feelings such as rejection, fatalism, unfaithfulness or deep longing for acceptance and union, I began to see spectres of loss, domination and mutilated longing (Freud [1915] 1971; Bragin 2005; Laub and Auerhahn 1993; Nordstrom and Robben 1995). I learned to see that I was 'playing a part in someone else's phantasy' (Bion 1959a, 149); that if allowed an unconscious porosity of communication, my feelings were a 'direct communication', unmediated by an interpretive frame (Winnicott 1971c, 54). Like the heaviness of the child sitting on the chest, I was coerced without a choice and felt controlled from within. The ability to contain the induced feelings by the listener, instead of throwing them back through a projective mechanism, carries a possibility for psychic reuptake. This intersubjective mode of containment through an interacting pair is the site or register of experience that made witnessing possible.

The mode of containment, however, that I experienced in the work of mourning in Kashmir implied 'tackling violence, terror and death through methods of somatic, sensory, affective, semiotic, symbolic, phenomenological, linguistic, performative and social historical constructions' (Feldman 1995, 226). The intersubjective field that mourner-survivors and I inhabited was grounded in the extremely unstable and dangerous condition of militarization, defining the relation between the stories found and how one finds them (Kovats-Bernat 2002; Sluka 2000; Willis 2000). Times when the lack of safety cut me off from methodological support—the theory and training that sustain us like oxygen does a living organism—I became conscious of wobbly feet of episteme, which is largely embedded in stable, predictable structures and dynamics in the field. As the field would have it, terror and violence did not contaminate the work, it was the work. The work of mourning unfolding before me was thawing slowly to reveal not just a violent separation or loss but a lack of separation between violence and loss (Robben 2000; Sluka 2000; LaCapra 2001; Das and Poole 2004). To go closer to a place of trauma or a wound entails acknowledging ambivalence involved in approaching pain that one might contact, a pain from which return might be unattainable. It is in this manner that witnessing experiences of loss and trauma is a political and ethical decision even though it feels like, at every step of the way, a reluctant act.

RADICAL SULLEN ATHEISTS OR DEVOTED PILGRIMS

In 'Black Sun', Julia Kristeva (1989) emphasizes the enigma of an ignoble, untenable melancholic retreat visible in the mourner's solitude. Deprived of meaning and values, the mourner turns inward, to regain audience with the thing lost, making her at once an atheist unmoved by other meanings or objects and a mute mystic or devotee adhering to the completeness of one's own 'inexpressible container' (14). Kristeva writes, 'In the tension of their affects, muscles, mucous membranes, and skin, they experience both their belonging to and distance from an archaic other that still eludes representation and naming, but of whose corporeal emissions, along with their automatism, they still bear the imprint' (ibid). While for Freud (1917), the presence of the private sanctum was vivified in the melancholic's self-reproach, invoking the presence of the archaic object into the threshold of consciousness. Kristeva, however, suggests the relation with the object as necessarily silent, an immutable devotion where depreciation and exaltation make the very fabric of a melancholy jouissance.

In the language of mourning—the mourning trails of Rasool Ahmed, Husaina, Samina and Aasa—the lost object, the disappeared person, is held cocooned in the self, or the ego, as a necessary condition of survival. The acknowledgement of loss, in disappearance, and the dangers posed by the 'giving up' of the object, help erect walls that protect and imprison the mourner in a state of exile from the outside, a world replete with opportunities of possible introjection. The exile from signs, images or relations independent of the loss, especially because it is widely negated, makes the mourners' enclave sullen and lacking in meaning. Their experience, however, suggests that the perpetual withdrawal is a requisite for hospitality to the archaic object, its demands, and a signal for the mourner's devoted care to fuel and fulfil the continuity of the object's tenure in the internal terrain. One significant aspect of the melancholic attachment is the reversible figure-ground relation between the object and the world—the turn inward provides the mourner a recovery of mystical fusion, a staple for devoted mourning; but the turn inwards, the very precision of the psychic demand, also cuts off the mourner from relating and attaching to newer objects. Like a staunch atheist, the lure of gods has little power or import for her.

With the mourner still joined to the object, the sadness associated with loss forces the aggressiveness and hate to run underground, exhibiting great restraint in the mourner's experience of loss. It is as though the self cannot put up with the experience of being abandoned, in loss, and the affect that comes with it. As we learned from the mourners' journeys in chapter 4, the disappeared persons are held dearly and lovingly, with their love and loyalty unquestioned. The agony and hardships revealed in the aftermath of disappearance do not alter the amorous ties with the disappeared nor are they blamed for the mourners' ill fate. The mourners, on the contrary, seem to use the melancholic attachment to the disappeared as vital to their continuity and meaning. While many mourners, in the context of disappearance, would perhaps correspond positively to the criteria of depression or post-traumatic stress disorder with lack of care or concern towards the external environment experienced as blatantly affectless or overwhelmingly uninteresting, their inner life is pervaded by the ritualistic return to the object installed within. The affective rhythm might change to muteness or the delights of suffering known to monks and ascetics, on the one hand; it may turn to omnipotence of an exalted language in a manic flight, underlying the erotic ties with the lost object as a vital life force, on the other. In the families that experienced the trauma of disappearance, each member carries a significantly differentiated response to the loss. While normality returned to re-establish a fledgling contact with the everyday for some, for the other members maintaining ties, returning to the memories of the disappeared at the risk of avoiding all else and the search for their return served as a private reservoir nourishing attachment, activism and personal memorialization. Devotion to the disappeared, carried by the 'sullen' mourners, fuelled their inner fantasies as well as their silent 'sit-ins', observing the suffering denied internally as well as externally, including politically. In our attempt to uncover the problematic of mourning, the terrifying melancholic rigidity and its simpler normal course, one possible casualty is a powerful psychic position, a profound device, of 'the turn inwards'. To what purpose does the mourner link her unending commitment to the singularity of memory? Is the plea of the melancholic a seduction hiding a radical refusal or resistance to mourn? What possible outcomes can emerge from the morbidity of pain? In the way that psychoanalysis and psychology both draw from and attenuate the melancholic position, we are caught in a Kafkaesque enactment of Ulysses and the Sirens. Scared of the songs of the Sirens, their mournful subterranean knowledge, like Ulysses, we have stuffed our ears with wax to prevent us from being pierced by the longing and wisdom of melancholia. Much more than the songs, or the mourners' lamentations, it was the Sirens' silence that was feared by the sailors scared to be disarmed in mortal combat. Reflecting on Ulysses' oversight, in 'The Silence of the Sirens', Kafka writes, 'But Ulysses, if one may so express it, did not hear their silence; he thought they were singing and that he alone did not hear them. For a fleeting moment he saw their throats rising and falling, their breasts lifting, their eyes filled with tears, their lips half-parted, but believed that these were accompaniments to the airs which died unheard around him. Soon, however, all this faded from his sight as he fixed his gaze on the distance, the Sirens literally vanished before his resolution, and at the very moment when they were nearest to him he knew of them no longer' (2002, 101–102). In the shifting of the gaze, like Ulysses, we forgo the recognition of the slowly vanishing Sirens, the subterranean language of melancholia, rendering it dangerous, or worse, banal. It is by going closer to the mourners, risking the certainty of fossilized positions, that we recover a new possibility to listen and understand the meaning of melancholy, its personal and social reverberations, without reproducing coercion and constraints on its expression.

In denouncing mourners as pathological and their suffering as inchoate or meaningless, we have overlooked the usefulness of the mourner's capacities to forge the continuity of relational ties to lived history. The avoidance of the mourner's inner worlds, their silences and their refusal to choose new objects manifest through quick prescriptions, and clinging on to expectations such as the return to normality or a pat for resilience, if it means adaptation. Such ideals pervade a wide range of theoretical discourses and therapeutic practices. The dismissal of the devoted turn to the figure of the disappeared might prove to be catastrophic in acknowledging the significance of melancholic attachment to recognize the mourner's annihilatory experience as well as collectively experienced social violation and erasure delivered through structures of power. In Freudian terms, in mourning and in melancholia, the turn of the ego upon itself becomes a place of identification with the lost object. Seen from the outside, what seems like the negation of loss is identification with the one lost, a memory or a life, in the service of psychic repair or restoration. In a similar vein, it is the loss annulled in the social that seeks and finds a refuge in the melancholic attachment. By doing so, the whole psychic (and the social) structure is changed from the bottom up, same way that decolonization changes the order of the world through a programme of complete disorder (Fanon 2001). An annulled loss incorporated in the melancholic can thus be the only topography for possible recovery.

RESISTANCE TO MOURN OR MOURNING AS RESISTANCE?

The mourner-survivors of the disappeared persons testify to the impossibility of successful mourning where loss has been rendered ambiguous. The unabated mourning in such contexts may meet the criteria of post-traumatic stress disorder, complicated grief or pathological mourning (Volkan 1981). The valence of the meaning that mourners themselves experience spills outside these narrow, even if useful, descriptions. In the manner that loss takes a permanent occupation in a mourner's mind, there may exist an inability to allow change or a turn to the future. While melancholia is imagined as a resistance to mourning, or an inability to 'introject the loss' (Abraham and Torok 1994), the lives of mourners in Kashmir suggest that the very characteristics of pain, the unbending rigidity that earns bad press, carry a purpose, a drive. In the context of political repression where lives are rendered ungrievable, mourning becomes an act of reclamation. To the extent that forgetting is linked to the disavowal of certain histories, the mourners' grief is a counter-resistance to the wounds afflicted on the ones dominated and forced to purge memory or to commit to forgetting. In one way, mourning is a response to social and political control, visibilizing implicit or presumably benign structures of power, as they act upon individual agency and vulnerability—a response one would not part with (Ogden 2005c). In ordinary terms, resistance is an act or a gesture, whether verbal, cognitive or behavioural, that discloses an intention to subvert functions or expectations of the powerful. Action or opposition remains the manifest form of resistance; what if resistance is not merely an act of protest but a quality of being unveiled by an actor? Like the singing spirituals who used singing as a method, or an internal preparation, to navigate the area between slavery and freedom, defying assumptions of inferiority asserted to oppress them, mourning carries the seed for assertion of worth and radical differentiation such that pain is a place of subjectivity (Sanger 1995, 179). The work of the oppressed constitutes overcoming the cycle of fatalism, helplessness and humiliation connected with the traumatizing experiences produced and maintained by structures of oppression. Shocked by the savagery of violence carried on the bodies of Sikh men, women and children in the massacre of 1984 in the city of Delhi, women mourners sat huddled outside their houses and camps, surrounded by blood-spattered walls and heaps of ashes. The women defiantly held on to their filth and pollution, embodying the catastrophic that they neither hid nor made tolerable, transforming their mourning into an active resistance against the state (Das 1990). In a situation of the normalization of body violence or the use of technology of domination, such as in Dirty Protest in Ireland against carceral violence, mourners and protestors actively betray rational aims (Aretxaga 1995). The unbending demand to mourn loss offers to reformulate the meaning of the social and the communal that is in danger of a violent and a pervasive severing. Personal loss may be put to political use for transformative action such that melancholia may not necessarily change its form, but may bleed its colour, or the concentration of its tedium, from location of the private into the public.

A reflection on the experience of enforced disappearance takes us to the questions: it is well known that a symptom has a social determinant, or origination in historical context, but can it have a political life? How would such knowledge affect our response to social suffering or collective trauma? Would we see the unconscious only as a repository of familial experiences or a mine of self-other collisions? The interaction between personal loss and collective trauma, in contexts of mass violence, offers a way to consider the private and the public not as separate, but as 'recoiling-refracting' mechanisms with which the social conditions and individual resistances interact (Sitas 2004). The mourners-survivors who take on the complex work of waiting for the return of the disappeared reimagine the work of mourning. By turning forgetting into a *taboo*, the mourners reclaim their attachment with the missing as a form of political protest. While state repression makes the body a hostage, it is one's ties with 'the missing' that cannot be erased. The mothers and wives, fathers and children, by incorporating the lost object, prevent the decay of the lives of the missing individual by embalming them in the inner crypts of their personal and collective memory. They articulate two appeals or two assertions—to be reunited with the missing or to come face to face with loss to reach a place of the 'futurelessness' of the fantasy of return or reunion.

At the community level too, the memory of the disappeared, sometimes as memory of the disappearance, is kept alive through fantasies, fears and concern about the past and the future. Like martyrs who sacrificed for the community, the disappeared persons and their family are imagined as permanently imperiled. The unearthing of mass graves, the unexamined question of disappearance, extrajudicial killings and torture carry the potential, and may sometimes serve as 'chosen traumas' and 'chosen glory', to galvanize the Kashmiri struggle (Volkan 1979). By keeping the disappeared present in the collective memory, just as they are in the everyday practices of the mourners, the disappeared remain 'unburied' (Cassia 2005; Galatariotou 2008). The search for the return of the disappeared is a strife for the restoration of justice and dignity. This mourning moves bodies, moves between bodies of the mourners, and moves from individual to collective containers. Mourning thus emulsifies, binds together and creates rituals of mourning. It is through the active labour of mourning that individuals and groups interpret the meaning of the past to reorient their future (Watkins and Shulman 2008; Vahali and Vahali 2019). From the realm of the visible located in the monthly sit-ins, the indiscreet plastic bag in the hands of the mourner carrying a careful assortment of the documentary evidence of disappearance and the continuous negotiation with the law and justice department to the private language of attachments to the body-memory of the disappeared relived through day's residue, mourning in the Kashmiri context argues for a 'non-redemptive' route that does not 'intend to finish with the past and return to "normal life" but rather to keep the past from slipping away in a present that continues to deny it' (Watkins and Shulman 2008, 123).

By fixing mourning along the lines of success and failure, as self-limited or as dark and regressive, a dynamic understanding of mourning as a psychic process has been stifled through disciplinary 'gatekeeping'. Like the hysteric whose desire and drive are infantilized by the doctor's authority, mourning too suffers the doctor's evaluation for over-identifying with the loss. As the hysteric is punished for overexcitement, the melancholic is banished for her morbidity. To the extent that such notions or the 'value-neutral' standard of professional participation are upheld, we are complicit in the adaptation of hegemonies and hierarchies that perpetuate oppression and human suffering (Gordon 2008). Living as we do in a context wounded by militarism, our psychic life unfolds in systems of suppression, exclusion, domination and exploitation. There is a danger that we may come to accept unconsciously the evil projected on us by the very structures and systems that also provide opportunities for creative living (Erikson 1974; Sonpar 2007). By excluding the political, historical or cultural embeddedness of individuals, we make loss alien and the lost ghostly. As newer categories, or phantasms, populate our consciousness as 'refugees', 'terrorists' or 'the disappeared', the meaning of such appearances are further complicated by gender, race, class and political life rife with the forces of ethno-nationalism and capitalism (Altman

2010). The exclusive engagement with loss in the process of mourning in the Kashmiri experience, as in the practice of psychoanalysis, offers a radical shift in imagining alternatives to violent histories and the contentious present. When as therapists we move outside the walls of offices to communities torn by uncontainable social suffering, we learn to feel and recover not just destructive potentials but also human vulnerability, fundamental to realizing an ethical response to pain. The future of all mourning lies in learning from the failures of the human and her failure to mourn the human.

THE PETITIONING UNCONSCIOUS

The search for the return of the disappeared in Kashmir reveals the possession of two temporalities by the mourners—a time for waiting and a time for searching. On the one hand is the iconic rigidity, a catatonic rejection of all else, exemplified in affective withdrawals in the private and to the domestic or its corresponding display in the public sphere through protests and participation. On the other hand, there is the harrowing movement of the mourners' body—a body forever in motion, in a state of restless readiness to find, or be disappointed, travelling from the house or the neighbourhood to police stations, detention camps, prisons, shrines, hospitals, courts and protests. In his paper, 'Remembering, Repeating and Working Through', known for his timeless innovation on the psychoanalytic technique, Freud posits going over or repeating of conflicts as a technique or logic inherent to the unconscious to revisit in order to rework, assimilate and ingest experiences left outside the realm of one's mind (Freud 1914). For Freud, repetition is haunted by what it is trying to escape—the fear of forgetting. One can only remember what one is able to repeat. As traumatic as repetitions may be, with little hope of 'working through' what remains incomplete or largely unchanged in the recesses of the mind, it is the last hope against the sin of amnesia or repression. Freud alludes to the force of such repetitions and its impact on the continuity of treatment. The force that animates the rigid body of the patient—the ghost that possesses the affectionate, servile subject—speaks in tongues that we as analysts are only beginning to comprehend. For Freud, it was an elderly woman, who entered analysis with 'affectionate transference' that increased in intensity with 'uncanny rapidity' (154). She repeatedly fled from her house and her husband in what Freud calls 'a twilight state' (154). She would go away, or disappear, without anyone knowing or becoming conscious of her motives. For me, it has been the mourners of the disappeared, who disappear into the twilight of despair, mourning losses while remaining unmourned. What would it mean to follow them into the twilight, to return changed? Can we imagine a Kashmir without acknowledging the ravaged lives of millions of people who are left behind to trace the unyielding monster of an insufferable mourning?

In the noise of repetition, one hears a petition. The unconscious appears to petition for acknowledgment. Of trauma normalized, losses denied and pain left unfelt. In every repetition—symptom, nightmare or transference—the unconscious knocks on the door of consciousness, with its foot in the door, hoping to be heard. In a petitioner's complaint, the last resort of an aggrieved party, there is an imagination of an audience or relief; that a sympathetic jury or a judge of reason will restore a lawful universe guided by shared humanity and justice. The search for the disappeared persons, the petitioning, changes from a massive and singularly disorienting rupture to a seat of inter-generational trauma engulfing mothers, fathers, wives, siblings and children. Each opportunity to recover the disappeared is also a tragic repetition of the same loss they are coping to recover from. This enactment of the search is a way to remember the unformulated aspects of the original trauma of disappearance. As Freudian suggestion holds, repetition here is transference of the forgotten past, of the state of breakdown in which mourner could not be a witness to herself or her strange predicament. It is the company of other mourners, the dissociated or estranged knowledge—the 'trans' state—that is finally inferred as transference to be worked through. The mourners in the Association of the Parents of the Disappeared Person help themselves overcome the enemy who has been rendered 'absent and not within range' by making it real, nameable and recognizable (Freud 1914). Seen from such a lens, the posture of the unconscious is necessarily that of mourning, petitioning vigorously to be felt, to be allowed a dignified entry and to be responded to. The praxis of mourning in Kashmir is an occasion for assertion, for a different register of pain. As witnesses to horrors endured by the land of Kashmir, the mourners' task exceeds their individual pain. At the heart of the spectacle of rage and mourning taking shape in the Kashmiri struggle for freedom is communication, tying the weapon to the wounded. It asks for a radical shift in the perspective on pain, involving giving up of one's 'natural' claims on pain stemming from notions of the worthiness of some lives and unworthiness of others. The semantics of pain reveal that to feel pain is to feel 'acted upon' by something or someone outside one's skin, or external to oneself. The anomie experienced by the Kashmiri experience suggests a need for a revision in our thinking on the site of pain and the language of its formulation. As suggests Joseph Beuys's imaginative sculpture of a knife blade bound in gauze, 'When you cut your finger, bandage the knife', we are called to feel in one's wound, the wound of the other; in one's own blood, the screams of someone else. Will something in this encounter yield or will we miss or skip, yet again, the appointment with the petitioner?

The experience of disappearances in Kashmir will carry long-lasting effects on the generations to come. The interplay between loss and absence created by disappearance could potentially offer itself as an open wound. Will the wound left by this collective trauma knock at us as a body in rage or a body in grief remains to be discovered? What is at stake is the Kashmiri people's right to memorialize lives and mourn the death of their beloved members. The denial of such ritual practices, the merciless attack on a community's beliefs and philosophical roots, have created holes in the very fabric that offers symbols of continuity. While the monstrous outcome of the historic trauma cannot be undone and the genie cannot be put back in the bottle, it is through containing, surviving and remembering historical trauma that one can hope to move forward and give the dissociated spectres of violence a place in lived history. The figure of the mourners of the disappeared persons in Kashmir pulsate in Kashmiri consciousness as a symbol and a response to the unrelenting oppression and the inchoate grief unleashed by three decades of brutal control and oppression. The work of mourning is made possible through their participation in the intersection of the psyche and the polis. As the disappeared continue to speak from a place of haunting, there emerges a conundrum of a new social category, of 'the disappeared', leading to an identity panic, characterized by 'irreconcilabilities in the ongoing assimilation' (Erikson 1968, 682). The hauntings are evidence of the effect of forgetting or the disavowal of the Kashmiri experience. The mourners of the disappeared speak from the great confinement caused by the disavowal of the trauma of the disappearance. In their laments and private proclamations, they pave way for renewal, continuity and healing in the context of social suffering. The willing opening of the wound, the re-experiencing of the memory of loss and abduction and the making explicit of a demand for justice reveal that at the heart of the unconscious, the backcloth of our psychic life, lies the impulse to petition for one's truth, to sit in the exquisite withdrawal of the disobedience of mourning. Even though one cannot return to the beginning, undaunted by the enormity of what is lost, it is the labour of the search that reveals the meaning of loss.

References

Abraham, Nicolas, and Maria Torok. 1994. *The Shell and the Kernel.* Chicago, IL: University of Chicago Press.

Adorno, Theodor W. 1950. *The Authoritarian Personality.* New York: Harper.

Agamben, Georgio. 2003. *The State of Exception.* Translated by Kevin Attell. Chicago, IL: University of Chicago Press.

Ahmad, Shafi. 2012. *The Half Widow.* Kolkata: Power Publishers.

Akhtar, Salman. 2005. *Real and Imaginary Fathers: Development, Transference, and Healing.* New York: Jason Aronson.

Akhtar, Salman, and Alexandra Powell. 2004. "Celluloid Fathers: The Depiction of Paternal Function in Some Recent Movies". In *Real and Imaginary Fathers-Development, Transference and Healing,* edited by Salman Akhtar and Henri Parens, pp. 73–94. New York: Jason Aronson.

Ali, Tariq, et al. 2011. *Kashmir: The Case for Freedom.* London: Verso.

Altman, Neil. 1995. *The Analyst in the Inner City.* Hillsdale, NJ: The Analytic Press.

Altman, Neil. 2008. "From Fathering Daughters to Doddering Father". *Psychoanalytic Inquiry* 28, 92–105.

Altman, Neil. 2015. *Psychoanalysis in an Age of Accelerating Cultural Change-Spiritual Globalization.* New York: Routledge.

Alvarez, Anne. 2012. *The Thinking Heart- Three Levels of Psychoanalytic Therapy with Disturbed Children.* New York: Routledge.

Amnesty International. 1980. *The Amnesty International Report.* London: Amnesty International Publications.

Amnesty International. 1981. *The Amnesty International Report.* London: Amnesty International Publications.

Amnesty International. 2012. *Amnesty International Report: The State of the World's Human Rights.* London: Amnesty International Publications. Retrieved from: http://files.amnesty.org/air12/air_2012_full_en.pdf

Amnesty International. 2018. *The Amnesty International Report.* London: Amnesty International Publications.

Aquinas, Thomas. *Summa Theologica.* Supplement to Part 3. 80.5.

Argentine National Commission on the Disappeared. 1986. *Nunca Más: The Report of the Argentine National Commission on the Disappeared.* New York: Farrar, Straus, and Giroux.

Arinto, Patrcia B. 1995. "Contours and Contents of Testimonial Narratives by Women in the Philippine National Democratic Movement". *Review of Women's Studies* 5, no.1, 64–87.

Asch, Solomon E. 1956. "Studies of Independence and Conformity: A Minority of One Against a Unanimous Majority. *Psychological Monographs: General and Applied* 70, no. 9, 1–70.

Barthes, Roland. 1978. *A Lover's Discourse: Fragments.* Translated by Richard Howard. New York: Hill and Wang.

Barthes, Roland. 2000. *Camera Lucida.* London: Vintage Books.

Barthes, Roland. 2010. *Mourning Diary.* New York: Farrar, Straus and Giroux.

Bauman, Zygmunt. 1995. *Life in Fragments: Essays in Postmodern Morality.* Cambridge, MA: Blackwell Publishers.

Benjamin, Jessica. 1988. The Bonds of Love- Psychoanalysis, Feminism and the Problem of Domination. New York: Pantheon Books.

Benjamin, Jessica. 2017. *Beyond Doer and Done To: Recognition Theory, Intersubjectivity and the Third.* New York: Routledge.

Benjamin, Walter. 1996. "On the Concept of History". In *Selected Writing*. London: Belknap Press.

Beshara, Robert. 2019. "Decolonizing psychoanalysis/ Psychoanalyzing Islamophobia". In *Islamic Psychoanalysis and Psychoanalytic Islam- Cultural and Clinical Dialogues*, edited by Ian Parker and Sabah Siddiqui, pp. 102–117. London: Routledge.

Bhabha, Homi. 1994. *The Location of Culture.* New York: Routledge.

Bhogal, Balbinder Singh. 2012. "The Animal Sublime: Rethinking the Sikh Mystical Body." *Journal American Academy of Religion* 80, no. 4, 856–908.

Bhutalia, Urvashi. 2002. *Speaking Peace: Women's Voices from Kashmir.* New Delhi: Kali for Women.

Bion, Wilfred. 1959. "Attacks on Linking". *International Journal of Psychoanalysis* 40, 308–315. London: Karnac Books.

Bion, Wilfred. 1961. *Experiences in Groups and Other Papers.* New York: Basic Books.

Bion, Wilfred. 1962. *Learning from Experience.* Northvale, NJ: Jason Aronson.

Bion, Wilfred. 1990. *A Memoir of the Future.* New York: Routledge.

Bishop, Elizabeth. 1983. "One Art". In *The Complete Poems 1927-1979.* New York: Farrar, Straus & Giroux.

Bloom, Leslie R. 1998. *Under the Sign of Hope: Feminist Methodology and Narrative Interpretation.* Albany, NY: State University of New York Press.

Blum, Harold P. 2003. "Psychic Trauma and Traumatic Object Loss". *Journal of American Psychoanalytic Association* 51, no. 2, 415–432. Retrieved from: http://apa.sagepub.com/content/51/2/415

Bollas, Christopher. 1987. *The Shadow of the Object: Psychoanalysis of the Unthought Known.* London: Free Association Books.

Bollas, Christopher. 1999. "Dead Mother, Dead Child". In *The Dead Mother: The Work of Andrè Green,* edited by Kohon, pp. 89-110. London: Routledge.

Bollas, Christopher. 2003. *Cracking Up*. London: Routledge.

Bragin, Martha. 2003. "The Effect of Extreme Violence on the Capacity for Symbol Formation: Case Studies from Afghanistan and New York". In *Terrorism and the Psychoanalytic Space: International Perspective on Ground Zero,* pp. 59–67. New York: Pace University Press.

Bragin, Martha. 2005. "To Play, Learn, and Think: Understanding and Mitigating the Effects of Exposure to Violent Events on the Cognitive Capacity of Children and Adolescents". *Journal of Infant Child* 3, 296–309.

Bragin, Martha. 2007. "Knowing Terrible Things: Engaging Survivors of Extreme Violence in Treatment". *Clinical Social Work Journal* 35, no.4, 229–236.

Britton, Ronald. 1998. *Belief and Imagination: Explorations in Psychoanalysis.* London: Rutledge

Butler, Judith. 1990. *Gender Trouble*. London: Rutledge.

Butler, Judith. 1997. *The Psychic Life of Power: Theories in Subjection.* Stanford, CA: Stanford University Press.

Butler, Judith. 2001. "Giving an Account of Oneself". *Diacritics* 31, no. 4, 22–40.

Butler, Judith. 2003. "Violence, Mourning, Politics". *Studies in Gender and Sexuality* 4, no. 1, 9–37.

Caruth, Cathy. 1995. *Trauma: Explorations in Memory*. Maryland: John Hopkins University Press.

Cassia, Paul S. 2001. "Waiting for Ulysses: The Committee of Missing Persons". In *The Work of the UN in Cyprus,* edited by Oliver P. Richmond and James Ker-Lindsay, pp. 193–235. Basingstroke: Palgrave Macmillan.

Cassia, Paul S. 2005. *Bodies of Evidence: Burial, Memory and Recovery of Missing Persons in Cyprus.* New York: Berghahn Books.

Chatterjee, Shraddha. 2018. *Queer Politics in India: Towards Sexual Subaltern Subjects*. London: Routledge.

Chenoy, Anuradha. 2002. *Militarism and Women in South Asia.* New Delhi: Kali for Women.

Chenoy, Anuradha. 2017. "Militarization Values, Attitudes and Practices in South Asia". In *Women and Politics of Peace- South Asian Narratives on Militarization, Power and Justice*, pp. 99–122. CA: Sage Publication

Clifford, James & Marcus, George E. 1986. *Writing Culture: The Poetics and Politics of Ethnography*. Berkeley, CA: University of California Press.

Cockburn, Cynthia. 2001. "The Gendered Dynamic of Armed Conflict and Political Violence". In *Victims, Perpetrators or Actors? Gender, Armed Conflict and Political Violence,* edited by Caroline O. N. Moser and Fiona C. Clarks, pp. 13–29. New Delhi: Kali for Women.

Danieli, Yael. 1988. Treating Survivors and Children of Survivors of Nazi Holocaust. In *Post- Traumatic Therapy and Victims of Violence,* edited by Frank M. Ochberg, pp. 278–294. New York: Bruner.

Das, Veena. 1990. "Our Work to Cry: Your Work to Listen". In *Mirrors of Violence: Communities, Riots and Survivors in South Asia*, pp. 345–399. New Delhi: Oxford University Press.

Das, Veena & Deborah Poole. 2004. *Anthropology in the Margins of the State*. New Delhi: Oxford University Press.

Das, Veena. 2006a. "The Act of Witnessing: Violence, Gender and Subjectivity". In *Life and Words: Violence and Descent into the Ordinary*. New Delhi: Oxford University Press.

Das, Veena. 2006b. "Language and Body: Transaction in the Construction of Pain". In *Life and Words: Violence and Descent into the Ordinary*. New Delhi: Oxford University Press.

Das, Veena. 2006c. "The Event and the Everyday". In *Life and Words: Violence and Descent into the Ordinary*. New Delhi: Oxford University Press.

Davidson, Julia O. & Derek Layder. 1994. *Method, Sex and Madness*. London: Routledge.

Derrida, Jacques. 1986. *Memoires for Paul de Man*. New York: Columbia University Press.

Derrida, Jacques. 1987. *The Post Card: From Socrates to Freud and Beyond.* Translated by Alan Bass. Chicago, IL: University of Chicago Press.

Derrida, Jacques. 2001. *The Work of Mourning*. Chicago, IL: The University of Chicago Press.

Derrida, Jacques, and Anne Dufourmantelle. 2000. *Of Hospitality*. Translation by Rachel Bowlby. Stanford, CA: Stanford University Press.

Devereaux, George. 1967. *From Anxiety to Method in the Behavioral Sciences*. Paris: Mouton & Co.

Donthi, Praveen. 2019. "Punjab Needs a Truth Commission: Satnam Singh Bains on New Evidence of Enforced Disappearances". *The Caravan*. https://caravanmagazine.in/conflict/satnam-singh-bains-punjab-disappearances

Dwyer, Leslie. 2009. "A Politics of Silence: Violence, Memory and Treacherous Speech in Post-1965 Bali". In *Genocide: Truth, Memory and Representation*, edited by Alexander L. Hinton, A. and Kevin L. O'Neill, pp. 113–139. London: Duke University Press.

Edelman, Lucila, Daniel Kersner, Diana Kordon, and Daria Lagos. 2003. "Psychosocial Effects and Treatment of Mass Trauma Due to Sociopolitical Events: The Argentine Experience". In *The Psychological Impact of War Trauma on Civilians: An International Perspective*, edited by Stanley Krippner and Teresa M. McIntyre. Westport, CT: Praeger Publishers.

Eigen, Michael. 1999a. *Psychic Deadness*. Northvale, NJ: Jason and Aranson Inc.

Eigen, Michael. 1999b. *Toxic Nourishment.* London: Karnac Books.

Eigen, Michael. 2007. "Incommunicado Core and Boundless Supporting Unknown". *European Journal of Psychotherapy and Counselling* 9, no. 4, 415–422.

Enloe, Cynthia. 2000. *Manoeuvres: The International Politics of Women's Lives.* Berkley, CA: University of California Press.

Erikson, Erik. 1958. *Young Man Luther: A Study in Psychoanalysis and History.* New York: W. W. Norton.

Erikson, Erik. 1964. "Identity and Uprootedness in Our Time". In *Insight and Responsibility,* pp. 81–108. New York: W. W. Norton.

Erikson, Erik. 1968. *Identity: Youth and Crisis*. London: Faber and Faber.

Erikson, Erik. 1978. *Life History and Historical Moment*. New York: W. W. Norton.

Erikson, Kai. 1995. "Notes on Trauma and Community". In *Trauma: Explorations in Memory*, edited by Cathy Caruth, pp. 183–199. Baltimore, MD: John Hopkins University Press.

Fanon, Frantz. (1967) 2001. *The Wretched of the Earth*. London: Penguine.

Fassin, Didier, and Richard Rechtman. 2009. *The Empire of Trauma: An Inquiry into the Condition of Victimhood.* Translated by Rachel Gomme. Princeton, NJ: Princeton University Press.

Fazili, Gowhar. 2016. "Familial Grief, Resistance and Political Imaginary in Kashmir". *Indian Anthropologist* 46, no. 2, 53–57.

Feldman, Allen. 1995. "Ethnographic States of Emergency". In *Fieldwork Under Fire- Contemporary Studies of Violence and Survival,* edited by Carolyn Nordstrom and Antonio Robben, pp. 224–253. Berkeley, CA: University of California Press.

Ferenczi, Sandor. 1949. Confusion of the Tongues between the Adults and the Child- the Language of Tenderness and of Passion. *International Journal of Psychoanalysis* 30, 225–230.

Ferenczi, Sandor. 1980. *Final Contributions to the Problems and the Methods of Psycho-analysis.* New York: Bruner/Mazel Publisher.

Fonagy, Peter, and Mary Target. 1999. "Towards Understanding Violence: The Use of the Body and the Role of the Father". In *Psychoanalytic Understandings of Violence and Suicide,* edited by Rosine Perelberg, pp. 51–72. New York: Routledge.

Foucault, Michel. 1977. *Discipline and Punish: The Birth of the Prison.* London: Penguin Books.

Foucault, Michel, and Jay Miscowiec. 1986. "Of Other Spaces". *Diacritics* 16, no.1, 22–27.

Frank, Arthur. 1995. *The Wounded Storyteller: Body, Illness and Ethics.* Chicago, IL: University of Chicago Press.

Freud, Sigmund. (1899) 1994. *The Interpretation of Dreams.* New York: Barnes & Noble Book.

Freud, Sigmund. (1914) 1958. "Remembering, Repeating and Working Through (Further Recommendations on the Technique of Psychoanalysis II)". In *Standard Edition of the Complete Psychological Works of Sigmund Freud* 12, edited and translated by James Strachey, pp. 145–156. London: Hogarth Press.

Freud, Sigmund. (1915a) 1971. "Instincts and their vicissitudes". In *Standard Edition of the Complete Psychological Works of Sigmund Freud* 14, edited and translated by James Strachey, pp. 117–140. London: Hogarth Press.

Freud, Sigmund. (1915b) 1971. "Thoughts for the Times on War and Death". In *Standard Edition of the Complete Psychological Works of Sigmund Freud* 14, edited and translated by James Strachey, pp. 275–300. London: Hogarth Press.

Freud, Sigmund. (1917) 1971. "Mourning and Melancholia". In *Standard Edition of the Complete Psychological Works of Sigmund Freud 14*, edited and translated by James Strachey, pp. 243–258. London: Hogarth Press.

Freud, Sigmund. (1919) 1955. "The Uncanny". In *Standard Edition of the Complete Psychological Works of Sigmund Freud* 17, edited and translated by James Strachey, pp. 217–256. London: Hogarth Press.

Freud, Sigmund. (1920) 1955. "Beyond the Pleasure Principle". In *Standard Edition of the Complete Psychological Works of Sigmund Freud* 18, edited and translated by James Strachey, pp. 7–64. London: Hogarth Press.

Freud, Sigmund. (1927) 1967. "Fetishism". In *Standard Edition of the Complete Psychological Works of Sigmund Freud* 21, edited and translated by James Strachey, pp. 147–157. London: Hogarth Press.

Freud, Sigmund. (1937) 1991. "Analysis Terminable and Interminable". In *Standard Edition of the Complete Psychological Works of Sigmund Freud* 23, edited and translated by John Strachey, pp. 216–253. London: Hogarth Press.

Freud, Sigmund. (1940) 1991. "An Outline of Psycho-analysis". In *Standard Edition of the Complete Psychological Works of Sigmund Freud* 23, edited and translated by James Strachey, pp. 139–207. London: Hogarth Press.

Freud, Sigmund, and Josef Breuer. (1895) 1955. "Studies on Hysteria". In *The Standard Edition of the Complete Psychological Works of Sigmund Freud 2,* edited and translated by James Strachey, pp. 1–335. London: Hogarth Press.

Fromm, Erich. 1976. *To Have or to Be?* New York: Harper & Row.

Galatariotou, Catia. 2008. "From Psychosocial Equilibrium to Catastrophic Breakdown: Cyprus 1955-1974". *International Journal of Psychoanalysis* 89, no. 4, 845–866.

Gampel, Yolanda. 2000. "Reflections on the Prevalence of the Uncanny in Social Violence". In *Culture Under Siege- Collective Violence and Trauma,* edited by *Antonious Robben and Marcelo Suarez- Orozco,* pp. 48–69. New York: Cambridge University Press.

Geertz, Clifford. 1983. *Local Knowledge: Further Essays in Interpretive Anthropology.* New York: Basic Books.

Gibson, Margaret, and Clarissa Carden. 2018. *Living and Dying in a Virtual World. Switzerland: Palgrave Macmillan Memory Studies.*

Giovacchini, Peter L. 1989. *Countertransferences: Triumphs and Catastrophes.* London: Jason Aronson.

Gordon, Avery F. 2008. *Ghostly Matters: Haunting and the Sociological Imagination,* 2nd edition. Minneapolis, MN: University of Minnesota Press.

Graham, Amanda Jane. 2012. "Assisted Breathing: Developing Embodied Exposure in Oscar Muñoz's Aliento." *Latin American Perspectives* 39, no. 3, 63–73.

Green, Andre. 1986. *On Private Madness.* London: Hogarth Press.

Green, Andre. 1999. *The Work of the Negative.* London: Free Association Books.

Green, Andre. 2005. *Key Ideas for a Contemporary Psychoanalysis: Misrecognition and Recognition of the Unconscious.* London: Rutledge.

Grotstein, James S. 2009. *But at the Same Time and on Another Level: Psychoanalytic Theory and Technique in the Kleinian/Bionian Mode.* London: Karnac Books.

Guru, Gopal. 2009. Rejection of Rejection: Foregrounding Self-respect. In *Humiliation- Claims and Context*, pp. 209–225. New Delhi: Oxford University Press.

Haq, Shifa. 2015. "Representing Absence- Survivor Art in Kashmir through Works of Masood Hussain". In *Proceedings of Indian Art History Congress, XXIII Session 2014, New Delhi,* edited by Shyamalkanti Chakravarti and Sudipa R. Bandhopadhyay, pp. 295–302. Guhati: Indian Art History Congress.

Haq, Shifa. 2020. "Surviving Destruction- Reading Gandhi in Winnicott". In *The Spiritual Psyche- Mysticism, Intersubjectivity and Psychoanalysis in Clinical Practice*, edited by Willow Pearson and Helen Marlo, 183-195. New York: Routledge.

Haq, Shifa, and Sabah Siddiqui. 2019. "Between Neutrality and Disavowal: Being Muslim Psychotherapists in India". In *Islamic Psychoanalysis and Psychoanalytic Islam: Cultural and Clinical Dialogues*, edited by Ian Parker and Sabah Siddiqui, pp. 60–69. London: Routledge.

Hegel, Georg W. F. 1993. *Introductory Lectures on Aesthetics*. Translated by Bernard Bosanquet. London: Penguin Books.

Herman, Edward S., and Noam Chomsky. 1988. *Manufacturing Consent*. New York: Random House.

Herzog, James. 1982. "On Father Hunger: The Father's Role in the Modulation of Aggressive Drives and Fantasy". In *Father and Child,* edited by Stanley H. Cath, Alan Gurwitt and J.M. Ross, pp. 163–174. Boston, MA: Little, Brown.

Herzog, James. 2001. *Father Hunger: Explorations with Adults and Children*. Hillsdale, NJ: The Analytic Press.

Hinton, Alexander, and Kavin L. O'Neill. 2009. *Genocide: Truth, Memory and Representation*. London: Duke University Press.

Hobfall, Stevan E. 2003. "Moving the Borders of Psychology to the Aid of Victims of War". In *The Psychological Impact of War Trauma on Civilians- An International Perspective,* pp. xi–xiv. Westport, CT: Praeger.

Hollander, Nancy Caro. 2010. *Uprooted Minds: Surviving the Politics of Terror in the Americas: Psychoanalysis, History, Memoir*. New York: Routledge.

Hollander, Nancy Caro. 2017. "Who is the Sufferer and What is Being Suffered? Subjectivity in Times of Social Malaise". *Psychoanalytic Dialogues* 27, 635–650.

Human Rights Watch. 2012. *Human Rights Watch World Report*. New York: Human Rights Watch.

Husain, Sahba. 2019. *Love, Loss and Longing in Kashmir*. New Delhi: Zuban.

International People's Tribunal on Human Rights and Justice in Indian Administered Kashmir and APDP Report. 2009. *Buried Evidence- Unknown, Unmarked, and Mass Graves in Indian-Administered Kashmir*. Srinagar.

International People's Tribunal on Human Rights and Justice in Indian Administered Kashmir and APDP Report. 2012. *Alleged Perpetrators: Stories of Impunity in Jammu and Kashmir. Srinagar.*

Janoff-Bulman, Ronnie. 1982." Esteem and Control Bases of Blame: 'Adaptive' strategies for victims versus observers". *Journal of Personality* 50, no. 2, 180–192.

Jegenathan, Pradeep. 2004. "Checkpoint: Anthropology, Identity, and the State". In *Anthropology in the Margins of the State,* edited by Veena Das and Deborah Poole, pp. 67–80. New Delhi: Oxford University Press.

Justice for Peace Foundation, 2012. *Enforced Disappearances in Thailand.* Bangkok: Justice for Peace Foundation.

Kabir, Ananya Jahanara. 2009. *Territory of Desire- Representing the Valley of Kashmir.* Minneapolis: University of Minnesota Press.

Kafka, Franz. 2002. *The Great Wall of China.* New York: Penguin Books.

Kakar, Sudhir. 1995. *Colours of Violence.* New Delhi: Penguine Books.

Kakar, Sudhir. 2008. *Culture and Psyche: Collected Essays.* New Delhi: Oxford University Press.

Kashani, Sarwar, Idrees Kanth, Gowhar Fazili, and Sahba Husain. 2003. *The Impact of Violence on the Student Community in Kashmir.* New Delhi: Publisher not identified.

Kaul, Ravender K. 2006. *Migration and Society: A Study of Displaced Kashmiri Pundits.* Ann Arbor, MI: The University of Michigan Press.

Kazi, Seema. 2010. *Between Democracy and Nation.* New Delhi: Oxford University Press.

Kernberg, Otto. 1967. "Borderline Personality Organization." *Journal of the American Psychoanalytic Association* 15, no. 3, 641–685.

Kernberg, Otto. 1976. *Object Relations Theory and Clinical Psychoanalysis.* New York: Jason Aranson.

Khan, Mohammed M. 1963. "The Concept of Cumulative Trauma". *Psychoanalytic Study of the Child* 18, no. 1, 286–306.

Kirkby, Joan. 2006. "Remembrance of the Future: Derrida on Mourning". *Social Semiotics* 16, no. 3, 461–472.

Klein, Melanie. 1946. "Notes on Some Schizoid Mechanisms". In *Envy and Gratitude and Other Works 1946-1963*, pp. 1–24. New York: Delacorte.

Klein, Melanie. (1928) 2002. "Early Stages of Oedipus Complex". In *Love, Guilt and Reparation and Other Works 1921-1945,* pp. 186–198. New York: Free Press.

Kovats- Bernat, J. C. 2002. "Negotiating Dangerous Fields: Pragmatic Strategies for Fieldwork amid Violence and Terror". *American Anthropologist, New Series* 104, no. 1, 208–222.

Krippner, Stanley, and Teresa McIntyre. 2003. "In the Wake of War". *The Psychological Impact of War Trauma on Civilians: An International Perspective,* pp. 1–14. Westport, CT: Praeger.

Kris, Ernst. 1956. "The Recovery of Childhood Memories in Psychoanalysis". *Psychoanalytic Study of the Child* 11, no. 1, 54–88.

Kristeva, Julia. 1989. *Black Sun: Depression and Melancholia.* New York: Columbia University Press.

Kumar, Manasi, and Atreyee Sen. 2018. "Disaster Diaries: Riot Affected Children in Ahmedabad and Hyderabad". In *Psychoanalysis from the Indian Terroir: Emerging Themes in Culture, Family and Childhood*, edited by Manasi Kumar, Anup Dhar and Anurag Mishra, pp. 119–141. Lanham: Lexington Books/ Rowman and Littlefield.

Kumar, Priya. 2013. "Beyond Tolerance and Hospitality: Muslims as Strangers and Minor Subjects in Hindu Nationalist and Indian Nationalist Discourse". In *Living*

Together: Jacques Derrida's Communities of Violence and Peace, edited by Elisabeth Weber, pp. 80–103. New York: Routledge.

La Capra. 2001. *Writing History, Writing Trauma*. London: John Hopkins University Press.

Lacan, Jacques. 1977. *The Four Fundamental Concepts of Psycho-Analysis*. London: Hogarth.

Laplanche, Jean. 1999. *Essays on Otherness*. London: Routledge.

Larkin, Philip. 2012. "High Windows". In Phillip Larkin: The Complete Poems, edited by Archie Burnett, pp. 280. London: Faber and Faber.

Laub, Dori. 1991a. "Bearing Witness, Or the Vicissitudes of Listening". In *Testimony: Crises of Witnessing in Literature, Psychoanalysis and History,* edited by Shoshana Felman and Dori Laub, pp. 57–72. New York: Routledge.

Laub, Dori. 1991b. "An Event Without a Witness: Truth, Testimony and Survival." In *Testimony: Crises of Witnessing in Literature, Psychoanalysis and History,* edited by Shoshana Felman and Dori Laub, pp. 72–92. New York: Routledge.

Laub, Dori. 1995. "Truth and Testimony: The Process and the Struggle". In *Trauma-Explorations in Memory,* edited by Cathy Caruth, pp. 61–75. Baltimore, MD: John Hopkins University Press.

Laub, Dori. 2017. "Listening to my Mother's Testimony". In *Wounds of History: Repair and Resilience in the Trans-generational Transmission of Trauma,* edited by Jill Salberg and Sue Grand. New York: Routledge.

Laub, Dori, and Nanette C. Auerhahn. 1993. "Knowing and Not-Knowing Massive Psychic Trauma: Forms of Traumatic Memory." *International Journal of Psychoanalysis* 74, no. 2, 287–302.

Layton, Lynne. 2006. "That Place Gives Me the Heebie Jeebies". In *Psychoanalysis, Class and Politics: Encounters in the Clinical Setting*, edited by Lynne Layton, Nancy C. Hollander and S. Gutwill. New York: Routledge.

Layton, Lynne. 2009. "Whose Responsible? Our Mutual Implication in Each other's Suffering". *Psychoanalytic Dialogues* 19(2), 105–120.

Levi, Primo. 1959. *Survival in Auschwitz: The Nazi Assault on Humanity.* Translated by Stuart Woolf. New York: Simon & Schuster.

Levi, Primo. 2007. *A Tranquil Star: Unpublished Stories.* Translated by Ann Goldstein, Alessandra Bastagli. New York: Penguin Books.

Lévinas, Emmanuel. 1990. *Nine Talmudic Readings.* Translated by Annette Aronowicz. Bloomington: Indiana University Press.

Lévinas, Emmanuel. 1991. Death and Time in Emmanuel Levinas. *Pris Cashiers de l'Herne* 60, 21–75.

Lévinas, Emmanuel. (1984) 1996. "Transcedene and Intelligibility". In *Emmanuel Levinas: Basic Philosophical Writings,* edited by Adriaan T. Peperzak, Simon Critchley, and Robert Bernasconi, pp. 149–160. Bloomington: Indiana University Press.

Lifton, Robert J. 1969. *Death in Life: Survivors of Hiroshima.* New York: Random House.

Lifton, Robert J. 1973. *Home from the War: Learning from Vietnam Veterans.* New York: Simon & Schuster.

Lifton, Robert J. 1983. *The Life of the Self: Towards a New Psychology*. New York: Basic Books.

Lifton, Robert J. 1993. *The Protean Self: Human Resilience in An Age of Fragmentation.* Chicago, IL: University of Chicago Press.

Loizos, Peter. 1981. *A Chronicle of Cypriot War Refugees*. Cambridge: Cambridge University Press.

Mahler, Margaret S. 1954. "Contribution to the Problems of Infantile Neurosis: A Discussion". *Psychoanalytic Study of the Child* 9, no. 1, 65–66.

Mahmood, Cynthia K. 2000. "Trials by Fire: Dynamics of Terror in Punjab and Kashmir". In *Death Squad: The Anthropology of State Terror,* edited by Jefferey A. Sluka, pp. 70–90. Philadelphia, PA: The University of Pennsylvania Press.

Malik, Inshah. 2019. *Muslim Women, Agency and Resistance Politics: The Case of Kashmir*. New York: Palgrave Macmillan.

Manchanda, Rita. 2001. *Women, War and Peace in South Asia: Beyond Victimhood to Agency*. New Delhi: Sage Publications.

Manchanda, Rita. 2017. "Gender, Power and Peace Politics- A Comparative Analysis". In *Women and Politics of Peace- South Asian Narratives on Militarization, Power and Justice*, pp. 31–57. CA: Sage Publication

Marks, Maureen, and Simon Lovestone. 1995. "The Role of the Father in Parental Postnatal Mental Health." *British Journal of Medical Psychology* 68, 157–168.

Matar, Hisham. 2011. *Anatomy of a Disappearance*. New York: Penguin Books.

Maxey, Ian. 1999. "Beyond Boundaries? Activism, Academia, Reflexivity and Research". *Area* 31, no. 3, 199–208. Retrieved from http://www.jstor.org/stable/20003985.

Mehdi, Zehra. 2019. "Politics of Secular Psychoanalysis in India: Hindu- Muslim as Religious and Political Identities in Sudhir Kakar's Writing". In *Islamic Psychoanalysis and Psychoanalytic Islam*, edited by Ian Parker and Sabah Siddiqui, pp. 48–59. London: Routledge

Mehrotra, Deepti P. 2009. *Burning Bright: Irom Sharmila and the Struggle for Peace in Manipur*. New Delhi: Penguin Books.

Meltzer, Donald. 2008. "The Apprehension of Beauty". In *The Apprehension of Beauty: The Role of Aesthetic Conflict in Development, Art and Violence,* edited by Donald Meltzer and Meg Harris Williams. London: Karnac Books.

Milgram, Stanley. 1964. "Group Pressure and Action Against a Person". *Journal of Abnormal and Social Psychology* 69, no. 2, 137–143.

Mitscherlich, Alexander, and Margararet Mitscherlich. 1980. *The Inability to Mourn.* Munich: R. Piper.

Nandy, Ashis. 2002. *Time Warps- Silent and Evasive Pasts in Indian Politics and Religion*. New Jersey: Rutgers University Press

Nandy, Ashis. 2003. *The Romance of the State and the Fate of Dissent in the Tropics*. New Delhi: Oxford University Press

Nordstrom, Carolyn, and Antonious Robben. 1995. *Fieldwork under Fire*. Berkeley, CA: University of California Press.

Ogden, Thomas. 1989. *The Primitive Edge of Experience*. London: Karnac.

Ogden, Thomas. 2000. "Borges and the Art of Mourning". *Psychoanalytic Dialogues* 10, no. 1, 65–88.

Ogden, Thomas. 2001. *Conversations at the Frontier of Dreaming*. Northvale, NJ: Jason Aronson.

Ogden, Thomas. 2005a. *This Art of Psychoanalysis: Dreaming Undreamt Dreams and Interrupted Cries*. New York: Routledge.

Ogden, Thomas. 2005b. "On Holding and Containing, Being and Dreaming". In *This Art of Psychoanalysis: Dreaming Undreamt Dreams and Interrupted Cries,* pp. 93–108. New York: Routledge.

Ogden, Thomas. 2005c. "What I Would Not Part With". In *This Art of Psychoanalysis: Dreaming Undreamt Dreams and Interrupted Cries*. New York: Routledge.

Ogden, Thomas. 2009. "A New Reading of the Origins of Object Relations Theory". In *On Freud's "Mourning and Melancholia",* edited by Leticia G. Fiorini, Bokanowski, Thierry, Sergio Lewkowics, pp. 123–144. London: Karnac.

OHCHR (Office of the United Nations High Commissioner for Human Rights). 2018. *Report on the Situation of Human Rights in Kashmir: Developments in the Indian State of Jammu and Kashmir from June 2016 to April 2018, and General Human Rights Concerns in Azad Jammu and Kashmir and Gilgit- Balistan.* Geneva: OHCHR.

Oliner, Marion M. 1996. "External Reality: The Elusive Dimension of Psychoanalysis". *Psychoanalytic Quarterly* 65, no. 2, 267–300.

O'Loughlin, Michael. 2012. "Trauma Trails from Ireland's Great Hunger: A Psychoanalytic Inquiry". In *Loneliness and Longing: Psychoanalytic Reflections*, edited by Brent Willock, Lori B. Bohm and Rebecca C. Curtis, pp. 233–250. New York: Routledge.

O'Loughlin, Michael. 2013. "Reclaiming Geneology, Memory and History: The Psychodynamic Potential for Reparative Therapy in Contemporary South Africa". In *Psychodynamic Psychotherapy in Contemporary South Africa: Context, Theories and Practices*, edited by Cora Smith, Glenys Lobban and Michael O'Loghlin. Johannesberg: Wits University Press.

Peer, Basharat. 2012. *Curfewed Night*. Noida: Random House.

Peterson, V. Spike. 2010. "Gender Identities, Ideologies and Practices in the Context of War and Militarism". In *War and Militarism,* edited by Laura Sjoberg and Sandra Via, pp. 17–29. Santa Barbara: Praeger Publishers.

Pollock, George H. 1971. "Temporal Anniversary Manifestations: Hours, Day and Holiday". *Psychoanalytic Quarterly* 40, no. 1, 123–131.

Ramphele, Mamphela. 1997. "Political Widowhood in South Africa: The Embodiment of Ambiguity". In *Social Suffering,* edited by Arthur Kleinman, Veena Das, Margaret Lock, pp. 99–118. New Delhi: Oxford University Press.

Rashid, Afsana. 2011. *Widows and Half Widows: Saga of Extra-Judicial Arrests and Killings in Kashmir.* New Delhi: Pharos Media.

Robben, Antonio. 1995. "Seduction and Persuasion". In *Fieldwork Under Fire- Contemporary Studies of Violence and Survival,* edited by Antonio Robben and Carolyn Nordstorm, pp. 89–104. Berkeley, CA: University of California Press.

Robben, Antonio, and Mario Suarez- Orozco. 2000. "Inter-Disciplinary Perspectives on Violence and Trauma". In *Culture under Siege: Collective Violence and Trauma,* Antonio C.G.M. Robben and Mario M. Suarez- Orozco, pp. 1–47. New York: Cambridge University Press.

Robinson, Geoffrey. 1995. *The Dark Side of Paradise: Political violence in Bali.* Ithaca, NY: Cornell University Press.

Roosa, John. 2006. *Pretext for Mass Murder: The September 30th Movement and Soharto's Coup of D'Etat in Indonesia.* Madison, WI: University of Wisconsin Press.

Rosaldo, Renato. 1989. *Culture and Truth: Remaking of Social Analysis.* Boston, MA: Beacon Press.

Rose, Gillian. 1997. "Situating Knowledges: Positionalities, Reflexivities and Other Tactics". *Progress in Human Geography* 21, no. 3, 305–320.

Said, Edward. 1978. *Orientalism.* New Delhi: Penguin Books.

Sanger, Kerran L. 1995. Slave resistance and Rhetorical Self-Definition: Spirituals as a Strategy. *Western Journal of Communication* 59, no. 3, 177–192.

Scarry, Elaine. 1985. *The Body in Pain: The Making and Unmaking of the World.* New York: Oxford University Press.

Schafer, Roy. 1968. *Aspects of Internalization.* New York: International University Press.

Scheper-Hughes, Nancy. 1993. *Death Without Weeping: The Violence of Everyday Life in Brazil.* Berkeley, CA: University of California Press.

Scheper- Hughes, Nancy. 1995. "The Primacy of the Ethical- Proposition of a Militant Anthropology". *Current Anthropology* 36, no. 3, 409–420.

Schweder, Richard. 1991. *Thinking through Cultures.* Cambridge: Harvard University Press.

Schweder, Richard. 1999. "Why Cultural Psychology". *Ethos* 27, no.1, 62–73.

Searles, Harold F. 1965. *Collected Papers on Schizophrenia and Related Subjects.* London: Hogarth Press.

Segal, Hanna. 1957. "Notes on Symbol Formation". *International Journal of Psychoanalysis* 38, 391–397.

Segal, Hanna. 1964. *Introduction to the Work of Melanie Klein.* New York: Basic Books Inc., Publishers.

Seeman, Don. 2008. "Ritual Efficacy, Hasidic Mysticism and 'Useless Suffering' in the Warsaw Ghetto." *Harvard Theological Review* 101, no. 3–4, 465–505.

Shafaie, Naseema. 2017. *Neither a Shadow, Nor a Reflection.* Translated by Indu Kilam. New Delhi: Sahitya Akademi.

Shakespeare, William. (1603) 2005. *Hamlet.* Cambridge: Cambridge University Press.

Shaw, Rosalind. 2006. "Displacing Violence: Making Pentecostal Memory in Postwar Sierra Leone". *Cultural Anthropology* 22, no. 1, 66–93.

Shukla, Rakesh. 2016. Murderous Rage, Public Lynching: A Look Under the Surface. Internal *Journal of Applied Psychoanalysis* 13, 367–370.

Siddiqui, Sabah. 2015. *Religion and Psychoanalysis in India.* New York: Routledge.

Sitas, Ari. 2004. *Voices that Reason- Theoretical Parables.* London: Brill Academic Publishers.

Sluka, Jeffrey A. 2000. *Death Squad- The Anthropology of State Terror.* Philadelphia. PA: The University of Pennsylvania Press.

Smith, J. H. 1975. "On the Work of Mourning". In *Bereavement: Its Psychological Aspects,* edited by B. Schoenberg, I. Gerber, A.H. Wiener, Kutscher, D. Peretz & A.C. Carr, pp. 1–25. New York: Columbia University Press.

Sonpar, Shobna. 2007. *Violent Activism: A Psychosocial Study of Ex-Militants in Jammu and Kashmir.* New Delhi: Aman Public Charitable Trust.

Spezzano, Chuck. 2013. *Affect in Psychoanalysis: A Clinical Synthesis.* New York: Routledge.

Spivak, Gayatri. 1999. *A Critique of Post-Colonial Reason: Towards a History of the Vanishing Present.* Cambridge: Harvard University Press.

Tahka, Veikko. 1984. "Dealing with Object Loss". *Scandinavian Psychoanalytic Review* 7, no. 1, 13–33.

Taina, Cecelia. 2014. "Mourning the Dead, Mourning the disappeared: The Enigma of Absence-Presence". *International Journal of Psychoanalysis* 95, 1087–1107.

Taussig, Michael. 1992. *The Nervous System.* New York: Routledge.

The International Convention for the Protection of All Persons from Enforced Disappearance, December 2008. 2008 C.N.1040.2008. Doc.A/61/488. Retrieved from: http://treaties.un.org/Pages/ViewDetails.aspx?src=IND&mtdsg_no=IV-16 &chapter=4&lang=en

Vahali, Honey O. 2009a. *Lives in Exile.* New Delhi: Routledge.

Vahali, Honey O. 2009b. *From Wild Grasslands to Nurtured Gardens: The Inward Journey in Buddhism, Psychoanalysis and Engaged Social Activism.* New Delhi: Indian Council of Philosophical Research Volume on Psychoanalysis in India.

Vahali, Honey O., and Diamond O. Vahali. 2019. "The (Im)possible Embrace: A Search for Non-Violent Possibilities in the Aftermath of Violent Uprootedness". *Psychology and Developing Societies* 31(1), 139–161.

Varvin, Sverre. 2012. "Islamism and Xenophobia". In *Psychoanalysis and Politics: Exclusion and the Politics of Representation*, edited by Lene Auestad, pp. 155–168. London: Karnac.

Volkan, Vamik D. 1972. "The Linking Objects of Pathological Mourners". *Archives of General Psychiatry* 27, no. 2, 215–221.

Volkan, Vamik. 1979. *Cyprus- War and Adaptation: A Psychoanalytic History of Two Ethnic Groups in Conflict.* Charlottesville, VA: University of Virginia Press.

Volkan, Vamik D. 1981. *Linking Objects and Linking Phenomena.* New York: International University Press.

Volkan, Vamik D. 2007. "Individuals and Societies as "Perennial Mourners" – Their Linking Objects and Public Memorials". In *On Deaths and Endings: Psychoanalysts' Reflections on Finality, Transformation and New Beginnings*, edited by Brent Willock, Lori C. Bohm, Rebecca C. Curtis, pp. 42–59. New York: Routledge.

Volkan, Vamik D. 2014. "Father Quest and Linking Objects: A Story of the American World War II Orphans Network (AWON) and Palestinian Orphans". In *Healing in the Wake of Parental Loss: Clinical Applications and Therapeutic Strategies*, edited by Phyllis Cohen, K. Mark Sossin and Richard Ruth, pp. 283–300. New York: Jason Aronson.

Volkan, Vamik D. 2018. Mourning, Large Group Identity and the Refugee Experience. In *An Uncertain Safety: Integrative Health Care for the 21st Century Refugees*, edited by T. Wenzel and B. Drozdek, pp. 23–35. New York: Springer.

Waheed, Mirza. 2019. "In Memory Lake". In *A Desolation Called Kashmir*, pp. 111–128. New Delhi: Harper Collins.

Watkins, Mary, and Helene Shulman. 2008. *Toward Psychologies of Liberation*. New York: Palgrave Macmillan.

Willis, Paul. 2000. *The Ethnographic Imagination*. Oxford: Polity Press.

Winnicott, Donald W. 1953. "Transitional Object and Transitional Phenomenon: A Study of the First Not-Me Possession". *International Journal of Psychoanalysis* 34, 89–97.

Winnicott, Donald W. 1956. "Primary Maternal Preoccupation". In *Through Paediatrics to Psychoanalysis*, pp. 262–277. New York: Basic Books.

Winnicott, Donald W. 1960. "Ego Distortion in Terms of True and False Self". In *Maturational Processes and Facilitating Environment*, pp. 140–152. London: Karnac.

Winnicott, Donald W. 1963a. "The Development of the Capacity for Concern". In *Maturational Processes and Facilitating Environment,* pp. 73–82. London: Karnac Books.

Winnicott, Donald W. 1963b. "Communicating and Not Communicating Leading to a Study of Certain Opposites". In *Maturational Processes and Facilitating Environment,* pp. 179–192. London: Karnac Books.

Winnicott, Donald W. 1965. *Maturational Processes and Facilitating Environment.* London: Karnac.

Winnicott, Donald W. 1967. "The Location of Cultural Experience". *International Journal of Psychoanalysis* 48, no. 3, 368–372.

Winnicott, Donald W. 1971a. "The Use of an Object and Relating through Identification". In *Playing and Reality*. New York: Tavistock.

Winnicott, Donald W. 1971b. *Playing and Reality.* New York: Tavistock.

Winnicott. Donald W. 1974. "Fear of Breakdown". *International Review of Psychoanalysis* 1, 101–107.

Winnicott, Donald W. 2016. *The Collected Works of D.W. Winnicott,* edited by Lesley Caldwell and Helen Taylor Robinson.

Wolman, Thomas. 2004. "The Failures of Paternal Function and their Compensations". In *Real and Imaginary Fathers- Development, Transference and Healing*, edited by Salman Akhtar and Henri Parens, pp. 95–106. New York: Jason Aronson.

Yasien-Esmael, H., and S. Rubin. 2005. "The Meaning Structures of Muslim Bereavements in Israel: Religious Traditions, Mourning Practices, and Human Experience". *Death Studies* 29, no. 6, 495–518.

Yin, Robert K. 1984. *Case Study Research: Design and Methods.* CA: Sage Publication.

Zepf, Siegfried. 2013. "A Note on the Application of the Term "Disavowal" in Psychoanalysis". *The Scandinavian Psychoanalytic Review* 36, no. 1, 35–42.

Zia, Athar. 2019. *Resisting Disappearance- Military Occupation and Women's Activism in Kashmir.* Seattle: University of Washington Press.

Zia, Athar, and Javaid I. Bhat 2019. *A Desolation called Kashmir*, pp. 1–26. New Delhi: Harper Collins.

Zizek, Slavoj. 2007. "Knight of the Living Dead". *New York Times*. http://www.nytimes.com/2007/03/24/opinion/24zizek.html

Index

Aasa's narrative: Ajeet's disappearance, 77–88; experience of dehumanization, 81; maternal preoccupation, 83–84; mourning, 82–87; overcoming alienation, 85; village life, 79
Abdullah, Sheikh, 29, 30
Abraham, Nicolas, 6–7
acid, xxx
Additional Protocols of 1977, 48n1
Agamben, Georgio, 43–44; *Homo sacer*, 44
Ahangar, Parveena, 41, 42, 51, 66
alienation, 17, 38, 65, 85–86
ambivalence, 7
Amnesty International, 37
analyzable, 14, 46–47, 68, 112
Anatomy of a Disappearance (Matar), 103
Anthropology in the Margins of the State (Das and Poole), 44
anti-metaphor, 19–22
Aquinas, Thomas, 57
Argentinian experience of military rule, 105
Ari, Ibu, 40–41
armed conflict, in Kashmir, xxvii
Armed Forces Special Powers Act (AFSPA), 30, 32; criticism against, 31; enforcement of, 30–31; extra-judicial killings and fake encounters, 30; procedures established by law, 30–31; in territories of Jammu and Kashmir, 30
association, 52, 56, 66, 73, 79
Association of the Parents of the Disappeared Persons (APDP), xxix, 28, 42, 45, 51–52, 113
attachment, 4
attitude, 2, 47
Auerhahn, Nanette C., 23, 58
avoidance, 9, 59, 108

baby's method of expressing separation, xxv–xxvi, 16
Balinese studies on violence, 40; disappearances, 40; Suharto's regime, 40
Barthes, Roland, 9
batin, 102
Bhabha, Homi, 89
Bion, Wilfred, 104
Bishop, Elizabeth, 5; *art of losing*, 5
bloodletting, 2
bond, xxiv, 5, 24, 72, 81
Bragin, Martha: survivors experience of 'othering,' 23; survivors of trauma, 22–23

burning, 8–9, 51

capitalism, 111
Caruth, Cathy, 21
cinematic representation of disappearance, 99; *The Dear Disappeared*, 99; *Haider*, 99; *Hamid*, 99; *No Fathers in Kashmir*, 99; *Tahaan*, 99; *Where Have You Hidden My New Moon Crescent*, 99
contained, 39, 48n1, 60, 104
container, 20, 38, 58, 60, 69, 102, 106, 111
'cops and robbers' play, 27
crypt, xxiii, 7–8, 12, 66, 77, 110
cryptic mourning, 7

damage, 23, 67, 91
death, xxii, xxiv, xxvii–xxviii, xxxii, 1, 4–6, 8–12, 14, 17–20, 30–31, 34–35, 41, 43–44, 46–47, 56, 58, 60–61, 63–68, 70–71, 75–76, 83, 86–87, 90–91, 93, 95–97, 99–101, 104, 106, 114
death symbolism, 47
demetaphorization, 7
denial, xxvi–xxvii, 7, 15, 18, 36–38, 42, 48, 54, 76, 80–81, 83, 114
Derrida, Jacques: *Memoires for Paul de Man*, 12; mourner's body, 12; on mourning, 11–13; response to Althusser's death in *The Work of Mourning*, 11
Devereaux, George, 105
Dirty Protest in Ireland, 110
disappearances, xxv–xxvii, 27; in Argentina, 38; in Bali, 40; body in context of, 34; in context of militarization, 45–48; in Cypriot, 38–39; disappeared Sikhs, 31; in Germany, 37; historical context, xxxi; involuntary, 52; in Kashmiri consciousness, xxxi–xxxii; mourning in the context of, xxvii; origin of, 37; proof of death, xxviii; as a torture technique, xxxi
disappearances in Kashmir, 28, 114; case of half-widows, 41–42. *See also* Sameena's narrative; forms of governance and, 42–45; involuntary nature of, 28; in militarized zone, 28; narratives, 53–88; state of exception, 42–45; Zia's account, 28
disavowal, 14–16, 56, 80–81, 109, 114
disciplinary, xxxi, 47, 111
disintegration, 36, 38, 91
disorganization, 49
dreams, 5, 101; for Freud, 8–10
Dwyer, Leslie, 40–41

Eigen, Michael, 16–17, 102
El Banco detention camp, 46
emancipation, 31, 47
enactment, 73, 84, 98, 105, 108, 113
enforced disappearance, 45, 84, 110
epistemological authority, 45
erasure, 14, 28, 34, 46, 76, 82, 96, 109
Erikson, Erik, 23, 24, 52
ethnographic repression, 105
ethno-nationalism, 84, 111
European nationalism, 38
extra-judicial killing, xxx, 28, 30, 78
eye witness, 45, 67

families of disappeared, 41–42, 51–52. *See also* Aasa's narrative; Javed's disappearance; Sameena's narrative
fantasies, xxx, 13, 21, 40, 53, 55–56, 58, 65, 74–75, 82–83, 98, 108, 110
Farooq, Mirwaiz Maulavi, 92
father, xxii, xxv–xxvi, xxxi, 8–10, 14, 42, 46, 51–53, 56–57, 60–63, 68, 70–72, 74–75, 82, 93, 98–100, 103, 110, 113
father hunger, 74, 98
Fatima, Iffat, 99
Ferenczi, Sandor, 6
fetishism, 14
FIND (Philippines), 52
First Information Report, 44–45, 51

Foucault, Michel: punishment, 33–35; rule of lateral effects, 35; rule of sufficient ideality, 35
Freud, Sigmund, 3–4, 103, 104, 106; 'Analysis Terminable and Interminable,' 16; *Beyond Pleasure Principle*, xxv–xxvi; distinction between 'repression' and 'disavowal,' 14; *The Interpretation of Dreams*, 8; introjection and incorporation, 6–8; *Mourning and Melancholia*, xxiii, 10; repetition, 112; theory on mourning and melancholia, 6; *Thoughts for the Times on War and Death*, 46; 'The Uncanny,' 17–18

Gaew Kadel massacre, 32
Gandhi, Indira, 43
Geneva Conventions of 1949, 48n1
'Ghost of the Christmas Past,' 17
Gordon, Avery F., 19
Greek Cypriots, 38–39

Hamlet (Shakespeare), 11
haunting, xxix, xxxi, 2, 18–19, 20, 49–50, 76, 90, 99–100, 114
Herzog, James, 98–99
hide-and-seek game, 27
Hindu nationalism, 32–33
Hiroshima bombing, 91
holocaust, 50, 58, 91
Husain, Masood, 92; 'Look Behind the Canvas,' 93; 'Submission,' 92; theme of absence and continuity, 93; 'Those Who Disappeared,' 93; use of mixed media and relief work, 92, 94

identification, 4, 16, 25, 25n1, 52; of ego, 3; narcissistic, 4; survivor, 24–25
Imroz, Parvez, 42
incorporation, 6–8, 12–13, 15, 25n1, 76, 82, 84, 102
Indian Independence Act of 1947, 29
Indian Muslim, xxx
Indian nation-state, 28, 32
Indonesian Communist Party (PKI), 40
internalization, 6, 71, 74
International Convention for the Protection of All Persons from Enforced Disappearances, 45
International Humanitarian Law, 37
introjection, 6–8, 25n1, 107
introjects, 5
involuntary disappearances, 52
Islamophobia, 31, 32

Javed's disappearance: BSF's story, 53–54; families' mourning, 53; Husaina's narrative of trauma, 60–65; psychological vulnerabilities of family, 59–63; Rasool Ahmed's fantasies about Javed, 56–57; Rasool Ahmed's reflection, 53–66
justice, xxvi, xxviii, 32, 34, 38–39, 41–42, 44–45, 55, 87, 111, 113–14

Kashmiri consciousness, 114
Kashmiri history: accession to India, 29–30; cultural life, 100–102; Dogra rule, 28–29; effects of militarization, 41; impact of terrorism, 33; Kashmiri people's right for self-determination, 29–30; Kashmiri struggle for autonomy, 31; mystic tradition, 100; narratives in mourning, 33. *See also* Aasa's narrative; Javed's disappearance; Sameena's narrative; privileges of permanent residents, 31; special status of state, Article 370, 29–31
Kashmiri identity, 52
Kashmiri Muslims, 29, 78
Kashmiri Sikhs, 78, 79
Kazmi, Sagera, xxx
Keitel, Field Marshal William, 37
knowing, 12, 14, 19–21, 23, 39, 58, 60, 63, 83, 85–86, 112
knowing terrible things, 22–23

KONTRAS (Indonesia), 52
Kristeva, Julia, 106

Lacan, Jacques, 9
Laub, Dori, 23, 50, 58
Levi, Primo, xxx; 'A Tranquil Star,' 19
Lifton, Robert J., 91
Line of Control (LOC), 30
linking objects, linking phenomena, 5
linking spaces, 51
losses, xxi–xxii, xxvii, 5–16, 18–19, 21, 23, 27, 33, 38, 40, 42, 47, 49–53, 55, 59–60, 62–65, 68–71, 73–74, 76, 78–80, 83–87, 90, 93, 95, 97, 99–107, 109–14; anxiety associated with a loved object, 9; denial of, 7; ethical in, 8–10; melancholic response, xxviii; surviving, xxiv
love, xxii–xxiv, xxvi–xxviii, xxx, 1, 3–11, 14, 19, 38, 42, 51, 57–59, 66, 69–70, 72, 74, 80, 85, 97, 101–2, 104, 107, 114
loved object, xxvi, 4–6, 9–10, 19, 104
'The Lovers' (Magritte), xxi

margins, 44
Massi, Mogul, 93
memorialization, 28, 41, 51, 75, 87, 108
memory distortion, 39
memory of disappearance, xxiii–xxiv, xxix, 20, 110
metaphor, xxii, xxviii, 20, 23, 40, 55, 67, 69, 91
methodology, xxix, xxx, 2, 15, 19, 34, 50, 82–83, 104, 106, 109
Militarism and Women in South Asia (Chenoy), 46
militarization, xxx, 45–48, 105
Modersohn-Becker, Paul, xxii
mortal, xxii, 9, 12, 83, 108
mother-mourners, 98
Mountbatten Plan. *See* two-nation theory
mourners, 49, 103–4, 104, 107–8, 111, 112, 114; knowledge of loss, 2; refusals and submissions, 3; transition of, 1–2
mourner-survivors of disappeared, 52–88, 105, 109
mourning, xxi–xxii, xxiii, 19, 37, 109–10, 111; aesthetic conflict in, xxiv; aspect of negative, 13–17; collective, xxvii; condition for, xxiii; in the context of disappearance, xxviii, xxxi; cryptic, 7; Derridian, 11–13; devoted, 102; diaries, xxiv–xxv; dreams, 5; expressions of, xxxii; in Freudian tradition, xxiv; image and conceptualization of, 10–11; in Kashmir, 106, 111–14; language of. *See* Aasa's narrative; Javed's disappearance; Sameena's narrative; as a metaphor for attachment, xxviii; normal, xxiii; *other within* of mourner, xxiii; perennial, 4–5; personal, xxvii; profound, xxiv; psychic purging associated with, 10; public, 43–44; relation between melancholia and, xxiii–xxiv, 2–6, 13–14, 107–9; 'relinquishing' one's ties, xxiii; as resistance, 109–12; self, 5; shape of, 104
Mourning Diary (Barthes), xxiii
Movement of Mothers of Plaza de Mayo, 38
moving on, xxiv
Muñoz, Oscar, 98

narcissistic identification, 4
narratives of disappearance: Abdul Hameed's case, 66–69; Ajeet's disappearance, 77–88; Javed's case, 53–66
nationalism, xxx, 24, 31–33, 38, 45, 84, 111
Nehru, Jawaharlal, 29
Nuremberg Laws of 1936, 31

object, xxii–xxvi, xxix, 1–17, 19, 35–37, 46, 59–60, 62–63, 65–66, 74–77, 84, 89–90, 99–100, 102–4, 106–10

objectification, 7
object loss, xxii–xxiv, xxvi, 1–8, 10–13, 15, 59, 102, 104, 107, 109–10
ontological, xxiii, 37
OPFMD (Sri Lanka), 52
other, xxi–xxv, xxix, xxx, 2, 5, 11–13, 22, 31, 48, 105, 113
othering, 23
otherness, 13, 49

pain, experience of, 35–37, 90
Pakistan formation, 29
Pariksa, 41
Post-Traumatic Stress Disorder, 109
Prevention of Terrorism Act (POTA), 84
profound mourning, xxiv
prohibited object, 6
psychic deadness, 17
psychoanalysis, xxxi–xxxii, 2, 18–19, 22, 108, 112
psychology, xxiv, 108
Public Safety Act (PSA), 32
punishment: in Christian theology, 34; experience of pain, 35–37; Foucault's view, 33–35
punishment–body relation, 34–35
Punjab Disturbed Area Act, 1983, 84
Punjab Documentation and Advocacy Project, 84

'qayamat,' 55

radical, xxxii, 7, 14, 20–21, 24, 52, 83, 86–87, 91, 94, 96, 108, 110, 112–13
remembering repeating, 28, 112
repetition, 21, 64, 90, 112–13
repression, 7, 14, 18, 21, 28–29, 33, 40, 42, 45–46, 98, 105, 109–10, 112
resilience, xxix, 22–23, 108
retraumatization, 80
return, xxii, xxv–xxvi, xxviii, 1, 3–5, 8, 11, 17, 21, 27, 31, 33, 40–41, 43, 45, 49, 55, 59, 62, 65, 69, 71–72, 74–78, 80, 86, 93, 95–98, 101–4, 106–8, 110–12, 114
Rilke, xxii; 'Requiem for a Friend,' xxii
Robben, Antonio, 105

Sameena's narrative, 66; Amna's health, 67; circumstances of Abdul Hameed's disappearance, 66–69; issue with mother-in-law, 72–73; mourning, 70–71, 75; pain and restoration of maternal love, 69–70; psychological vulnerabilities of family, 72–76
Scarry, Elaine, 35–36
Schafer, Roy, 25n1
schizoid patient, 16
Schmitt, Carl, 43
self, theory of, 6
semantic, xxxi, 76, 113
Shafaie, Naseem, 94; *Baakh*, 94; image of wandering mother, 97; Neither Shadow Nor Reflection, 94; Open Windows, 94–96; *The Return*, 95; symbolism of melancholia, 96; tone of maternal lament, 96–97; transition and transformation of Kashmiri women, 97
Shimla Agreement, 30
Singh, Maharaja Hari, 29
spiritual struggle, 91
state of exception, 42–45
sufferer, 36
suffering, xxviii, xxx, xxxii, 7, 11, 15, 17, 22, 36, 38, 47, 49, 53, 55, 65, 75, 82–83, 85–87, 90, 92, 94, 100, 107–8, 110–12, 114
survivor art, 91; Kashmiri artists, 91–92. *See also* Husain, Masood; Shafaie, Naseem; use of mixed media and relief work, 92

Terrorist and Disruptive Activities (Prevention) Act (TADA), 84

Torok, Maria, 6–7
torture, xxx
transference, xxix, 19, 23, 49, 90, 100, 105, 112–13
transitional space, 51
trauma/traumatic event, 20–22, 22; impact on community, 23–24; recovery from, xxiv; remembering, 23; structure of experiences, 23; survivors of, 22–23
Treaty of Accession, 29
Turkish Cypriots, 38–39
two-nation theory, 29

unconscious (other related terms), xxix, xxxi–xxxii, 2, 10, 18, 21–23, 53, 62, 67, 69–71, 74, 82–83, 86, 94, 97, 105, 110, 112–14

Violence, Mourning, Politics (Butler), 48
Volkan, Vamik, 5, 10, 39, 51; introjects, 5; 'linking objects' or 'linking phenomena,' 5; melancholic response in mourning, 4–5; '*On Death and Ending*', 4
vulnerability, 44, 47–48, 51, 53, 56, 60, 62, 66, 76–77, 81, 84, 99, 109, 112

Warhol, Andy, 21
Winnicott, Donald W., 89, 98; culture, 90; 'The Location of Cultural Experience,' 89; 'Primary Maternal Preoccupation,' 97
witnessing, 22
working through, 23, 112
wounds, xxvii–xxviii, 13, 16, 23, 36–42, 51, 63, 66–67, 79, 86, 93, 101, 106, 109, 113–14

zahir, 102
'zulm,' 55

About the Author

Shifa Haq is a psychoanalytic psychotherapist and assistant professor in psychology-psychotherapy, School of Human Studies, Ambedkar University, Delhi. She writes on gender, mourning and psychoanalysis.

www.ingramcontent.com/pod-product-compliance
Ingram Content Group UK Ltd.
Pitfield, Milton Keynes, MK11 3LW, UK
UKHW041843031026
15587UKWH00002B/980

9 781498 582483